MOTHERS, CHILDREN, AND THE BODY POLITIC

ANCIENT CHRISTIANITY AND THE RECOVERY OF HUMAN DIGNITY

NADYA WILLIAMS

IVP
Academic
An imprint of InterVarsity Press
Downers Grove, Illinois

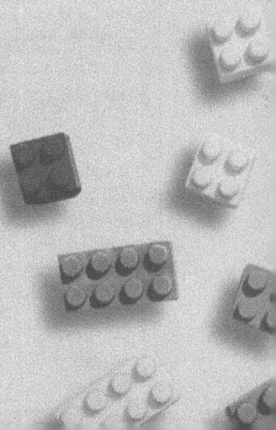

InterVarsity Press
P.O. Box 1400 | Downers Grove, IL 60515-1426
ivpress.com | email@ivpress.com

InterVarsity Press® is the publishing division of InterVarsity Christian Fellowship/USA®. For more information, visit intervarsity.org.

All Scripture quotations, unless otherwise indicated, are taken from The Holy Bible, New International Version®, NIV®. Copyright © 1973, 1978, 1984, 2011 by Biblica, Inc.™ Used by permission of Zondervan. All rights reserved worldwide. www.zondervan.com. The "NIV" and "New International Version" are trademarks registered in the United States Patent and Trademark Office by Biblica, Inc.™

The publisher cannot verify the accuracy or functionality of website URLs used in this book beyond the date of publication.

Cover design: David Fassett
Interior design: Jeanna Wiggins
Images: © Javier Zayas Photography / Moment / Getty Images, © clu / DigitalVision Vectors / Getty Images, © Antonio M. Rosario / Tetra images / Getty Images, © wjarek / iStock / Getty Images Plus

ISBN 978-1-5140-0912-3 (print) | ISBN 978-1-5140-0913-0 (digital)

Printed in the United States of America ∞

Library of Congress Cataloging-in-Publication Data
Names: Williams, Nadya, 1981- author.
Title: Mothers, children, and the body politic : ancient Christianity and
  the recovery of human dignity / Nadya Williams.
Description: Downers Grove, IL : IVP Academic, [2024] | Includes
  bibliographical references.
Identifiers: LCCN 2024011107 (print) | LCCN 2024011108 (ebook) | ISBN
  9781514009123 (paperback) | ISBN 9781514009130 (ebook)
Subjects: LCSH: Motherhood–Religious aspects–Christianity. | Child
  rearing–Religious aspects–Christianity. | Human beings–Religious
  aspects–Christianity. | Image of God. | BISAC: RELIGION / Christianity
  / History | RELIGION / Christian Living / Family & Relationships
Classification: LCC BV4529.18 .W53 2024 (print) | LCC BV4529.18 (ebook) |
  DDC 248.8/431–dc23/eng/20240508
LC record available at https://lccn.loc.gov/2024011107
LC ebook record available at https://lccn.loc.gov/2024011108

31 30 29 28 27 26 25 24 | 13 12 11 10 9 8 7 6 5 4 3 2 1

To the Lion, the Whale, and the Unicorn.

With gratitude for all the

books and cookies we

have already shared,

and with anticipation

for many more to come.

CONTENTS

ACKNOWLEDGMENTS

IT SEEMS APPROPRIATE THAT WRITING the first draft of this book took nine months, but the ideas gestated for much longer before and after that stage. Family life shapes us in ways that we may not fully see. Everyday life of a homeschooling family is busy. Any writing on the walls in my life is of the literal variety and is not done by me. It feels more stressful—or at least requires more immediate busywork—than any writing that I might have been able to do if I didn't have to clean up walls or floors. And then, someone is always hungry (even five minutes after a meal), laundry is always piled up (even if I was doing it all day. I don't get this), and I do not get to read and write as much as I might like (but then, who does?). But what I am clumsily trying to say here is: I am grateful for this beautiful gift—the privilege of life with these people, my people!—and the ways this life forces me as a parent to have a heart for the suffering of others. It is no coincidence that a mother would write a book like this one, although one key takeaway of writing this book for me was seeing the treasuring of human life in the New Testament come most powerfully and emphatically through Jesus' care for unmarried and widowed women. To love others, we must see them as they are, suffering included. And that's hard. If we truly see them, it will bring us to tears of compassion too.

But while this book's subject matter looks inward in some ways—motherhood is, after all, so deeply personal!—it also looks outward in engaging in dialogue with writers and scholars, ancient and modern. I am grateful for the following wonderful scholars, many of whom are also cherished friends, who so generously shared their time (that most scarce of resources!) and expertise to read all or some of the manuscript in draft form and offer comments—and I want to emphatically claim any remaining errors in this book as mine.

Erika Bachiochi and Agnes Howard's comments on drafts of the first four chapters were wonderfully helpful in revising the portions of the story with which, as a classicist by training, I was the least familiar. Jennifer Banks's in-depth comments on chapter five offered key insights that proved useful for revising other portions of the book as well. Eric Miller, writer and editor extraordinaire, provided helpful comments on chapter ten, drawing on his considerable expertise in the work of Wendell Berry.

Agnes Howard's monthly Zoom group of writers on motherhood discussed chapter five, an occasion that offered the collective expertise of several gifted writers and scholars to improve that particular chapter. I want to thank Agnes Howard, Bria Sanford, Jennifer Banks, and Jessica Hooten Wilson for that discussion.

It was a joy to work on this project with the editorial team at IVP Academic. I am grateful for Jon Boyd's excitement for this "one-of-a-kind" book, as he described it early on, and for Rachel Hastings's wide-ranging expertise as scholar and editor. Jeff Bilbro served as a peer reviewer for the manuscript, providing thorough and helpful comments and suggestions for revisions. I also want to express my thanks to the second peer reviewer (who remains anonymous), the third reader, and the copyeditor who read the manuscript in its entirety and took the time to engage with it thoughtfully and constructively. Their comments greatly improved this final product.

Some ideas that have made it into this book have appeared in various forms in the following publications: Anxious Bench, *Christianity Today*, Church Life Journal, Fairer Disputations, Front Porch Republic, and *Plough*. I am so thankful for all these venues for encouraging my work and for supporting human flourishing as part of their larger mission. But the greatest thanks are to my main intellectual home these days: Current and the Arena blog I have the privilege of stewarding on Current's site. The chance to work on Current with John Fea, Jay Green, and Eric Miller continues to be a joy and a wonderful learning experience.

Dixie Dillon Lane and Ivana Greco, fellow homeschool moms and writers on issues connected to motherhood, offered near daily jokes and crazy kid stories, pie inspo, and the sort of moral support that is so important for human flourishing in the daily slog—yet is, well, scientifically immeasurable.

My husband, Dan, provided me with near-weekly Saturday "writing retreats" by taking the kids to the zoo, parks, playgrounds, and this really creepy Bible wax museum in the next town over. I will never understand my children's obsession with this last one, but I am grateful for the time to write, although it may mean using all future book royalties for the kids' therapy fund.

Finally, no list of gratitude for the opportunity to write a book like this one can be complete without acknowledging the beauty of the body of Christ, of Christians who model the sacrificial love of Christ for all in their midst and in the community. We moved from our longtime home in Georgia to Ohio as I was finishing the first draft of this book. I am deeply grateful for both King's Chapel Presbyterian Church, which had been my family's home for seven years before the move, and for Christ Community Church, our new church home.

1

INTRODUCTION

In July 2023, I walked away from academia and tenure after fifteen years as a professor. This decision in and of itself was not so unusual. It is the twenty-first century, and plenty of people change careers, after all—especially in this post-2020 age of the Great Resignation. What shocked both friends and strangers alike, however, was what I decided to do instead. Instead of opting for the more typical alternative career choice for ex-academics, such as a consultant or UX researcher, I decided to stay at home full time (aside from some freelance writing and editing) to homeschool my children. "What a loss to the profession," several friends and former colleagues commented. A couple of friends made tradwife jokes, all in good humor, about my becoming a stereotypical housewife. For what better image to evoke as the exact opposite of a serious academic professional, that stereotypical disheveled creature of crumpled tweed, elbow patches, and eyes perennially red from grading far too late into the night, powered by an excess of caffeine and peanut butter consumed straight out of the jar. With a spoon.

For the record, while everything else applies, unlike most male colleagues, I never did own a tweed jacket with elbow patches. Yet I am no tradwife frolicking in flower fields in a sundress and milking cows for cameras, rest assured. For one thing, sundresses are really not practical for either hanging out at flower fields or milking cows, I hear. But aside from the tradwife social media cosplays, too many married women today, evangelical and secular alike, have generally internalized the message that feminist writer and cultural icon Betty Friedan first articulated in her 1963 bestselling book *The Feminine Mystique*—even if they have never read Friedan or even heard of her.[1] Friedan was a writer and journalist who was fired from her job for pregnancy, back when this was normal. She saw her contemporary stay-at-home moms (and, of course, herself) as bored, oppressed, and depressed. In response, she wrote her book as a manifesto for miserable modern married women's liberation.[2] (She had hoped that her therapist would cowrite the book with her. Alas, he turned down this irresistible offer.)[3] An educated woman, in Friedan's view, could never be truly fulfilled or happy if her life sphere were restricted to the domestic life. But what does such a view suggest about the value of motherhood and its essential companions—children?

DEVALUING CHILDREN AND MOTHERHOOD

Fast-forward sixty years. In August 2022, Bloomberg broke a sensationalizing news story, confidently asserting that "women not having kids get richer than men."[4] There it was, set forth already in the title of the article, a bold economic argument that put a price on human relationships and human life, leaping far beyond what Friedan, who was no absolute enemy of marriage and motherhood, had originally advocated. Marriage, the article aimed to show, cost something to women. And, of course, so did having children. In other words, if you are a woman and your chief aim is building up wealth and personal security (as the article presumes it surely should be), then your best course of action is clear. First, do not have children, and second, maybe marriage is not a good idea either. Here is an argument for a life of singlehood (albeit presumably not celibacy), and one that conflates

---

[1]Betty Friedan, *The Feminine Mystique* (New York: Norton, 2013).

[2]For a sympathetic yet complex biography of Friedan, see Rachel Shteir, *Betty Friedan: Magnificent Disrupter* (New Haven, CT: Yale University Press, 2023).

[3]Shteir, *Betty Friedan*, 79.

[4]Molly Smith, "Women Who Stay Single and Don't Have Kids Are Getting Richer," Bloomberg, August 31, 2022, www.bloomberg.com/news/articles/2022-08-31/women-not-having-kids-get-richer -than-men.

economic wealth and career success with that more elusive and less easily measurable goal—flourishing.

I read this article a few months before I had finalized my decision to walk away from academia, but I did read it as a married mother of three children. To be honest, it made me angry. The argument boldly put on trial women like me—married and mothers—and found our lives and choices lacking. To be clear, it did not affect my joy in my family, but it was upsetting to learn that the article's author might look at women like me with pity mingled with outright hyper-Friedanian disdain. I can only imagine what she would have said about my career change.

Before I go on to address responses to this article by experts, I must acknowledge an important point. There is often a perception in evangelical circles that church life is rigged to include and support mothers and exclude single women, making them feel lacking in much the same way as the Bloomberg article did for me. There is certainly some truth to this perception—although the precise degree varies depending on the specific congregation, theological tradition, location, and so on. There is no denying that single women experience significant challenges, and the church should do more to support their flourishing.[5] And yet, there is also no denying that our surrounding culture is increasingly more hostile to motherhood and family.[6] The cultural hostility to one group of women, in other words, in no way negates the existence of similarly intense hostility to another group. This brings us back to the Bloomberg article and the obvious question: Is this true? Are childless women really wealthier and happier than mothers?

Critics swiftly debunked the article's false premises and misleading methodology, which did not include any married women in the study. Compelling data exists, in fact, that it is married women with children who are the best off economically of all categories of women in modern American

---

[5]I appreciate the work of Danielle Treweek in this area. See her book *The Meaning of Singleness: Retrieving an Eschatological Vision for the Contemporary Church* (Downers Grove, IL: InterVarsity Press, 2023).

[6]Timothy Carney, *Family Unfriendly: How Our Culture Made Raising Kids Much Harder Than It Needs to Be* (New York: HarperOne, 2024).

society.[7] Study after study shows that while single unwed mothers are not flourishing economically, people in happy marriages are financially better off, happier, and healthier.[8] The happiness and health effects seem especially noticeable for men, who live longer if in a happy marriage, but women benefit too—in terms of both finances and health.[9] Indeed, Brad Wilcox, who directs the National Marriage Project, has echoed Pope Francis in describing marriage as "a matter of social justice."[10]

The veracity or falsehood of the Bloomberg article's arguments, however, is less important than the mere fact of its existence and subsequent popularity. The very attempt in this work to propose the argument that it makes, and to do it so boldly, is a symptom of a pervasive problem in American society: the problem of devaluing motherhood and children in every sphere of modern life. That is the problem that I seek to confront in all its ugliness in the present book, with the conviction that it is impossible to address a problem whose existence and full repercussions in our world and our own lives we do not recognize or acknowledge openly. It is a problem that is symptomatic of a larger devaluing of human life in our society more generally.

The choice of someone to conduct "research" and write the piece, not to mention the willingness of a prominent media corporation such as Bloomberg to publish it, shows a desire in our society, one that is hidden in plain sight, to devalue motherhood and children by pricing human life. In any attempts to make such pricing happen overtly and in distinctly economic terms, the value of mothers (the ones who produce children) and

---

[7]W. Bradford Wilcox, "Two Is Wealthier Than One: Marital Status and Wealth Outcomes Among Preretirement Adults," Institute for Family Studies, December 1, 2021, https://ifstudies.org/blog/two-is-wealthier-than-one-marital-status-and-wealth-outcomes-among-preretirement-adults-. Erika Bachiochi also provides a historical overview of these trends in *The Rights of Women: Reclaiming a Lost Vision* (Notre Dame, IN: University of Notre Dame Press, 2021). See especially chap. 9.

[8]Richard Fry and Kim Parker, "Rising Share of U.S. Adults Are Living Without a Spouse or Partner," Pew Research Center, October 5, 2021, www.pewresearch.org/social-trends/2021/10/05/rising-share-of-u-s-adults-are-living-without-a-spouse-or-partner/.

[9]Brad Wilcox and Nicholas Wolfinger, "Hey Guys, Put a Ring on It," *National Review*, February 9, 2017, www.nationalreview.com/2017/02/marriage-benefits-men-financial-health-sex-divorce-caveat/.

[10]Brad Wilcox, "Marriage as a Matter of Social Justice," *The Atlantic*, September 26, 2015, www.theatlantic.com/politics/archive/2015/09/pope-francis-marriage-family/407494/. Wilcox further expands on this concept as the central argument of his new book *Get Married: Why Americans Must Defy the Elites, Forge Strong Families, and Save Civilization* (New York: Broadside Books, 2024).

children (the products that mothers nurture at various costs—first and foremost to themselves) invariably seems to come up short. Even if the main claim of the article is faulty, there are real costs attached to children and motherhood—costs that Anna Louie Sussman has declared have led to "The End of Babies."[11]

First, the health-care costs associated with pregnancy and childbirth alone are staggering—even for a perfectly healthy pregnancy and delivery. As one recent study notes, "Women who give birth incur almost $19,000 in additional health costs and pay about $3,000 more out-of-pocket than women of the same age who do not give birth."[12] Then there is the cost of work hours lost to the employer, if a working mother takes leave according to the Family and Medical Leave Act (FMLA), and the cost of wages lost to the employee. If the child has any disabilities that require assistance in school or later in life, then there is further economic cost to both the parents and society. In addition, the costs for disaster situations, such as those that require children to be placed in the foster-care system, require yet more financial resources from the state.

Numbers, one could say, do not lie. Children in this day and age are expensive, which means that motherhood is as well. This makes both children and motherhood luxury goods by economic default. It seems callous and crass to speak of motherhood and children in terms of plain economics, even as this has been the implied reality since the original legalization of abortion in 1973. The legal right to abortion made having children an economic choice, and the reversal of *Roe v. Wade* has not reversed this deeply embedded societal belief. Arguments for abortion as a necessary measure of poverty relief continue unabated.

At the same time, we know instinctively deep down—or, at least, we should know it, if we reflect—that this is not how it is meant to be. This is

---

[11] Anna Louie Sussman, "The End of Babies," *New York Times*, November 16, 2019, www.nytimes.com /interactive/2019/11/16/opinion/sunday/capitalism-children.html.

[12] Matthew Rae, Cynthia Cox, and Hanna Dingel, "Health Costs Associated with Pregnancy, Childbirth, and Postpartum Care," Health System Tracker, July 13, 2022, www.healthsystemtracker.org /brief/health-costs-associated-with-pregnancy-childbirth-and-postpartum-care/.

not how God looks at any of us—in his eyes, every single image bearer is priceless. Nevertheless, so often in our society, we conduct this kind of pricing of human "goods" without even thinking. The deadly storm over the past two years of the converging trifecta of the Covid-19 pandemic, reactions to the repeal of *Roe*, and the Russian invasion of Ukraine, to mention just some relevant examples, has brought such conversations and questions to the fore more openly than before.

What is a human life worth? Are some lives more economically beneficial to society than others? And are there not ways of estimating the worth of a life that are not economically driven at all? As a historian of the ancient world and the early church, I am reminded of the way the earliest Christians challenged the longstanding values of the pagan world around them to display a love of all humanity that was utterly radical—and costly. The early Christians' pro-life stance included, at the economic level, a radically different and selfless use of money for the benefit of others.[13] That we do not do so in our society today is a powerful reminder that the values of our society at large, including those of many confessing Christians within it, are values of the post-Christian culture all around rather than the church.

> Without God and without the understanding of the *imago Dei* within each human being, what is a human life worth? The pre-Christian Mediterranean world gives us a terrifying answer: it depends.

Those same values were also the values of the pre-Christian culture. Without God and without the understanding of the *imago Dei* within each human being, what is a human life worth? The pre-Christian Mediterranean world gives us a terrifying answer: it depends. We are living in a crisis of devaluing all human life, and especially the lives of children, even as the June 2022 repeal of *Roe* is lending a false veneer of security or even victory for the pro-life cause.

---

[13]Nadya Williams, "Pricing Human Life," *Current*, September 20, 2021, https://currentpub.com /2021/09/30/pricing-human-life/.

GOD'S ECONOMY VERSUS THE MODERN SECULAR ECONOMY

In March 2020, the conversations around the shutdown of the economy brought up questions about the value of human life in direct and tangible ways. In those days, as the pandemic was cruelly carrying off one in every one hundred Americans over the age of sixty-five (a milestone achieved by December 2021), Texas lieutenant governor Dan Patrick openly called for older people in society to sacrifice themselves so that the economy could get back on track. Meanwhile, in an NPR conversation, economists brought up a very straightforward number, shifting the question from the metaphysical to the literal: a human life is worth around $10 million, although the cost of death, more precisely, for a family breadwinner could be calculated more along the lines of $800,000.[14] Then, in September 2021, in another instance of pricing human life, a Texas law proposed a $10,000 reward for those who successfully prosecute abortion providers. Precious lives, again, reduced to mere numbers.

But, again, it is not these figures that should shock us as much as their sheer existence. It is a disturbing reflection of our society's disordered vision of human beings vis-à-vis money that it occurred to so many people to sit down and determine complex formulae that would enable such calculations. What is a human life worth? The answer can, it turns out, be presented as a simple, albeit quite large, number. In contemporary America, making these calculations has become just regular business—a good business practice sometimes, as long as *good* is defined by sheer profit numbers. Here's another example.

In the 1970s, the Ford Motor Company decided not to make safety improvements to its subcompact car model Pinto based on financial calculations. The car manufacturers knew that a safety flaw existed in the Pinto: the positioning of its fuel tank made an explosion likely even in a low-speed rear-end collision. The manufacturers knew how it could be fixed. But calculations based on costs concluded that while recalling the car and providing the necessary safety improvements would have saved lives, the safety

---

[14]Sarah Gonzalez, Kenny Malone, and Betsey Stevenson, "Lives vs. the Economy," NPR, April 15, 2020, www.npr.org/transcripts/835571843.

improvements would have cost more than paying the families of a few people who were expected to die in this defective car model (*Grimshaw v. Ford Motor Company*, 1981). In other words, the company made a profit-driven decision after pricing the safety features needed vis-à-vis the price of paying for the deaths of a few drivers.

Ford's calculations are far from the only time a modern company has used cost-benefit analysis about human life to reach similar conclusions. I could continue listing examples, but the point is clear. Whenever calculations of pricing human life come into the equation, it turns out that people and their well-being are generally not worth as much as industrial or corporate profit. This economics-driven, practical approach to estimating the value of life may seem to make sense in a utilitarian society, in which the chief goal is to do what is most useful and the least costly for the greatest number of people around. But is the United States today a utilitarian society?

Ford's economics-driven approach to pricing human life—an approach that invariably results in devaluing human beings—is an example of a secular company prioritizing profits. Companies do this all the time, we might say and dismiss this example as irrelevant to the present conversation. And yet, while evangelical Christians claim to be staunchly pro-life, both evangelical individuals and institutions are no less guilty on a regular basis of promoting utilitarian policies that, if we analyze them more closely, amount to pricing human life and devaluing motherhood and children. I was shocked to learn, for example, that many evangelical colleges have maternity-leave policies for employees that are even worse than at the secular state university where I taught.

Seeing such inconsistencies grieves me as an evangelical woman and the mother of three image bearers. Christ-followers are people who believe in God's incredible love for all human beings, who are made in his very image, in Christ's atoning death on the cross for this sinful human race, and in his resurrection, which changed everything and is a radical call for Christ's followers to live transformed lives of caring for others. If this is who we are, we need to recognize the clash of values that our identity in Christ presents with the worldly value of pricing human lives in economic terms.

In God's economy, children (and, really, all people) are not goods. Rather, in God's vision of creation, children are *good* in that absolute sense that goes back to the very beginning of creation, in which God expressly pronounced that blessing, the proclamation of goodness. But without God's proclamation that everything and everyone in creation is good, there is no worth except that which people arbitrarily bestow on goods (including people). Without the idea of every single human being as bearing the *imago Dei*, an economically driven universe—the sort that secular economists gleefully ordain with their complex formulae—makes perfect sense.

My goal in this book is to push back against the acceptance of this clash of worldly and Christ-centered values regarding human life, especially the lives of children and by implication mothers, in our society today, particularly in evangelical circles. Indeed, the devaluing of children is inextricably connected to the disdain our society conveys for the work of mothers— from the process of pregnancy to the work and resources expended on child rearing and education. In other words, our society has a built-in disdain for motherhood as a concept. So, I want to begin with an examination of the symptoms that we overlook in our body politic—those nagging body aches and mysterious rashes that we have lived with for so long as to not notice them. We have suffered them so long that we do not realize that anything is wrong, even as the body so desperately tries to tell us that something really has gone terribly awry. This was not how we were created to live, think, and perceive our own worth and the worth of other human beings.

These general themes, of course, are nothing new. Catholic theologians, including Pope John Paul II in his encyclical *Evangelium Vitae*, have been leaders in this conversation about the sanctity of human life for a long time.[15] Evangelical thinkers have not lagged far behind. The work of Francis Schaeffer readily comes to mind, as he spent much of his career charting this very history of the devaluing of human life and worth in Western civilization, and warning against

---

[15]Pope John Paul II, *Evangelium Vitae* (1995), www.vatican.va/content/john-paul-ii/en/encyclicals /documents/hf_jp-ii_enc_25031995_evangelium-vitae.html.

consequences yet to come if these trends were to continue.[16] More recently, over his prolific writing career spanning six decades and counting, Wendell Berry has also considered similar questions in connection to local culture and agriculture. Human dignity and worth, for Berry, are under extreme threat in our industrialized and viciously and unnaturally industrializing world.[17]

I cannot improve on their works, but this book has something new to add to the conversation yet. My focus is specifically on ways in which the problem of devaluing human life manifests itself so insidiously and pervasively in our society's widely accepted attitudes toward children and those who invest so much into children, beginning with the very investment of their own bodies—mothers. Through this focus I pursue the attendant historical and theological question—What difference does the belief in *imago Dei* make?—and also aim to propose countercultural answers, likewise rooted in a historical exploration.

There are important new implications and applications that emerge from this narrower starting focus on devaluing of children and motherhood in our culture, if considered from the perspective of a mother who holds evangelical theological views. It seems that too often, after all, reflections on children and motherhood come from a worldview that is thoroughly secular and feminist, a tradition ranging from Virginia Woolf's writings to Betty Friedan's *The Feminine Mystique* to, most recently (to name just a few representative examples), Sophie Lewis's books *Full Surrogacy Now: Feminism Against Family* and *Abolish the Family: A Manifesto for Care and Liberation*, and Julie Phillips's *The Baby on the Fire Escape: Creativity, Motherhood, and the Mind-Baby Problem*.[18]

In such examinations and manifestos, children are forced to give way and get written out of the narrative exalting mothers' creative impulses. There

---

[16]Francis Schaeffer, *How Should We Then Live: The Rise and Decline of Western Thought and Culture* (Wheaton, IL: Crossway, 2005), and, to note a less famous book in which he also addresses this, *Back to Freedom and Dignity* (Wheaton, IL: Crossway, 1972).

[17]See, for example, Wendell Berry, *What Are People For?* (Berkeley, CA: Counterpoint, 2010), and *Remembering* (Berkeley, CA: Counterpoint, 2008).

[18]Virginia Woolf, *Orlando: A Biography* (Boston: Mariner Books, 2006); Sophie Lewis, *Full Surrogacy Now: Feminism Against Family* (Brooklyn, NY: Verso, 2019); Lewis, *Abolish the Family: A Manifesto for Care and Liberation* (Brooklyn, NY: Verso, 2022); and Julie Phillips, *The Baby on the Fire Escape: Creativity, Motherhood, and the Mind-Baby Problem* (New York: Norton, 2022).

are other equally worthy—or, Lewis contends, much worthier—competitors for the mother's affections than children. This, as I will show, is yet another symptom of the devaluing of both children and motherhood in our society. In God's economy, even the most amazing works of art will never compete with people, every single one of them made in his very image. Besides, as Jennifer Banks shows in her book *Natality: Toward a Philosophy of Birth*, it is reflections on birth and on being born, even if not always in connection with motherhood proper, that define the creative thought and writing of many leading thinkers of the modern world, from Mary Shelley to Hannah Arendt and Toni Morrison.[19]

To be clear, several thoughtful voices have recently advocated for the recovery of a different kind of feminism from that presented by Woolf, Friedan, and Lewis. In her book *Rights of Women: Reclaiming a Lost Vision*, Erika Bachiochi presents a poignant call to growth in virtue for both men and women based on the philosophical writings of Mary Wollstonecraft.[20] Women's full flourishing, Wollstonecraft argued over two centuries ago, requires supporting their full intellectual development and access to education. It also requires seeing marriage and the work of child rearing as a joint project of men and women together, growing in virtue as parents. Wollstonecraft's vision of feminism—and we would be remiss to not recognize it as feminism!—involves celebrating mothers and furthermore viewing women's education in moral and intellectual spheres as essential for their ability to fulfill their calling as mothers, wives, and productive members of society.

In her book on the history of pregnancy, *Showing: What Pregnancy Tells Us About Being Human*, Agnes Howard makes a similar case for the natural growth in the virtues that pregnancy fosters in expectant mothers.[21] Meanwhile, in her book *Motherhood: A Confession*, Natalie Carnes tracks this personal growth that a mother experiences through her journey into this

---

[19]Jennifer Banks, *Natality: Toward a Philosophy of Birth* (New York: Norton, 2023).
[20]Erika Bachiochi, *The Rights of Women: Reclaiming a Lost Vision* (Notre Dame, IN: Notre Dame University Press, 2021).
[21]Agnes Howard, *Showing: What Pregnancy Tells Us About Being Human* (Grand Rapids, MI: Eerdmans, 2020).

unfamiliar land by rewriting Augustine's *Confessions* from her own perspective as a new mother.[22] Finally, the new journal launched in 2023, Fairer Disputations, and its contributors—including Bachiochi, Leah Libresco Sargeant, and Mary Harrington, among others—argue effectively that contrary to its claims, modern secular feminism has been decidedly antiwoman in its treatment of women's bodies and psyches.[23]

This book contributes to the valuable dialogue that these and other thinkers have started, but my chief contribution to this conversation comes in my capacity as a classicist and historian of the ancient world. The contrast between the pre-Christian Roman world and the values of the early church provides a striking argument for the role of Christianity in creating a wholly countercultural valuing of human life, no matter age, gender, social status, family connections, or ability level. This story, in turn, shows ways in which the recovery of these values of the early church could yet reshape our own society's blighted discourse on human life.

It is ironic indeed to acknowledge that at this moment, following the repeal of *Roe*, the number of abortions in the United States has not diminished significantly. In fact, in states where abortion is legal, it has increased dramatically.[24] The numbers may be even higher than reported, as increasingly more abortions are completed by medication.[25] Acrimonious divisions only foment further polarization over the subject of abortion access in different states and smaller locales. Meanwhile just to the north of the United States, in Canada, euthanasia continues to grow and expand. It is only through the recovery of the valuing of all human life, so deeply countercultural in our world, that there is a chance to change the broader culture, at

---

[22]Natalie Carnes, *Motherhood: A Confession* (Stanford, CA: Stanford University Press, 2020).

[23]Fairer Disputations, https://fairerdisputations.org; Leah Libresco Sargeant, Other Feminisms Project, https://otherfeminisms.substack.com/; and Mary Harrington, *Feminism Against Progress* (Washington, DC: Regnery, 2023).

[24]So reports the Guttmacher Institute, a pro-choice organization that actively supports access to abortion: "New State Abortion Data Indicate Widespread Travel for Care," September 7, 2023, www.guttmacher.org/2023/09/new-state-abortion-data-indicate-widespread-travel-care.

[25]Rachel K. Jones et al., "Medication Abortion Now Accounts for More than Half of All US Abortions," Guttmacher Institute, February 24, 2022, www.guttmacher.org/article/2022/02/medication-abortion-now-accounts-more-half-all-us-abortions.

least in some circles. How we talk about human life has the potential to reshape the current conversations that have largely stalled.

PRICELESS: RECOVERING THE COUNTERCULTURAL VALUING OF ALL HUMANITY

There are three main questions I want to answer in this book. First, in what ways does this devaluing of motherhood and children in our own society manifest itself? Just how deep does this problem go? Second—and this is where my historical expertise will particularly come into play—how might the history of the extraordinary and unconditional valuing of human life in the early church help us to get back on track?

The early church, while not always living up to its own teachings, aimed to be deeply countercultural in the cruel setting of the ancient Mediterranean. We need to restore this countercultural valuing of all humanity in our own world. While this means not thinking of human life primarily in economic terms, it also means recognizing, as the early church did, that we sometimes must redeem others at a cost to ourselves. Cost-benefit analysis is not a Christian approach to thinking about human beings. The work of Charlie Camosy, among others, in advocating for family-friendly policies in contemporary America as the key to reducing abortions thus directly responds to some of the calls of the earliest Christians to fight against the dominant culture that was as antilife as it is in our own world.[26]

> We need to restore this countercultural valuing of all humanity in our own world. While this means not thinking of human life primarily in economic terms, it also means recognizing, as the early church did, that we sometimes must redeem others at a cost to ourselves. Cost-benefit analysis is not a Christian approach to thinking about human beings.

---

[26]Charles Camosy, "Why Believe Better Family Policies Will Reduce Abortions? Well, There's the Data," Religion News Service, June 7, 2022, https://religionnews.com/2022/06/07/why-believe-better-family-policies-will-reduce-abortions-well-theres-the-data/.

Third, where do we go from here? In responding to this final question, I consider the ideas of three select thinkers, two ancient and one modern, who have been pushing us to see the preciousness of all humanity in ways that acknowledge the challenges of this present life while insisting on the eternal truth about the priceless value of every human life.

With these overall questions in mind, part one of the book focuses on the symptoms of the disease in the body that is modern American society. Each chapter offers a close examination of those symptoms, which suggest that something truly is wrong and that our society at large, including Christians and non-Christians alike, has absorbed the view that motherhood and children are too costly and insufficiently valuable in economic terms. I argue that different people may not project this assumed disdain for motherhood and children in exactly the same ways. Yet, regardless of who we are, where we live, and even how many children we have (or don't have), this devaluing of children and motherhood has become so deeply and universally ingrained that we project it in some way, thought, or behavior.[27]

Chapter two looks at the death of the dream of becoming a parent, which used to be a natural part of expectations of a fulfilling life as recently as the mid-twentieth century but no longer. In examining the signs of the death of this dream, which show the devaluing of motherhood in our world, I consider the modern approach to pregnancy and delivery. For instance, what messages do expecting mothers encounter when they go to a typical doctor's office for prenatal care? You'd be surprised.

In the third chapter, I turn to the objectification of children as commodities, as seen in fertility practices and the educational system. I argue that in both cases, there is a desire to engineer the ideal child, and this desire ultimately ignores personhood and the uniqueness of God's own design for each child. Ultimately, the modern view of children proposes an assembly-line life that denies any personhood and individuality, preferring instead to

---

[27]A Catholic economist who has most recently and poignantly analyzed this tendency in our society is Timothy P. Carney in his book *Family Unfriendly: How Our Culture Made Raising Kids Much Harder Than It Needs to Be* (New York: HarperCollins, 2024).

commodify children to their parents' and society's preferences. Faulty models at all stages of the assembly line ought not to be tolerated.

To conclude part one of the book, I consider in the fourth chapter the most personal of all the symptoms of devaluing motherhood and children, at least for me as a wife and mother who also happens to be a writer. This symptom is the encouragement of women, over the course of the second half of the twentieth century on, to think of themselves as writers, intellectuals, artists, and capitalist producers, all at the expense of thinking of themselves as mothers. Instead of thinking of these identities as overlapping and supplementing each other, the emphasis is rather on competition for a woman's time and energy. In this particular economy, children yet again come up short in the writings of such leaders as Roland Barthes, Betty Friedan, and Julie Phillips. All three writers' arguments in favor of women's liberation and empowerment as creative doers ironically dismantle women's value as women and mothers. In the process, their arguments reflect a devaluing of children in favor of the idol of self-gratification. Furthermore, I argue, the mother becomes reduced in the process to the role of mere surrogate.

Taken together, the chapters in the first part of the book show remarkable similarity in our world's devaluing of children and motherhood to that in the pre-Christian pagan Roman world. So, shifting gears to dig deeper into the historical background, part two of this book examines the contrast between the overwhelming devaluing of life in pre-Christian antiquity with the revolutionary embracing of the value of life, and especially of mothers and children, in the early church. While the undervaluing of life in the pre-Christian Roman world is obviously not an exact correlation to the modern American experience, the similarities to our increasingly post-Christian society should nevertheless give us pause. Without the doctrine of *imago Dei*, what is the perception of humanity and the worth of any life, including those of women and children? The answer that emerges is clear: without an understanding of the value of humans as made in God's image, there is no reason to regard them as priceless.

Chapter five turns to the devaluing of women and children in the pre-Christian ancient Mediterranean. The surviving sources from classical Greece and into the Roman Empire show clearly that in the socially and economically stratified communities of the ancient Mediterranean, misogyny was rampant, women were largely valued as mere sex objects, and children's value depended on their status and perceived health. As table IV of the earliest Roman law code, the Twelve Tables, states, the father of the household had the duty to kill a deformed infant upon birth.

Chapter six will consider the perception of the members of ancient Mediterranean society who did not fight in war—meaning women, children, and the elderly—as *achrestoi*, the useless ones. The connection between the value of people for the military and their value in society was definitive in antiquity. Citizenship was only available to those eligible to serve in the military as well. At the same time, civilians were most likely to be victimized by war in various ways—from systematic rape and genocide to sale into slavery. Julius Caesar's own account of the Gallic Wars will be one of our chief guides in considering this phenomenon. In addition, the treatment of captive women as portable trophies to be traded at will, seen already as early as in Homer's *Iliad*, further underscores the objectification of women and the devaluing of their lives in the pagan worldview.[28] Overall, this is what a world without Judeo-Christian theology of personhood looks like. Last but not least, however, ancient warfare practices also show that valuing life is connected to stewarding the land. By contrast, devaluing life is connected to destroying the land in which people live. This has implications for today, to which I will turn in the concluding chapter of the book.

Chapter seven highlights some of the ways in which the early church overturned these deeply ingrained values by seeing all people as precious and valuable, because they were made in God's image. One particularly key point that emerges is that valuing single people, the childless, and other

---

[28]Strikingly, a recent so-called vitalism movement of right-wing intellectuals seeks to recover this very sort of pagan view of women. See John Ehrett, "The Impossible Bronze Age Mindset," *American Reformer*, April 15, 2023, https://americanreformer.org/2023/04/the-impossible-bronze-age-mindset/.

"rejects" in ancient society sets the stage for valuing all other human life, including mothers and children. In Christ, every human life is precious, and this valuing stands in sharp contrast to the ancient world, where one's value depended on family of origin, marital status, and childbearing, among other factors.

The concluding part of the book aims to present more practical reflections that might heal our world and encourage the church to be countercultural in its treasuring of mothers, children, and all humanity. In the third part of the book, I examine closely the arguments of three thinkers, two ancient and one modern, who offer exemplary voices of life. All three push us in different ways to embrace a comprehensive and consistent pro-life ethic of valuing children and motherhood and all humanity as good in an absolute sense. All three have relevant answers for us in considering where to go from here, if we want to advocate for the kind of countercultural valuing of life that the early church defended. This means embracing a slower-paced life that provides comfort in the difficulties of raising children, challenges the idolization of technological progress, consistently condemns war and violence, and, finally, recovers the importance of rootedness in a specific place as an essential aspect of valuing human life and flourishing.

The first of these three thinkers, whose writing I examine in chapter eight, is the martyr Perpetua, who was killed along with an enslaved Christian woman, Felicity, in Carthage in AD 203. Perpetua's prison journal while she was awaiting martyrdom brings up questions of priorities, earthly and eternal, for Christian mothers, presenting a powerful answer to the anti-motherhood ethos of modern feminist manifestos.

In chapter nine, I turn to Augustine. For him, valuing life involved acknowledging the horrors of war head-on, as we see especially in the brutal Gothic sack of Rome in AD 410, which inspired his *City of God*. Augustine's emotional retelling of Roman history in the wake of this tragedy that rocked the Roman Empire shows his conviction that a proper understanding of history is essential for a theologically accurate valuing of human lives in all periods, including in the present. Augustine's response to the sack of Rome gives us powerful tools for processing modern traumas of devaluing human life. Finally, Augustine's love of writing for the church reminds us of the importance of maintaining Christian community through writing that convicts, encourages, and transforms. This is what the redemption of writing looks like. It is not just an act of self-fulfillment but a transformational act of evangelism and love.

I conclude the book with a chapter examining the thoughts on personhood and the valuing of life by Wendell Berry, a writer who has devoted his life to writing about ways we could honor and value humanity in connection to God and the land. He speaks of the power of words and seemingly simple actions to heal and make whole bodies, hearts, and souls that have been wounded by life in the modern world. Ultimately, valuing mothers and children for who they are, rather than bemoaning their economic cost, is about celebrating the preciousness of human life in the context of family and community. This means stripping away all the extras that we sometimes make into idols that move us more than the real image bearers all around, who need and deserve our love.

We live in a time of crisis. In fact, we live in a time of many crises, but as has been the fate of the weak in all of human history, this crisis, revolving around the valuing of children, has simply not been taken as seriously as some others. It is a social and ethical crisis that encompasses such hot-button issues as the nature of the family, the definition of marriage and its purposes, abortion and fertility treatments, and larger questions about human flourishing in a world that reduces people to machines while elevating machines to the status of persons. But we cannot forget that at its heart, this is a theological crisis. Without acknowledging the existence of this crisis and seeing it for what it is—the seeping of societal values into the church—God's people will only continue to lose their saltiness. Ultimately, a society that lives as though the *imago Dei* is not true has a crisis of unbelief.

PART 1

SYMPTOMS OF DISEASE

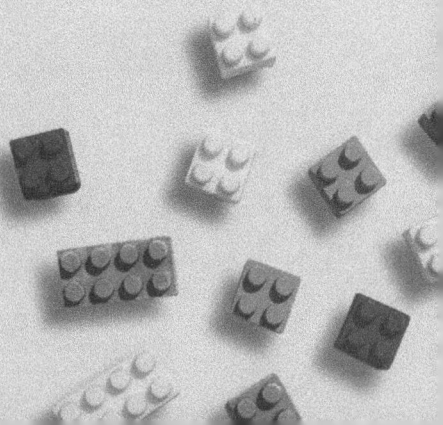

2

DEVALUATING PREGNANCY, CHILDBEARING, AND THE MATERNAL BODY

NESTLED IN RICHARD SCARRY'S 1968 COLLECTION, *Best Storybook Ever*, assembling under one binding eighty-two stories that had also been published as self-standing Golden Books, is Patricia Scarry's "The Bunny Book." It is a sweet story about a daddy bunny who is joyfully playing with his baby at the end of the day as he wonders what his baby will grow up to become.[1] Various relatives eagerly present their thoughts about possible careers for the baby bunny, as relatives are wont to do with any baby—perhaps he could become a mailman, or a candy decorator, or a railroad engineer, or a pilot, or even a farmer.

But as the reader turns to the final page in the story, a surprising revelation awaits. As it turns out, the baby bunny, who spends this conversation quietly munching a carrot, the way a good baby bunny should, already knows what he would like to grow up to be. But it is not any of the career

---

[1]Richard Scarry, *Best Storybook Ever* (Racine, WI: Western, 1968), 208-16.

options his loving relatives have suggested. Instead, "He will have lots of little bunny children to feed when they are hungry. He will read them a story when they are sleepy, and tuck them into bed at night. And that is what the baby bunny will grow up to be. A daddy rabbit."[2]

I did not grow up in the United States. Richard Scarry's books came into my life with my husband, who has wonderful memories of reading them with his parents growing up and who made sure to get our children this particular collection. But the story about this particular baby bunny got my attention when my second son, while still quite young, once remarked after hearing it that he too would like to grow up to be a dad, just like his own daddy. The reason this comment stuck in my mind has to do with its rarity. This is not a comment we hear often today. And that should give us pause. Why don't more children today dream of becoming parents themselves?

THE DREAM THAT DIED

When Richard Scarry originally wrote his stories, with their focus on family values and their delight in large families, whether of mice or rabbits or chipmunks, it seems that there were a lot of Americans for whom this was indeed the dream goal of life. This was the Baby Boom age immediately after World War II, when so many Americans were getting married young, having lots of babies—an average of 3.62 per family in 1960!—and enjoying a greater degree of economic prosperity than ever before, which certainly helped with raising all those babies.[3] So when did the baby bunny's dream die in our society, or at least became the dream of only the very select few?

The answer that the demographic data suggest is soon after 1960. After reaching their zenith around 1960, birthrates were in steady decline until 1980, when the average US family had only 1.84 children. The average number of children per US family has stayed relatively stable ever since, only briefly rising above two around the new millennium, then dipping down to

[2]Scarry, *Best Storybook Ever*, 216.
[3]"Average Number of Children Per U.S. Family (Historic)," Population Connection, 2020, https://populationeducation.org/wp-content/uploads/2020/04/average-number-children-per-us-family-historic-infographic.pdf.

a new historic low of 1.73 per family in 2018. The age of parents at the birth of their first child has been rising for a while, but a 2021 survey showed that a "growing share of childless adults" in the United States "don't ever expect to have children."[4]

But demographics can tell only one part of the story. Of greater significance here are the cultural shifts that produced a sea change in how society valued children—and what it takes to raise them. Indeed, already by the time Richard Scarry's *Best Storybook Ever* appeared in print, the dream of growing up to have a large family of one's own was starting to give way to a new dream, the product of the wild side of the 1960s. It was a dream of never growing up—or, at least, never settling down to have a family. In this new dream, there was no room for children or the task of parenting, which was a hindrance to all the fun one could be having instead.

To be fair, seeds of this dream were planted much earlier. In considering the rise of reproductive rights and in particular the vision of Margaret Sanger's Planned Parenthood, Angela Franks explains: "Sanger developed a worldview that I call the 'ideology of control,' which promoted three types of control: birth control, population control, and eugenic control. All of these were put in service of Sanger's other passion, an untrammeled pursuit of sexual pleasure."[5]

Sanger opened her first birth control clinic in New York City in 1916, but it took another half century for her vision to take deeper root and come to fuller fruition. The eugenic control of the movement, manifest in forced sterilization of women of color, was an early chapter in making this vision come true.[6] The 1960s at last provided fertile ground for the explosive growth

---

[4]Anna Brown, "Growing Share of Childless Adults in U.S. Don't Ever Expect to Have Children," Pew Research Center, November 19, 2021, www.pewresearch.org/short-reads/2021/11/19/growing-share -of-childless-adults-in-u-s-dont-expect-to-ever-have-children/.

[5]Angela Franks, "*Humanae Vitae* in Light of the War Against Female Fertility," Church Life Journal, July 7, 2018, https://churchlifejournal.nd.edu/articles/humanae-vitae-in-light-of-the-war-against -female-fertility/. See also Franks's authoritative study of Margaret Sanger and her legacy, *Margaret Sanger's Eugenic Legacy: The Control of Female Fertility* (Jefferson, NC: McFarland, 2005).

[6]Paola Alonso, "Autonomy Revoked: The Forced Sterilization of Women of Color in 20th Century America," 2020, https://twu.edu/media/documents/history-government/Autonomy-Revoked--The -Forced-Sterilization-of-Women-of-Color-in-20th-Century-America.pdf.

of Sanger's vision. The concomitant rise of feminism and panic about global overpopulation in the 1970s only contributed additional reasons for devaluing children and the task of parenting as anything worthwhile. Children and those who dared bring them into the world, instead of being valued, became the enemy of the environment, the ones who were deliberately killing this overpopulated planet. Indeed, Paul Ehrlich's *The Population Bomb*, perhaps the most famous book on this topic, appeared in 1968, the same year as Richard Scarry's book.[7] The bunny's dream, nostalgically looking back to an imagined better past, became already by the time it was published the enemy of the world—literally so in the eyes of some contemporaries. The 1973 legalization of abortion on demand in *Roe v. Wade* provided a proverbial final nail in the coffin for the respectability and desirability of the bunny's dream.[8]

Over half a century after the publication of the bunny's story, many more repercussions are readily visible, some directly stemming from the 1960s and others arising more recently. Taken together, to use the analogy of a vicious disease that affects every part of the body without altogether killing the patient, these are the symptoms of systemic and pervasive illness in the American body politic. These symptoms show a surprising truth that we may find difficult to believe following the repeal of *Roe* in June 2022.

The difficult truth that this first part of the book uncovers is that contemporary US society utterly devalues children, motherhood, and the dignity of human life more generally. This devaluing is an invisible cancer within our society that has pervaded every system of the body politic, including even the church. It is so ever-present that we do not realize that all the symptoms we experience in our life rhythms tell a horrifying tale: in our society, we have embraced thoroughly pagan values about the worth of

---

[7]The book that arguably started a cottage industry of publishing on the topic of overpopulation and the environment is Paul R. Ehrlich, *The Population Bomb: Population Control or Race to Oblivion?* (New York: Ballantine Books, 1968).

[8]See Erika Bachiochi, *The Rights of Women: Reclaiming a Lost Vision* (Notre Dame, IN: Notre Dame University Press, 2021), for a full legal and social history of these debates from the Industrial Revolution to the present.

human life. And it is making all of us feel correspondingly worthless and miserable—feelings that have led to the skyrocketing rates of depression in people of all ages.

Some of the symptoms of this insidious disease, as noted already in the previous chapter, include evaluating the worth of motherhood and children in economic terms, by which they are guaranteed to come up wanting. But additional, related symptoms involve distorted patterns of thought concerning every area of life—beginning with the subject of this chapter, the expectations for and messages to women about pregnancy and childbirth.

These symptoms, utterly ingrained in our minds and taken for granted by Christians and non-Christians alike, are myriad and show the tragic ways in which we ourselves and those around us reflect the scars of living in this postmodern secular world. All is not well, but we have lived in sickness for so long that we do not even realize we are sick. This is our normal, but it does not have to be.

The early Israelites, and then the early Christians, were in utter awe of one idea that was so outrageous that no one else in the ancient world could believe it: God delights in humanity! In our modern world, without even noticing that we have done this, too many Christians live as though this were not true. In our regular values and actions, we have somehow exchanged the truth for a lie. Let us consider some ways in which we live out this lie with full and shameless boldness when it comes to devaluing pregnancy, childbirth, and the maternal body.

> The early Israelites, and then the early Christians, were in utter awe of one idea that was so outrageous that no one else in the ancient world could believe it: God delights in humanity! In our modern world, without even noticing that we have done this, too many Christians live as though this were not true. In our regular values and actions, we have somehow exchanged the truth for a lie.

DEVALUING PREGNANCY

The baby bunny's dream to become a daddy has one more dimension we have not yet explored. While Richard Scarry is the author of most of the stories included in the collection in which the baby bunny's story was also published, the author of this particular book was Patricia Scarry. A noted children's book writer in her own right, she authored quite a few books that her husband illustrated. Her authorship of this particular story is significant: for this woman writer, the dream of the baby bunny not only reflects the desire of boys to become fathers but implicitly includes the desire of little girls to grow up to become mothers.[9] This dream, which so many women still feel instinctively today, is under attack on every side. One example of such an attack can be found even in those medical practices whose ostensible purpose is to support pregnancy and motherhood. Let me explain.

A few years after moving to Georgia, when I was expecting my second son, I was faced with the perfectly standard decision of finding an obstetrics-gynecology practice to oversee my pregnancy. Since my town had a hospital less than fifteen minutes away from my house, I initially selected the OB/GYN practice located right next to the hospital. Boasting several highly experienced doctors, the practice emphasized its expertise in every area of women's health care. But what struck me the most every time I visited was the waiting room decor.

Covering much of the available wall space around the waiting room were colorful posters advertising two types of products. First, there were advertisements for various types of birth control, including different varieties of the pill and the intrauterine device. Second, there were advertisements for Botox injections. In combination, the messaging was striking: the worth of women lies in their ability to carefully control their bodies both through preventing any unwanted pregnancy and also through maintaining eternal youth—or, at least, slowing down the ravaging effects of

---

[9] Another children's book on these themes with which Patricia Scarry was surely familiar is DuBose Heyward's *The Country Bunny and the Little Gold Shoes* (New York: Clarion Books, 2014). Originally published in 1939, it has been continuously in print since and is considered a feminist and antiracist argument for motherhood and large families.

time on one's face. Indeed, one poster recommended Botox as the best birthday gift a woman could receive. The contradiction of terms latent in this ideal is staggering.

Age, especially when combined with motherhood, leaves scars, wrinkles, and stretch marks on a woman's body. One does not, after all, carry and nourish another human being for nine months, perhaps gaining as many as fifty or more pounds in the process, without incurring permanent reminders of the experience on one's body. A difficult delivery might add yet more scars. Breastfeeding further changes the body. As any woman who has experienced childbirth could confirm, even if one succeeds in returning to one's "prebaby figure" or clothing size, it does not actually mean that everything is exactly the same.

In this office, whose waiting room was habitually filled with expecting mothers, the cosmetic procedures boldly advertised promised to prevent motherhood altogether or to erase at least some of these imprints of motherhood. Taken as a single narrative, the overall decor presented a secular medical profession's default view on women and motherhood. Children, in this worldview, are problems to prevent. Beauty and youth should be each woman's dream instead.

Eight months into my pregnancy, I switched practices. Worried about the doctors' negative attitude about my desire for a natural childbirth, I reluctantly chose to forgo the convenience of a doctor's office and hospital in my town and drove instead to a midwives-run practice a little over an hour away, attached to a major hospital in Atlanta. The decor there could not have been more dramatically different.

Portraits of infants covered the walls. Infants in hats, infants in baskets, infants artfully posed in various settings, sleeping peacefully or yawning in that delightful full-face yawn that only infants make look so incredibly adorable. The contrast told a powerful story: this practice was all about babies! Imagine holding this sweet little one in your arms in just a few months or weeks, the images reminded. This is the goal for which you are bearing these discomforts right now, the decor encouraged the expecting mothers to remember, right along with the midwives themselves. The work of pregnancy—and, as historian Agnes Howard encourages us to remember, it truly is hard work!—bears this fruit.[10]

The decision to switch there ultimately ended up being the best one I could have possibly made for my health and that of my baby. The same wonderful midwife ended up delivering both my son and, almost four years later, my daughter. Both deliveries were healthy, and in both I felt that my voice and preferences were respected, even as my safety and that of my babies was carefully monitored. Indeed, that respect toward expecting mothers is something not to take for granted. It was refreshing after my interactions with traditionally trained obstetricians before, who told me exactly how my delivery was going to go without ever listening to my thoughts on the matter. But, strikingly, even in this baby-centered practice, the first question I was asked when I came back for my standard six-week postpartum checkup was: What birth control would I like to rely on now? Now that my healthy baby was successfully out, it was time for me to employ the right technology to manage my (re)productivity.

If it seems that our society has at best an ambivalent attitude toward children—those great economic resource–busters—its attitude toward pregnancy and impending motherhood is much, much worse. In her book *Showing: What Pregnancy Tells Us About Being Human*, Howard unpacks the problematic attitudes toward women at their most vulnerable and most productive period of life—the nine months of growing a baby. Pregnancy takes significant physical labor, and in the process of transforming a woman's body, it also has the potential to form a woman's character, educating her in the virtues. Yet, there is little societal recognition or respect for this important work.

Through her analysis of doctors' writings and prenatal literature directed at expecting mothers themselves, Howard shows the condescending devaluing of pregnant women's labor over the course of the twentieth

---

[10]Agnes Howard, *Showing: What Pregnancy Tells Us About Being Human* (Grand Rapids, MI: Eerdmans, 2020).

century. The expectant mother is, it seems, passive in her work. The baby will just keep on growing. Yet, this devaluing is paradoxically accompanied with harsh advice for women about every aspect of life during pregnancy, from nutrition to exercise habits to patterns of thought. The unfortunate implication, as Howard notes, is that if all goes well in the pregnancy and it results in a healthy baby, the mother deserves only a fraction of the credit. If there are any complications, however, the mother deserves all of the blame.

But many of the experiences that Howard describes, and indeed those I had, reflect privilege. At least I had access to maternity care and was able to choose where to give birth. These privileges are not to be taken for granted, considering the utterly broken state of the American health-care system, which regularly fails expecting mothers and their babies. When my husband's cousin and his wife adopted a baby a few years ago, the baby's mother, it turned out, had been homeless for the entirety of her pregnancy and had never been to a doctor's appointment before arriving at the hospital to give birth.

Maternity care deserts, furthermore, proliferate in a number of areas, as increasingly more hospitals have chosen in the recent past to close their labor and delivery wards, forcing women in those areas to commute increasingly farther away to access maternal care and give birth. As Ivana Greco, a writer who analyzes family policy, notes, there are obvious cost calculations involved in making such decisions: "The US health-care system is under tremendous financial and political pressure to become more cost-effective. In obstetrics, this often means a preference for consolidating deliveries at urban hospitals with sophisticated technology and a large medical staff. This consolidation comes at the expense of women in rural areas."[11]

But, alas, there is more. Just as our society, sometimes implicitly and sometimes quite openly, devalues pregnancy, there is also a further

---

[11]Ivana D. Greco, "Why Rural Maternity Wards Are Disappearing," Compact, May 3, 2023, https://compactmag.com/article/why-rural-maternity-wards-are-disappearing.

devaluing of the very act of childbirth through the process of abortion and its recategorizing in certain circles, even if small ones, as health care. Such language—the words we use to talk about others—matters.

DEVALUING CHILDBIRTH: ABORTION AS HEALTH CARE

Once upon a time, sometime in the fifth century BC, there was a doctor in the Greek-speaking world named Hippocrates. Well, we think that he existed, although in reality, the figure of Hippocrates is as murky and uncertain as that of Homer, the supposed author of the greatest epics of Western civilization, who also may never have existed. But the debate over Hippocrates's existence and his authorship of various texts that have survived under his name is really not that important for the argument at hand. What matters, rather, is that preserved as part of the Hippocratic corpus is a curious oath that doctors already in the classical Greek world took. Up until fairly recently, so did their modern counterparts. Swearing by Apollo the healer and his son Asclepius, they promised, as part of a list of basic precepts, that they would not perform surgery (surgery originally was a different profession from the work of doctors). And, most relevant to our argument at hand, they promised that they would not carry out an abortion.

I noted in the introduction that one of the key contrasts that this book investigates is the antilife ethos of the ancient pagan world and the pro-life ethic of the early church. But it is more complicated than that. Even while the ancient world did not value people's lives unconditionally, a revulsion about abortion appears to have been common, at least for doctors. The Hippocratic oath provided for centuries an ideal of morality in medicine, a sort of gold standard on which all doctors could agree.

Of course, the original oath's connection to the pagan gods required reconfiguring it in the Middle Ages as a Christian document, but allowing for this culturally necessary modification, the oath was still recited by doctors up until the twentieth century. Lydia S. Dugdale, a physician and ethicist, recently asked in a poignant article in *Plough* what is lost now that the oath no longer is a foundation for the medical profession.[12] In a nutshell, Dugdale shows that this loss of a standardized medical oath across the profession means that there is no longer a commonly shared ethical understanding of the goals of medicine. Medical students may know how to perform certain procedures, but they cannot explain why some or others of these procedures may or may not be ethical in any given circumstances. And in few (if any) areas is this demise of medical ethics as salient as in the case of abortion, now redefined as a bona fide medical procedure and, furthermore, a fundamental part of health care. The repeal of *Roe* has only made the state of affairs more difficult, as procedures that were never even considered bona fide abortions—for example, treatment of ectopic pregnancy—became militarized, as some doctors have ironically refused to perform this procedure for risk of being accused of performing illegal abortions.[13] To be clear, these necessary medical procedures, traditionally not considered abortions, are not the ones I am condemning. My concern, rather, is with abortion on demand being categorized as health care.

Even as statistics grimly rank the United States first in the industrialized world for infant mortality and maternal delivery deaths, the slogan "abortion is health care" has continued circulating in the past few years, as national conversations leading up to the repeal of *Roe* grew only more heated.[14] This choice to prioritize conversations about whether abortion is a form of health care, instead of directing further resources to support expecting mothers and their babies, is a dramatic statement about our society's undervaluing of babies and mothers, regardless of where one stands on the political spectrum.

Congress considered the Abortion Is Health Care Everywhere Act in 2020 and 2021. While in both cases it failed in the Senate after securing approval

---

[12]Lydia S. Dugdale, "Bring Back Hippocrates," *Plough Quarterly* (Autumn 2022): 22-27, www.plough .com/en/topics/community/education/bring-back-hippocrates.

[13]For example, see Frances Stead Sellers and Fenit Nirappil, "Confusion Post-Roe Spurs Delays, Denials for Some Lifesaving Pregnancy Care," *Washington Post*, July 16, 2022, www.washingtonpost.com /health/2022/07/16/abortion-miscarriage-ectopic-pregnancy-care/.

[14]Joshua Cohen, "U.S. Maternal and Infant Mortality: More Signs of Public Health Neglect," Forbes, August 1, 2021, www.forbes.com/sites/joshuacohen/2021/08/01/us-maternal-and-infant-mortality -more-signs-of-public-health-neglect/?sh=fe23dc93a508.

in the House, both the name of these bills and the philosophy behind them are telling. Instead of presenting abortion as the killing of an embryo, these bills presented the procedure rather as routine health care that should be supported and covered by health insurance as casually as if it were an annual wellness check or a flu shot. To be sure, there are emergency situations, such as ectopic pregnancy, in which the embryo must be removed, since a sure death awaits both mother and child otherwise. But these emergency interventions are not the scenarios that inspired the claim that abortion is health care.

Implicitly defining health and health care as the state of being not pregnant—as this slogan does—presents a specific value statement on the worth of the baby involved. There are many medical procedures that involve the removal of something from the patient's body—whether a cancerous tumor, an embedded foreign object, or even an appendix or a gallbladder that has ceased to be useful. But none of these objects, of course, will be capable of independent life outside a woman's body. Yet, it is to these objects that a baby is implicitly likened in framing abortion as health care. Without a mother's desire to carry a child to term, a baby becomes nothing but a disease and a diseased object. Only once *it* is removed, can she be medically whole again.

But framing the removal of a baby from the womb as health care is, of course, also a statement on motherhood. A healthy woman, by this definition, is one who is not with child. And just as the opposite of health is sickness, so is wellness the opposite of pregnancy. What does this mean for our secular society's perception of motherhood? A logical interpretation is a pitying and condemning view of mothers as those who have willfully chosen to engage in something that will make them terribly, horribly, and irreversibly sick (and poor!) for a long time—pregnancy and then motherhood. They were warned repeatedly—just look at the obstetrician office posters!—but chose to ignore these warnings, just like smokers who continue to ignore the surgeon general's health warnings. The science is there, but they just will not listen. So, just as a two-pack-a-day smoker or a drug addict who keeps taking in dangerous foreign substances that erode her very body and mind over time, a woman who chooses to remain pregnant and become a mother engages in dangerous and unhealthy behavior, whose effects and repercussions will last a lifetime both for her (bad!) and for the society into which she brings a child (even worse!).[15]

Whether a woman chooses to become a mother or not—and the societal emphasis is, of course, on this choice—she is affected by these expectations that openly glorify a world that pretends to have no children or mothers within it. Indeed, this is the damage that the sexual revolution, made possible by the birth control pill, and the more recent rhetoric of choice surrounding motherhood have wrought.[16] By glorifying personal, individual choice, ironically, our society has devalued motherhood by making it just one possible choice, and a choice made by one person (the woman), as opposed to valuing personhood within the context of a larger family, community, and society.

> Whether a woman chooses to become a mother or not—and the societal emphasis is, of course, on this choice—she is affected by these expectations that openly glorify a world that pretends to have no children or mothers within it.

As Erika Bachiochi notes in documenting the history of this language of choice in the latter half of the twentieth century, the greatest damage that the culture of choice and the related discourse around a woman's right to privacy has done is to provide a woman with no choice other than the right to choose.[17] As a result of the lack of any support structures for

---

[15]Such assumptions have been the driving force behind the work of Sophie Lewis in her books *Full Surrogacy Now: Feminism Against Family* (Brooklyn, NY: Verso, 2019) and *Abolish the Family: A Manifesto for Care and Liberation* (Brooklyn, NY: Verso, 2022). In addition, this is the assumption underlying the TurnAway study: What happens to women who are denied an abortion? The presumption is they are worse off, especially financially. See Diana Greer Foster, *The Turnaway Study: Ten Years, a Thousand Women, and the Consequences of Having—or Being Denied—an Abortion* (New York: Simon & Schuster, 2020).

[16]For an overview of the devaluing of women more generally since the advent of the pill, see Mary Eberstadt, *Adam and Eve After the Pill: Paradoxes of the Sexual Revolution* (San Francisco: Ignatius Press, 2012), and Louise Perry, *The Case Against the Sexual Revolution* (Cambridge, UK: Polity, 2022).

[17]Bachiochi, *Rights of Women*, 258-59.

motherhood, ultimately every message around a woman's right to choose silently screams: the correct choice is to forgo motherhood altogether, except under perfectly curated circumstances, or erase all of its traces from her body.

DEVALUING THE MATERNAL BODY:
ERASING MOTHERHOOD AND FAMILY

Few have gone as far in their argument against motherhood, parenting, and even family altogether as social scientist Sophie Lewis. Dedicated to presenting what she terms a queer, feminist, cyborg, transhumanist, and most of all antifamily stance, she argues for the abolition of motherhood and family altogether as the only way to eliminate the injustices that, she argues, these concepts have historically encouraged and perpetuated.[18] I will examine Lewis's arguments in greater detail in chapter four—they are important for understanding how the world around us has made such arguments seem not only plausible but decisively persuasive for some. But in the meanwhile, I conclude this chapter with a consideration of cultural messaging in popular media culture about erasing all signs of motherhood from a woman's body and life. This cultural messaging also highlights what happens in the absence of another key for human flourishing—the virtues for character formation and for healthy relational bonds, both in the family and in society at large.

What if a mother gives in to the societal messaging devaluing the maternal body and lifestyle after she has already birthed children? As it happens, one of our best primary sources for this phenomenon has been unfolding in reality television. A number of enormously popular shows about housewives have depicted women in their thirties, forties, and older aiming to look significantly younger, turning to plastic surgery and extreme dieting to make their bodies fit into a decidedly unmaternal mold. Of course, their behavior merely takes to the public sphere what my OB/GYN office was advertising for individuals living a more private life.

---

[18]See, in particular, Lewis, *Abolish the Family*.

In his book *The Housewives: The Real Story Behind the Real Housewives*, self-described Real Housewives anthropologist Brian Moylan analyzes the train-wreck franchise, showing the intricate ways in which media attention has only contributed to heightening the drama of the show's subjects while shaping the minds of viewers—clearly and undoubtedly, we may conclude, even if Moylan does not, for the worse.[19] Things can and do, however, get more problematic once motherhood is more expressly brought to the fore for the sake of entertainment.

Recently, a new reality-television show took a step further in its glorification of decidedly unmaternal bodies. But it chose to do so while paradoxically casting mothers as its main subjects. The show *MILF Manor* took as its foundational concept the quintessential vulgar ideal of a term decidedly not fit to use in polite company—but crossed it with a dating show. In this case, the "MILFs" living in the manor are all eligible single women looking for love. Vying for their affections are men who are literally half their age and therefore young enough to be their sons.[20]

First and foremost, looking at the advertising images, one would never be able to tell from these women's bodies that they ever birthed children. As they are perfectly slender, sculpted, and tan, the show's advertising suggests that they spend their time on camera clad in scanty bikinis and tight-fitting dresses, their hair and makeup perfect. But unnaturally inflated lips and bosoms on some of these women show the truth: these bodies of mothers in their forties or beyond have undergone significant work, some of it of the surgical variety, in order to look the way that they do and to erase all trace of motherhood from their appearance. Furthermore, their presence on the show also testifies that their children's fathers have likewise been erased, allowing these women, in what is truly their middle age, to seek to recover a wild youth.

---

[19]Brian Moylan, *The Housewives: The Real Story Behind the Real Housewives* (New York: Flatiron Books, 2021).

[20]I should note a disclaimer here before proceeding to the rest of this analysis: I have not watched the show and am not planning to do so. The analysis that follows proceeds from the assumption that the premises of the show are abundantly clear from the promotional materials.

But what kind of relationships would *MILF Manor* generate? What kind of matchmaking would yet another seedy dating reality-television show accomplish? One can assume that the absolute best-case scenario that the producers foresee is successful pairings. Sure, a show like this is predicated entirely on the possibility of fostering steamy hookups among the participants. But maybe, upon the show's conclusion, one or two of the women will settle into some sort of long-term dating relationship with the young men they met. Naturally, no talk of marriage is likely to occur, but maybe cohabiting is on the proverbial table. Unwedded bliss may be theirs for a while, but of course, no children will be forthcoming from it, even if they had wanted such fruit. We must remember, after all, that no matter how much Botox one's face or body can take, women's reproductive systems act their true age even if their bodies do not look it.

A paradoxical fascination with mothers as strange, zoo-like exhibit objects drives this show forward. It is the women's identity as mothers, after all, that is in the show's title, fetishizing their identity as once-upon-a-time birthers of life, even as all traces of that reality have been expunged now from their well (re)constructed bodies. Aldous Huxley's 1932 dystopian novel *Brave New World* suddenly seems not so far away. Indeed, the moral stance on relationships that this show presents is one that would be at home in the society Huxley describes in his novel. It is a world where motherhood is but a dirty word, babies are grown and hatched in incubators in a lab, and all individuals, ever preserved in their youthful state until they are of age to be euthanized, can devote their lives to the radical pursuit of sexual pleasure, unrestrained by commitment or any possibility of pregnancy.

CONCLUSION: EDUCATION IN ANTIVIRTUES

The outspoken reactions of abortion-rights activists to the repeal of *Roe* in June 2022 made Alasdair MacIntyre's book *After Virtue: A Study in Moral Theory* seem downright prophetic.[21] Without the historically Judeo-Christian

---

[21] Alasdair MacIntyre, *After Virtue: A Study in Moral Theory* (Notre Dame, IN: University of Notre Dame Press, 1981).

moral values that for millennia had governed relationships within the family, home, workplace, community, and beyond, so many acts previously illicit suddenly seemed possible and defensible. Who was to say they were not? And, indeed, this is the story that Bachiochi as well documents in considering the history of women's rights from the late eighteenth century to the present.[22] For Mary Wollstonecraft, credited by some as the original feminist, one's entire life ought to be a process of education in the virtues. Through lifelong growth in virtues such as temperance, patience, and self-control, both men and women could become good husbands and wives and good fathers and mothers. But, to ask MacIntyre's question, what if these moral virtues no longer function as the foundation of society?

The devaluing of mothers and the devaluing of the children who are nourished in their pregnancies go side by side. Regarding the "product" as unnecessary and harmful devalues the "producer." And devaluing the one type of work that women's bodies can biologically do is a powerful attack on their preciousness and personhood. Ultimately, the kind of freedom provided by erasing all traces of childbearing, real or potential, has been made possible by the dismantling of the traditional Christian virtues that Wollstonecraft or MacIntyre extolled as the ideal undergirding for healthy society. But it is not only that our society has rejected these values over the past half century. The current ways in which our society overtly devalues motherhood, pregnancy, and thus maternal bodies also serve to provide continued education in antivirtues to all who are exposed to the culture around them. Here is one particularly poignant example.

In her most famous essay, first published in 1971, American philosopher Judith Jarvis Thomson offers a memorable analogy for abortion rights: imagine that a woman's circulatory system has been connected to that of a famous violinist, whose life she now must sustain for nine months. For Thomson, the situation is clear: no one should be forced to do something for which they did not sign up. Just as the hypothetical woman in her thought experiment would be perfectly warranted to cut

---

[22]Bachiochi, *Rights of Women*.

off the famous violinist, so would a woman who finds herself pregnant but does not wish to be.[23]

While Thomson's goal was to promulgate the rights of women vis-à-vis abortion, her example is telling about the absolute devaluing of human life in modern society. It does not matter whether someone is a noted violinist or otherwise famous—this specificity in the case study is a red herring. What matters is the existence of someone. If we unconditionally value humanity and human life, it would be appropriate to say, if unexpectedly placed in a situation where we could preserve someone's life: yes, this human being matters, even if I did not sign up for this duty. The hyperindividualistic stance that no one's life or existence is valuable if I personally did not choose to support it is a horrifying commentary not about pregnancy and child-bearing alone but about our society's overall devaluing of human beings. The question to ask has to do with how we see our nature: Is each human being a precious image bearer of God? If we answer yes, this admission places obligations on us to act accordingly.

My focus in this chapter has been specifically on the symptoms in our society that exhibit clearly the devaluing of motherhood. As the example of Thomson's arguments shows, however, this devaluing is in many ways inseparable from the devaluing of human persons in our culture more generally. After all, just as *MILF Manor* commodifies its female subjects, reducing single mothers with grown children to sexual objects, it does no less to the young men cast in the show. Instead of being perceived as young men with potential abilities, talents, and life dreams, they, too, are one-dimensionally reduced to entertainment fodder that borders on sexual exploitation. Such are the fantasies popular culture pushes on its victims, suspecting or unsuspecting alike.

Gone is the Richard Scarry–esque ideal of family life, centered on loving fathers and mothers and children, spending quality time together and dreaming of a future generation that replicates the same ideal. Of course, we must remember that real families in the midcentury did not always live up

---

[23]Judith Jarvis Thomson, "A Defense of Abortion," *Philosophy and Public Affairs* 1 (1971): 47-56.

to Scarry's ideal, and we should beware excessive nostalgia. In his essay "The Mirage of the 1950s," historian Adam Jortner summarizes the devastating anxieties that plagued that particular decade in American life, from fears of nuclear war from abroad to domestic race tensions.[24] And yet, at least the ideal that Scarry presents is one that acknowledges happy, functional families as best for all, individuals and society alike.

What came to replace that ideal? In its place, as family life and all traces of motherhood are erased, we find hyperindividualism that idealizes selfish relationships that require no commitment. Any commitment instead is to be reserved for one's career, as we will see in considering the erasure of motherhood from the discussion of women's creative work in chapter four. But we should not forget the focus on the daddy bunny and his son's dreams in Patricia Scarry's story. It is a reminder that this dismantling of motherhood, while the focus of my observations here, has implications that are no less important for the devaluing of fatherhood. Men's dreams and goals and lives, too, have been affected by the capitalist pressures, even if less so than those of women.

The culture in which one is emmeshed is like secondhand smoke, historian Christopher Shannon recently noted in an essay on the modern (il)liberal order, focusing in particular on shifting societal values regarding sexual mores.[25] Modern media culture, from social media to television and beyond, has created a secondhand smoke like no other. At the same time, though, this media culture is remarkably honest in setting forth the majority views and beliefs of a society. Even if many people would never admit that these are their views, they passively absorb them through consumption. We have traded Patricia Scarry's bunny family for *MILF Manor* and didn't even notice.

Yet, even as our society continues in so many ways to exchange the truth about the value of motherhood for lies, the fundamental desire for children

---

[24] Adam Jortner, "The Mirage of the 1950s," Current, June 26, 2023, https://currentpub.com/2023/06/26/the-mirage-of-the-1950s/.
[25] Christopher Shannon, "Forum: Post-liberal America," Current, December 12, 2022, https://currentpub.com/2022/12/12/forum-post-liberal-america/.

still beckons for so many. But the societal devaluing of motherhood and of children has disfigured even this desire in ways that I will examine in the next chapter. Instead of precious image bearers, children in our society—a society that idolizes individualism and yet does not value individual children qua persons—have become reduced to products to engineer and perfect by ever-improving modern technologies and educational research. In a society that devalues human life, children's existence has been reduced to an assembly-line life, from conception to the grave.

3

YOUR ASSEMBLY-LINE LIFE

ONCE UPON A TIME, there lived a talented sculptor. He loved his art, but he also seems to have agreed with that universally acknowledged truth "that a single man in possession of a good fortune must be in want of a wife."[1] He really wanted to find such a wife, but he was repeatedly repulsed by the depraved moral character of women—or so he said, so it must be true. Disappointed with women made of flesh and blood, he spent his days with, well, people made of marble. At least they could never disappoint his high standards. In his sorrow, or maybe simply in his love for his art, one day he decided to sculpt the perfect woman. And so he did. Made of ivory, she was perfect in every way—not only in her appearance but also (it appeared to her maker) in her moral state. She seemed to have that perfect modesty that so suits a virgin. But while she, a statue, continued to behave with perfect ivory-clad restraint and modesty, her maker lost it all.

Our sculptor, Pygmalion, fell completely and hopelessly in love with this ivory woman, the creation of his own hands. He brought her gifts of various

---

[1] This is the opening line of Jane Austen's novel *Pride and Prejudice*. See Austen, *The Annotated Pride and Prejudice* (New York: Vintage, 2007).

sorts, dressed her in finery, and could not resist caressing her beauty. At last, overcome with desire for the ivory maiden, he prayed to Venus, the goddess of love, for a wife who would be just like his statue. The goddess knew, however, that what he really wanted was for the statue to come to life. So, as Pygmalion kissed the statue again, she came to life, married him, and nine months later gave birth to their child.

In this myth, part of the Roman poet Ovid's famed epic *Metamorphoses*, we find a happy ending—at least as far as the sculptor is concerned.[2] The wife Pygmalion crafted for himself turned out to be perfect in every way. One might note that she never speaks or expresses any opinion of her own, but then she was not made to speak or have opinions. Pygmalion custom-made her to suit his preferences in every way, and so she did. Any of us who have ever had to deal with the complexities of family holiday schedules might also quip that Pygmalion eschewed any in-law considerations in the process too. Perhaps this was part of the wife's perfection.

CREATING THE PERFECT HUMAN

This tale is the best-case scenario for the timeless dream of humans since antiquity to overcome nature and fashion the perfect human according to their own preferences. But while it worked out great for Pygmalion, this test case ought to be accompanied with an important warning: results not typical. Indeed, this is one apt way to summarize Adrienne Mayor's book on robots and automata in ancient myths, *Gods and Robots: Myths, Machines, and Ancient Dreams of Technology*.[3] One could also note that no person is created solely for the joy of another person, but this was not part of Pygmalion's worldview. In a world that ran on slave labor and viewed some people as indeed made and intended for the enjoyment of others, this last objection is not one he would have comprehended.

---

[2] For a translation of the myth of Pygmalion in Ovid's *Metamorphoses*, see Ovid, *Metamorphoses*, ed. and trans. Brookes More (Boston: Cornhill, 1922), available at https://www.perseus.tufts.edu/hopper /text?doc=Perseus%3atext%3a1999.02.0028. For a complete translation, no one can beat Stephanie McCarter, trans., *Metamorphoses* (New York: Penguin Classics, 2022).
[3] Adrienne Mayor, *Gods and Robots: Myths, Machines, and Ancient Dreams of Technology* (Princeton, NJ: Princeton University Press, 2018).

By the early nineteenth century, dreams of designing the perfect human had grown more cautionary, as we see in Mary Shelley's novel *Franken-stein*, an updated Pygmalion tale of sorts but one in which the designer is not crafting a love interest. Rather, he aims to create the perfect human just to see whether he can. But while the original Pygmalion's experiment results in a passive and therefore morally perfect, subservient wife, Dr. Frankenstein's experiment results in a physically perfect (when it comes to strength and physical abilities) but aesthetically hideous creature, whom Frankenstein cannot even call human. This being is furthermore utterly corrupt and devoid of all moral compass. Rather than blame the monster, however, Shelley's intent is to show the flawed nature of the human creator—anything we touch is flawed because of our own fallen and imperfect nature.

The alluring dream of creating the perfect human remains no less ir-resistible as we get into the twentieth century, cautionary tales be cursed. These most recent dreams, however, no longer involve the creation of perfect men or women, with the notable exception of Ira Levin's *Stepford Wives*. Instead, the modern idea of creating the perfect human centers on engineering the perfect baby.[4] This dream is seen in exquisite detail in Aldous Huxley's *Brave New World*, a novel that features a state-of-the-art baby hatchery to replace traditional human reproduction. It has now come to fruition through advances in modern technology that allow one to create the baby one wants in a petri dish—if only one has the money to do so.[5]

This desire brings to the fore a curious phenomenon. A tension continues to exist: despite the frequent messages devaluing motherhood and children, our society cannot entirely write them out of existence. But it can, as it turns out, commodify them just as we commodify nearly every other good or concept, from food, to entertainment, to housing, to travel, and more.

---

[4]Although one could make the argument that this same issue of engineering the ideal human is also afoot now with transgender ideology and the modern plastic-surgery industry.

[5]One useful summary is Robert L. Klitzman, *Designing Babies: How Technology Is Changing the Ways We Create Children* (New York: Oxford University Press, 2020).

Indeed, in March 2023, a circuit court judge in Virginia cited old slavery laws to rule that frozen embryos are property or "chattel."[6]

This consumer attitude toward children begins already with messaging to women about preventing pregnancy, as we saw in the previous chapter: as with any other goods in modern life, when it comes to having a child, you can get one if you want, but do not get one if you do not want to. If you choose to get one, though, why not get the absolute best one that you can, just as you might when making any other major purchase? We live in a world of you-get-what-you-pay-for consumer mentality. The latest scientific advances and in vitro fertilization technology—whereby the best preselected and pretested embryo is implanted—now allow prospective parents who can afford it to customize the features of an embryo, much like we might do in customizing features for a car or a home. Gone are the days of leaving such matters entirely up to God or chance. Our consumerist culture does not gamble with such major purchases.

What interests me is not that so many people approach the different stages of creating and raising children in this way. This has become the privileged reality of some pockets of the modern world, even if most people do not use every step of the assembly-line process. Rather, my question is: What does it say about us and our society that we objectify children and childhood in this way? In this chapter, we will walk through select phases of this assembly-line life, from conception to adulthood, before considering the alternative to the assembly-line view of children that the gospel uniquely provides. But first, one key point to keep in mind: when I speak of the assembly-line desires and procedures in this chapter, I am not speaking of parents struggling with in-fertility. Rather, the discussion that follows considers parents who could have a baby the old-fashioned way but decide to harness science and fertility treatments not because they must but entirely by choice—to help optimize the baby.

The desire to create perfect babies, who will grow, with each successive move in the assembly line, into perfect children, students, and adults, can come from

---

[6]Matthew Barakat, "Judge Uses a Slavery Law to Rule Frozen Embryos Are Property," AP News, March 9, 2023, https://apnews.com/article/embryos-slavery-chattel-custody-virginia-82e1f36ecbc f35ec4659e8e2c3443c4f.

a good place. The desire to have children who flourish is natural for parents. As Jesus asks, who would choose evil for their child if they could choose good? (Mt 7:9-11). But taken to the assembly-line extreme, this approach displays a utilitarian approach to human life and a devaluing of the beauty and diversity of God's creation. It is not surprising, therefore, that we see this very approach now in the phenomenon of secular technophilic pronatalists, of whom the most famous is Elon Musk.[7] Their ideal is to fill the earth with the best progeny. In describing this dream, the language of saving the planet through this eugenic endeavor is salient, made possible with the help of technology.

Such use of technology in reproduction is a powerful expression of unbelief. It is an overt declaration: I do not trust God to have good plans for me and my child, so I will take the reins for myself. Most troubling of all is that this assembly-line process tolerates no flaws or imperfections. There are only two options for a defective product: be fixed or be eliminated.

This is no mere hyperbole. Utilitarian ethicist Peter Singer expressly argues that handicapped infants ought to be killed for their own good and that of others.[8] Indeed, in a world that readily accepts such options as (ironically) viable solutions for the fetus in utero, the only difference between Singer and many mainstream pro-choice individuals is simply that Singer extends the license to kill to outside the womb. In such a material

Such use of technology in reproduction is a powerful expression of unbelief. It is an overt declaration: I do not trust God to have good plans for me and my child, so I will take the reins for myself. Most troubling of all is that this assembly-line process tolerates no flaws or imperfections. There are only two options for a defective product: be fixed or be eliminated.

---

[7]Bart van den Dikkenberg, "Three Women, Ten Children; How Elon Musk Tries to Save the World," Christian Network Europe, May 12, 2022, https://cne.news/article/2163-three-women-ten-children-how-elon-musk-tries-to-save-the-world.

[8]Peter Singer and Helga Kuhse, *Should the Baby Live? The Problem of Handicapped Infants* (Oxford: Oxford University Press, 1986).

approach to building humans, the desire to create perfect children through the perfect assembly line is the ultimate sign of both the devaluing of human life and the rejection of God.

OPTIMIZING BABY

There was once a royal family that was blessed with healthy twin sons—an heir and a spare all at once! They were, of course, overjoyed. They swiftly learned, however, that one of these baby boys was rather unusual. One night, vicious snakes mysteriously invaded the infants' crib. Hearing their cries, their mother ran to the crib to discover that while one infant was crying (a perfectly typical infant response), the other son had caught and strangled the snakes with his bare hands (not a typical infant response). This story about baby Heracles, who grew up to become the most physically powerful demigod in Greek mythology, reminds that an integral part of engineering the perfect baby hero begins with good genes.

According to Greek myth, Zeus, the king of the gods himself, was the father of Heracles. The mortal husband of the twins' mother, Alcmene, was the father of the other (fraternal) twin. From infancy, this distinction be-tween the two babies' genetic makeup was clear from the super-level strength of one and the ordinary abilities of the other.

Still, there were ways, the Greeks believed, to enhance the superpowers of both ordinary mortals and even of the demigods. In another myth, a minor goddess gives birth to a baby boy whose father is mortal. Determined to give her baby the best advantage in life, she dips him into Styx, the powerful river running through the underworld. As a result, he becomes forever immune to all wounds, except for his heel—for it is by the heel that the mother held the baby during his medicinal immersion. This baby was the epic hero Achilles.

These two myths highlight a basic awareness in antiquity of something we now understand better through science. The best of nature is great, but medical interventions can be harnessed to improve on nature. Some eager parents rely today on this combination of nature and state-of-the-art medical science to create the perfect baby. This process begins with crafting the perfect embryo, which will then be implanted in the mother or a gestational surrogate. But what constitutes the perfect embryo or baby? While there may be basic requirements on which most parents can agree, generally concerning the embryo's health and ensuring the lack of genetic disorders, there are also additional extra preferences that can be entirely individual.

One company, Fertility Institutes, offers interested parents the option of selecting their child's sex and eye color.[9] This service reminds us just how quickly the field is advancing, by the way, as in 2020 Robert Klitzman noted that such design was not yet possible.[10] Pictures of happy babies and parents on the company's website show the happy products, their smiles belying the complicated process by which such selection of options happens. After all, this genetic engineering cannot occur in the womb. The process instead involves an artificial creation of embryos and the editing of genes in them prior to the implantation of the best candidates in the mother. Genetic screening for IQ—done by testing for traits associated with high or low IQ—is the next frontier and is now in development as well.[11]

Far from a natural process, in other words, this baby making happens entirely in a lab and the doctor's office. Furthermore, no fertility clinic brochure discusses what happens to the unlucky embryos that do not meet the checklist criteria. The aim of these businesses—which is, of course, what they are—is to provide their customers the perfect product, made to the customer's preferences. Customer satisfaction matters, we repeatedly hear in the modern world. The customer is always right. If you do not sell the customer the desired product, the customer will simply go to another vendor. This is just how business works—and this business is estimated to hit $41 billion by 2026.[12] In the process, the assembly line is continuously perfected.

[9]"Choose Your Baby's Eye Color," Fertility Institutes, www.fertility-docs.com/programs-and-services/pgd-screening/choose-your-babys-eye-color/.

[10]Klitzman, *Designing Babies*, 120-21.

[11]Antonio Regalado, "Americans Are Ready to Test Embryos for Future College Chances, Survey Shows," MIT Technology Review, February 9, 2023, www.technologyreview.com/2023/02/09/1068209/americans-test-embryos-college-chances-survey/.

[12]Heather Landi, "Fertility Support Startups Banked $345 Million in 2021. Here's Why the Business of Family Planning Is Booming," Fierce Healthcare, May 17, 2022, https://www.fiercehealthcare

Genetic testing is now routine for all pregnancies, especially for older mothers. While testing can save lives, too often it is used to flag conditions that merit destruction. If the product on the assembly line is faulty, it is best to destroy and start over—indeed, this is what happens on the assembly line. Quality control, a common industrial standard, involves throwing away and destroying any items in the process of mass production that do not meet the high industry standards. Even the most ardently pro-choice mother might flinch at this language of quality control in the baby-making industry. Still, the argument for this very quality control, couched in terms of sparing the (flawed) child future suffering, has become common.

In some ways, this is brilliant rhetoric, for instead of relying on the argument for the convenience of parents—who wants to parent a child who will always need extreme care and will never be able to live a self-sufficient and healthy life?—it shifts the concern to the child. It is, the argument goes, for the child's best to destroy him or her, rather than let this child live such an imperfect life. As Richard Dawkins once publicly tweeted to a woman who wondered what she would do if she were expecting a baby with Down syndrome: "Abort it and try again. It would be immoral to bring it into the world if you have the choice."[13]

Dawkins's comment received significant backlash, but the only line he truly crossed, in the eyes of many, was saying something like this out loud so crassly. This view is unfortunately common, as Down syndrome diagnoses result all too often in abortion. But as Matthew Loftus notes in a powerful essay, such a view of fetal life also devalues all other lives—those of people of all ages.[14] It makes sense: if we think that an unborn child with a particular condition should be put out of his or her misery before birth, why would we value someone of any age who happens to have a horrible disease that might make "regular"—meaning, self-sufficient—life impossible? At

.com/health-tech/fertility-support-startups-banked-345m-funding-2021-heres-why-workplace-perk-becoming/.

[13] Erna Albertz, "Pursuing Happiness: Down Syndrome, Richard Dawkins, and Human Joy," *Plough*, March 21, 2019, www.plough.com/en/topics/justice/culture-of-life/pursuing-happiness.

[14] Matthew Loftus, "Does Abortion Spare the Child Pain?," *Plough*, April 17, 2023, www.plough.com/en/topics/justice/culture-of-life/does-abortion-spare-the-child-pain.

what point, in other words, do we tell someone their life has no meaning or value?

But let us say that you do get everything you desire at this stage in the assembly-line process: the perfect newborn! He (or she, if you elected a girl) is perfectly squishy, smart, cute, and healthy, with the eyes in the exact color you checked on the order form—unlike some of those sweaters you can order online that turn out to be an entirely different color in person from on the webpage. Anyway, you get the point—here's the perfect baby, hurrah! The problem is: this child will still disappoint. Any attempts to customize children deny the reality of human flesh. Children, like all people, are unpredictable individuals and are not made for the convenience of their parents. Customizing the body will not allow for customizing the heart, mind, and soul—and that is a good thing. Parents who had hoped to play Pygmalion vis-à-vis their children are simply setting themselves up for disappointment— if not now, then later.

This struggle to design the ideal baby ultimately reduces human beings— in this case, children—to objects to be shaped and molded to our own will and for our own happiness, rather than image bearers entrusted to our stewardship for a season.[15] Furthermore, this objectification, this desire to design children, comes with the same danger that exists with other things we design for our own pleasure: when an object no longer sparks joy, the principles of the KonMari method remind us to get rid of it.[16] "And Mom and Dad can hardly wait for school to start again," merrily declares a popular Christmas song, originally written in 1951. Sometimes, getting rid of children in our world looks like sending them to school. At least, we get to justify it as simply the essential next step in the assembly line.

It seems like quite a jump at first glance: surely sending children to be educated is not the same thing as resorting to extreme technological methods

---

[15]See, for example, Gloria Furman, *Missional Motherhood: The Everyday Ministry of Motherhood in the Grand Plan of God* (Wheaton, IL: Crossway, 2016), and Teresa Whitehurst, *How Would Jesus Raise Your Child?* (Grand Rapids, MI: Revell, 2007).

[16]The KonMari method is the trademark of Marie Kondo, a minimalist consultant, organizer, and author of several bestselling books that encourage people to take control of their lives by getting rid of everything that does not "spark joy." See https://konmari.com/.

to engineer the perfect baby? To be clear, I am not criticizing here the practice of sending children to school in general. Rather, as we will see, I exhort us to consider culturally ingrained motivations that perhaps we may not even realize we have: the desire to continue the necessary high-impact engineering to create that perfect child at each stage of the growing process.

SENDING CHILDREN TO SCHOOL

Sometime in the first century AD in Rome, a child disgruntled over educational drudgery etched a curious graffito on the wall of his schoolroom. A delightfully executed donkey turns a millstone, grinding grain, while the accompanying inscription states with all the sarcasm this young scholar could muster, "Work, little donkey, as I have worked, and it will be for your benefit." To be fair, there are reasons to suspect that our reluctant scholar may have been enslaved, and his bitter words may have therefore been a response to the harsh physical labor that he endured, in addition to mere schoolwork.[17]

His misery nevertheless gives us a rare perspective on schooling from a child in a world where children's perspectives did not matter. And it brings to the fore the ways in which adults during each back-to-school season sometimes show disordered desires, ones that do not reflect valuing children whom we send off to be educated.

There are so many worries and concerns and big feelings at the beginning of each new year. But too often the things we as parents worry about are not the right ones, and our big feelings in this season are as disordered and distorted by sin as in any other season. My concern here is with locating a theologically well-ordered view of sending children away to school, a view that does not view them as products to mold or inconveniences to remove but souls to cherish. At the same time, I want to consider a way of reflecting about schooling that does not yet again reduce children

---

[17]This section and several others in this chapter draw on my essay, "A Post-classical Perspective on Valuing Children During the Back-to-School Season," Church Life Journal, September 12, 2022, https://churchlifejournal.nd.edu/articles/a-post-classical-perspective-on-valuing-children-during-the-back-to-school-season/.

to products on the assembly line. Neither of these comes easily, even to thoughtful Christian parents.

Throughout one summer a couple of years ago, many a half-jest I heard in Christian circles, including at church, revolved around parents' longings to see their children finally go back to school. Some mentioned count-downs. There was widespread parental dismay when schools in the city decided to postpone the first day of classes by two weeks that year. When that first day of school finally arrived, at long last, one dad joyfully and publicly expressed his gratitude at church on Sunday. Many an *amen* rang back from the congregation.

It is not that Christians making such jests do not love their children—quite the opposite is true. Still, this anecdotal evidence reminds us that even for loving parents, it can be difficult to rejoice over their children's company all day, every day, all summer long. Why? Because the assembly-line process most often (although not universally) assumes that the assembly line ex-tends well outside the home into the public or private school environment. After all, just as you rely on the experts to help you conceive and birth the best baby, so do the experts then help you optimize that product at each successive stage.

Yet, outright rejoicing over seeing children back in school should give us pause. To go from constant togetherness to separation for much of the day entails a severing of bonds and should feel like a real fracture. In some ways, the intensity of emotions should echo another drastic separation: the birth of a child, which too marks a moment severing a bond of the ultimate togetherness—the child hidden within the mother's womb—into existence as two visibly separate beings, individuals with separate desires and thoughts. But the separation brought about by childbirth is natural and foreordained. By contrast, the separation brought about by the end of summer does not have that same sense.

To be fair, for many parents, the joy of sending children back to school is mixed with sorrow, even if they feel that send them away they must. There are several studies that underline this tension in feelings. For example, one

2016 study shows that parents in the United States now spend more time with their children than their 1960s counterparts.[18] But the increased pressure that the modern assembly-line pressure-cooker life places on parents in every sphere of life—at work and at home—has made this increased time with children feel more stressful for parents than in previous generations.[19] As a 2007 study put it, "Today's U.S. mothers and fathers spend at least as many hours caring for their children each week as parents did four decades ago during an era that in the popular imagination was a golden age of family togetherness. It may seem contradictory, then, that many parents complain of feeling rushed and of not having enough time with their sons and daughters."[20]

It is possible for the same parents to feel relief at seeing the kids back at school and to feel nostalgia and a certain tightening in the chest as they watch them depart. If we value our children, the emotions we experience around the return to school show at their best that raising children touches a thoroughly premodern nerve in our souls. We feel a hint that maybe parenting was not meant to be this way. The assembly line, while having ancient predecessors, is thoroughly modern, after all, in its obsessions with forming this perfect child our own way and for our convenience.

This mixture of longings—to see them depart and to see them stay—reminds us of a world not so long ago, when this particular stage of the assembly line was not so strongly defined and when children did not just leave home for seven to ten hours a day. Indeed, this mixture of longings should convict us of an eternal truth about the value of children, a truth that the modern, secular view of children as inconveniences, mere hindrances to our real and proper paid work and creative desires, so readily contradicts with

---

[18]Esteban Ortiz-Ospina, Charlie Giattino, and Max Roser, "Time Use," Our World in Data, November 29, 2020, https://ourworldindata.org/time-use#are-parents-spending-less-time-with-their-kids.

[19]This is indeed a central part of the argument Timothy Carney presents in his book *Family Unfriendly*. Carney notes a number of contributing factors beyond those I mention here, including, to name just one example, the very physical environment in which we dwell—the antifamily (and procar) design of modern neighborhoods.

[20]D'Vera Cohn, "Do Parents Spend Enough Time with Their Children?," PRB, January 17, 2007, www.prb.org/resources/do-parents-spend-enough-time-with-their-children/.

every breath. That default view in our society that sees children as the opposite of fun and productivity has become ingrained even in the church, as declining birthrates among churchgoers reveal.[21]

It is striking that while we as a society worship productivity in our own work lives, we have this same unrealistic and soul-crushing expectation of productivity of our children as well. This idol is thoroughly modern, one of our own making. The polytheistic ancient world, which had gods, major and minor, for what seems like everything—for instance, Cloacina, the goddess of the sewers of the city of Rome—did not have any gods in charge of productivity or work in general. As part of embracing the idol of productivity, we use schools, to which we send our children to enhance our own efficiency in the workplace, to engineer our children as the best of the Americans.

THE BEST OF THE AMERICANS

It all starts with really good genes, as we saw already. Take the hero Heracles, who was already showing his superhuman strength while still in diapers. But every hero then must get schooled, and so Heracles was. The pressure got to him one day in music class. When his lyre teacher mocked his inadequate playing, Heracles killed him in a fit of rage. The pressure to be the best at everything, it appears, was very real. That same pressure dominated the life of another hero, the one whom Homer dubbed "the best of the Achaeans." That hero was none other than Achilles, he whose mother had dutifully dipped him in the Styx to make him invulnerable. Achilles did well in music class, but by the time we meet him as an adult in the *Iliad*, he has one goal only in life: to be "the best of the Achaeans."[22]

One of the foundational concepts in Greek heroic epic is the idea of being the best. While Homer's *Iliad* describes events that take place during the mythical Trojan War, none of the heroes seem to see victory as their main goal in the war. Instead, we see repeatedly as the epic unfolds that the chief

---

[21]Lyman Stone, "Baby Blues: How to Face the Church's Growing Fertility Crisis," *Christianity Today*, August 8, 2022, www.christianitytoday.com/ct/2022/august-web-only/birth-rates-church-attendance -decline-fertility-crisis.html.

[22]Gregory Nagy, *The Best of the Achaeans* (Baltimore: Johns Hopkins University Press, 1979).

goal of each Greek hero, at least, in going to this epic-worthy war was to become the "best of the Achaeans." No, there was no second best. No silver or bronze medals were expected to be awarded. The competition among the heroes was truly all or nothing. Just how badly did the heroes want to win this? When the widely recognized "best of the Achaeans," Achilles, is killed in battle by an arrow to his heel, there is cutthroat competition among several leading heroes for his armor.

Heroes were generally happy about hand-me-down armor. Armor was expensive, after all, and stripping the armor of a defeated enemy as spoils had both material benefits and those of prestige. In the case of Achilles's armor, however, the desire was more symbolic than anything else, even if Achilles did have really good armor—the metalsmith god Hephaestus himself had made it.[23] But the point was: since Achilles was the best of the Achaeans, whoever was going to inherit Achilles's armor was unofficially going to be recognized as inheriting his status. When one of the leading contenders, the hero Ajax, is not chosen for this prize, he dramatically commits suicide, considering his life to be over in dishonor.[24] There is an important cautionary tale here about such all-or-nothing competitions: if there can be only one winner, this means that all but one will be losers. How do you learn to value yourself and your worth in the world as a loser? Is this how you should view yourself? Is this how parents should view their children?

Creating one's child to be the American counterpart to the "best of the Achaeans" is now the goal of many parents who have fully embraced the assembly-line model to molding their perfect baby into the perfect adult. Homeric-style excellence is expected in every activity, and second best is not an option—just ask the Tiger Mom.[25] It begins already with expensive pre-schools and waitlists to get into them. Just ask anyone you know who has sent their child to the local Montessori preschool. It continues with the obsession with just the right model of schooling for the growing student—and,

---

[23]The shield of Achilles is described in very close detail in *Iliad* 18.478-608.
[24]This story forms the plot of Sophocles's tragedy *Ajax*.
[25]Amy Chua, *The Battle Hymn of the Tiger Mother* (New York: Penguin Books, 2011).

by the way, homeschooling can be a part of this assembly-line vision just as much as public or private schooling. One does not have to send one's child away to put them on the assembly line. We are perfectly capable of creating idols out of good things right here at home, thank you very much.

Indeed, the current debates—or, if we are honest, outright culture wars—over education are really disagreements over what different parents consider to be the best assembly line for shaping our children. In the case of public education, in particular, the concern is with optimizing mass production. Children in public schools are objects to be shaped and molded into a particular product in a decidedly procrustean fashion. Don't want this kind of assembly line? Parallels exist, including increasingly more expensive private schools or homeschooling. In some ways, we could even consider the culture wars surrounding the different kinds of schooling, and the content to be allowed or banned in them, as wars over control of the assembly line.

What is the ideal final product supposed to look like, think like, believe like? We cannot quite agree as a society, but we can agree on one thing: we want to control it, because it matters. Education, we see, is never neutral because knowledge is not. Whatever children absorb at this stage on the assembly line is going to mold their bodies, minds, and souls. So, the project of optimizing baby continues year after year, as the stakes in achieving this ideal product only get higher. Historian Dixie Dillon Lane notes that the common culture of excellence and emphasis on grades creates such a crippling fear of failure as to drive even the best of students to cheat in school.[26]

But if all has gone well, congratulations! Sometime around age eighteen or so, this baby, who has just the right eye color and no bodily disabilities (thanks, science!) and all the correct schooling and learning and excellent grades, is ready for the next stage in the assembly line: college. This is where the "best of the Americans" are truly selected, as colleges have rankings that are well-known and revered. Getting into the right college is like being awarded the armor of Achilles: you know you have been marked as the

---

[26]Dixie Dillon Lane, "A.I. Doesn't Cause Cheating. Fear Does," Front Porch Republic, May 24, 2023, www.frontporchrepublic.com/2023/05/a-i-doesnt-cause-cheating-fear-does/.

crème de la crème, so your life after college will obviously be amazing. Except, what if your child does not get into the right college? Will they be damaged goods?

A few years ago, Hollywood reeled from an unusual scandal. No, nothing of the usual sort (sex or drugs or harassment). In this scandal, rather, two mothers could not stand the possibility of their children not getting into the top colleges that they had wanted to attend. So, the mothers bribed their children's way in, concocting rather elaborate (not to mention expensive) schemes to achieve this goal.[27] Many members of the public were shocked, and yet perhaps the secret is: if they had the finances to do it, many more parents would likely do the same. Ensuring that one's child will become the best of the Americans, someone successful in life, demands as much. Colleges themselves only feed this frenzy further, with their own competition over the best students and the highest rankings. Such competition is, after all, good for business.

Except, what is that success to which Hollywood parents and their millions of much more normal counterparts seek to launch their assembly-line-perfected offspring? In AD 14, shortly before his death, the Roman Emperor Augustus launched the classic public-relations stunt considering this very question in connection with his own life: What is success? He wrote his own autobiography with the aim that it be inscribed on his mausoleum after his death, thus serving double duty as his tombstone inscription as well.

Augustus's definition of success in this document is one that comes naturally to us as well. He glides expertly over any potentially problematic episodes in his career—such as proscriptions early in his career, in which he sanctioned the assassination without trial of prominent Roman citizens, emphasizing instead the victories he had achieved, both military and political. In a nutshell, he shows, he became the best of the Romans—quite literally, as his title noted, *princeps*, the leading citizen. But any reader with

---

[27]For coverage of this story, see Sopan Deb, "Felicity Huffman and Lori Loughman: How College Admission Scandal Ensnared Stars," *New York Times*, March 12, 2019, www.nytimes.com/2019/03 /12/arts/huffman-loughlin-college-scandal.html/.

a knowledge of Roman history might ask, At what cost? How many bodies had to pile up for Augustus to build his success?

Augustus's definition of success as a list of his own victories over all others and at the cost of countless lives comes to mind as I reflect on the individualistic definitions of success that too many parents but also colleges and universities use in evaluating their students, current and former. Put simply, the successful alumni about whom parents and institutions brag are typically working at prestigious places and earning a lot of money. They are politicians, doctors, lawyers, filmmakers, journalists, and so on. No one brags about graduates who are missionaries overseas, volunteering or serving somewhere remote and unglamorous, or (worst of all) are homemakers and homeschooling mothers. When it comes to the latter, even the government will weigh in to tell you that all they are doing is dragging down the economy.[28]

It seems that in our society, the assembly line, with its competitive ethos, does not end with college. It only keeps going for the rest of our lives. Selfish to the core, this ethos puts the idol of success first, far ahead of any family relationships, actual or potential. Is it any wonder that so many from the most recent generation of young people raised on the assembly line are bypassing marriage and children? Achilles and Augustus built their successes on corpses. Today's best of the Americans might not do that, but their view of the value of human lives, including their own, is not that much better. In competition, after all, there can be only one winner.

The much-maligned American concept of participation trophies ironically exists side by side with this competitive ethos that so many parents hold, pushing their children to achieve more and more, and do so earlier, all with the goal of getting into the best college and then, of course, living the best life. And yet, perhaps we should celebrate these participation trophies just a bit more. The alternative, as the stories of both Achilles and Ajax remind us,

---

[28]See Ivana Greco, "Biden Administration Claims Full-Time Mothers Hurt the Economy," The Federalist, May 10, 2023, https://thefederalist.com/2023/05/10/biden-administration-claims-full-time-mothers-hurt-the-economy/; and Greco, "A Home Security System," American Compass, September 21, 2022, https://americancompass.org/a-home-security-system/.

is ugly in its reduction of people to the demeaning categories of winners and losers, placing a value (possibly with real dollar signs involved) on real flesh and blood, mortal creatures with immortal souls.

Stepping off the assembly line requires us to admit, first and foremost, that maybe the assembly-line approach to raising image bearers is not God-honoring or, as even secular mental health experts would say, healthy. Maybe the goal should not be to create the perfect baby or child or adult but to delight in each image bearer's unique ways of reflecting God's goodness and beauty, all while recognizing the built-in, all-too-human limitations. Yes, we are beloved children and image bearers. But as theologian Kelly Kapic reminds in his beautiful book *You're Only Human: How Your Limits Reflect God's Design and Why That's Good News*, we are indeed "only human."[29] Only if we fully accept both truths can we—and our children—step off the assembly line.

> **Stepping off the assembly line requires us to admit, first and foremost, that maybe the assembly-line approach to raising image bearers is not God-honoring or, as even secular mental health experts would say, healthy.**

STEPPING OFF THE ASSEMBLY LINE

In an iconic episode of *I Love Lucy*, the show's heroine takes a job at the chocolate factory. Packing products at a conveyor belt that keeps moving faster and faster, she finds that she just cannot keep up. Hilarity ensues. But such assembly-line processes are less funny in real life—especially when we ourselves or our own children are the products on the assembly line, moving ever faster just to keep up with unrealistic expectations of this modern life.

The quest for perfecting humanity is ever advancing, right along with medical science. Can we produce humans who are healthier, stronger, taller, leaner, prettier, smarter, and longer-lived? What will it take to make such a modern-day Frankenstein's monster? These are questions that the public

---

[29] Kelly Kapic, *You're Only Human: How Your Limits Reflect God's Design and Why That's Good News* (Grand Rapids, MI: Brazos, 2022).

asks, and science answers—although this is a bit of a chicken-and-the-egg kind of conversation. Leading the way in these quests is the burgeoning field of transhumanism, which seeks to optimize humans with the help of technology and artificial intelligence. But there are costs, as writers such as Mary Harrington and Jennifer Egan warn in their respective explorations of these optimization experiments on the physical body and on the human mind.[30]

In her critique of the cost of transhumanism for the human body, Harrington notes that it is women's bodies most of all who bear the cost—indeed, using the term *bear*, traditionally associated with a bearing of a different sort, is ironic here. In her public speaking, Harrington repeatedly dubs the pill "the first transhumanist technology." But it is merely the first of many other technological advances that allow people today to turn their bodies into build-your-own dreams. The process, Harrington argues, is deeply anti-woman, as optimizing the body involves erasing everything that had made women unique, especially their ability to carry and birth a baby. Egan presents similarly strong cautioning of the dreams of optimizing the human mind in her novel *Candy House*. In this story, characters explore a technology, "Own Your Unconscious," that allows everyone who opts in to download their memories—every memory they have ever had—to common storage and share these memories with other subscribers to the service. Say it with me: What could possibly go wrong?

Harrington and Egan show that the obvious cost of the assembly line is, well, our humanity. This cost has significant metaphysical implications. It seems that optimizing the self through modern technology will cost you your soul—a Faustian bargain, we call it, after Goethe's protagonist who sold his soul to the devil in exchange for just such optimizations. In Faust's case, the warning might say: results all too typical.

If we are honest with ourselves, we will admit that seeking the kind of perfection that the assembly line process promises will only drive us to despair. Why? Because no matter how perfect we try to be—or how perfect we

---

[30]Mary Harrington, *Feminism Against Progress* (Washington, DC: Regnery, 2023); Jennifer Egan, *Candy House* (New York: Scribner, 2022).

try to make our children—we are all broken in myriad ways, some more visible than others. But the good news is that God fixes broken things and welcomes broken people. Instead of urging us to strive to create perfection right now, God promises to bless the broken and heal their bodies someday. That is the real hope of the gospel promises. We do not have to outdo God. He is in control all along, and the plans he has for us and for our children are much more beautiful than we can imagine. In light of these promises, what would it look like to step off the assembly line right now?

It could start with filling our minds with more edifying content than the modern entertainment industry and social media encourages. We have internalized, perhaps without even realizing it, not just the assembly line's rule over our lives but also the need to brag about how much faster our personal conveyor belts are moving—done on social media and in Christmas family newsletters. I am reminded of the satirical family Christmas letter that writer and counselor M. Elizabeth Carter wrote in the voice of an imaginary mom bragging about the incredibly exaggerated achievements of her children in a holiday newsletter, trying to put a positive spin even on the negative developments and concluding with sappy prayer requests.[31]

Our bodies are what we eat, but sometimes we forget that our minds and souls are also what we consume. Reading God's Word and cultivating our spiritual health will help us draw closer to God. So, we should read edifying books, look at beautiful art, listen to beautiful music, and enjoy God's creation in all its goodness.[32] The list can keep going. Reorienting ourselves and our children toward eternity will help us value humanity in God's image not just as something we claim but as something we live out every day.

But, of course, the vast majority of Christian parents in antiquity, just as today, do not represent these polar extremes of pagan values or martyrdom.

---

[31]M. Elizabeth Carter, "'Tis the Season!," Current, November 8, 2022, https://currentpub.com /2022/11/08/tis-the-season-2/.

[32]A number of recent books serve as guides for doing this. To name just a few that I have appreciated, see Elissa Yukiko Weichbrodt, *Redeeming Vision: A Christian Guide for Looking and Learning from Art* (Grand Rapids, MI: Baker Academic, 2023); Jessica Hooten Wilson, *Reading for the Love of God: How to Read as a Spiritual Practice* (Grand Rapids, MI: Brazos, 2023); and Makoto Fujimura, *Art and Faith: A Theology of Making* (New Haven, CT: Yale University Press, 2021).

At our best, rather, we would like to be more like Monica, the mother of Augustine, who sent her child away to different schooling experiences reluctantly, embracing the assembly-line version of her own day while hoping for social and economic advancement for him. But through it all, she prayed for his salvation for many years, even as he walked in darkness. Prayer, we too often forget, to our own detriment and that of our children, is the most powerful tool that we have for resisting the assembly line.

Prayer, we too often forget, to our own detriment and that of our children, is the most powerful tool that we have for resisting the assembly line.

What would it look like for us to step off the assembly line, and to parent like Monica today, to view our children, these sinful but oh-so-beautiful image bearers, the way she viewed Augustine, whether as a colicky infant, as a recalcitrant, pear-stealing teen, or as a willful young man, eager to deceive, sin, and do life his own way? This valuing of our children should begin with praying for our children and rejoicing each day over their existence.

We need to pray not just for them but also for transformation in our own hearts, so hardened by life in secular modernity and its decidedly corrupt messaging about priorities in the here and now. Only then might we send them out, whether to school now or into life as adults, not as products on the assembly line but as the cherished children of our own flesh and blood as well as of the God whose image they bear.

In this chapter, we examined the symptom of devaluing children as precious image bearers, reducing them instead to assembly-line products for parents' enjoyment or not—their choice. This symptom, we saw, logically flowed from the symptom examined in chapter two, the devaluing of the physical and emotional work latent in the process of women's pregnancy. Taken together, these two phenomena show the hostility of our society to motherhood and the work of nurturing children, these now-devalued products of pregnancy.

But the question remains: What would our modern world of progress have a woman do instead of the work of mothering and valuing a baby? Or, if she does have the baby that she so desperately wants, against society's warnings, how might she redeem her life afterward? The answer to these questions involves our society's ingrained idealization of work in a way that marginalizes or even excludes children and motherhood. Let us turn next to this final symptom of devaluing children and motherhood and the insidious work of this symptom in our world. Our gateway into this world will revolve around women's creative work, such as writing. The framework of thought around this kind of work, however, applies more broadly to our society's general discomfort with the idea of working while mothering, or perhaps mothering while working.

4

MOTHERHOOD AND CREATIVE WORK; MOTHERHOOD VERSUS CREATIVE WORK

IN 1957, RENOWNED FRENCH LITERARY and social critic Roland Barthes published a collection of essays, *Mythologies*.[1] In these short and poignant essays, Barthes unpacks popular, everyday phenomena and objects, teasing out in the process their nature as powerful symbols or myths representative of social values. Among a wide range of topics, he considered the national obsession with wrestling—how lowbrow! Another essay analyzed the consumption of steak and fries—the bloodier the steak, the better, but what does that mean? Yet another essay deconstructed advertisements for laundry detergents—welcome to the modern life of luxury! But the essay from this collection that concerns us right now is "Romans et enfants" ("Novels and Children").

---

[1]For a recent translation, see Roland Barthes, *Mythologies: The Complete Edition, in a New Translation*, trans. Richard Howard and Annette Lavers (New York: Hill and Wang, 2013).

GLORIFYING WORK AND WRITING OUT MOTHERHOOD

In his mordant essay, Barthes takes to task the women's magazine *Elle* for its profiles of women novelists. In introducing these writers, the magazine used the following formula: name, number of children, number of novels. Barthes was not impressed. He found the ready and inevitable inclusion of the two statistics side by side for each woman novelist to present condescending and damaging messaging about the societally expected connection of women's productivity in their writing and their child production. Women, sputtered Barthes, are presented in these profiles as creatures who give birth to novels and children in alternation—*quel scandale!* Further implied is the no less scandalous (in Barthes's view) societal expectation that their novel making had better not impede their baby making.

Elle's profiles, for Barthes, were ultimately backward and harmful in their emphasis that each novelist was always a mother as much as a writer. Would it not be enough instead to cast these women merely as writers, he wondered, as we do for men? But Barthes's objections, which seem at first glance to stand firmly in favor of women's empowerment as equal partners in the publishing world and the modern workplace more generally, also reflect the problematic implications of this messaging.

It is not Barthes's fault, but this desire to entirely decouple motherhood from work, with a firm emphasis on the supreme value of the latter, is deeply ingrained in the modern labor market. One might quibble that in the modern workplace, men, too, are expected to be workers first and thus face the same expectations. The problem is that the biological requirements that pregnancy and breastfeeding place on women make it impossible for mothers to effectively separate their maternal identity from all else. Unfazed by biology, in the modern workplace our society writes children and motherhood out, casting the resulting sanitized view of women worker bees as a measure of empowerment. But such empowerment is nothing but an illusion. Instead, the result is the devaluing of children and motherhood in favor of more economically valuable productive outputs. Novels? They are tangible products, and (hopefully) they sell well. Artwork? Likewise.

Children? Not so much. They just drain the time and mental and emotional energy that a woman could have been devoting instead to her art or other work. They are always a cost, never a profit.

Other self-identified feminist thinkers, from Betty Friedan in *The Feminine Mystique* to, more recently, Julie Phillips in *The Baby on the Fire Escape: Creativity, Motherhood, and the Mind-Baby Problem*, have continued to wrestle with the challenge of what it means to be a mother who loves writing or her work more generally. Ultimately, secular writers on this theme invariably reach the same conclusion, although degrees of force differ: children are important, but they are not more important than a woman's creative desires. In fact, they are not even more important than a woman's basic desire to work outside the home, although Friedan was willing to give children shared place of prominence with these other works that a mother could be doing.[2]

For Friedan, motherhood was not the competitor for a woman's affections per se; rather, the lack of sufficient intellectual activity and meaningful work was. Others who followed and continue to follow in the same vein nevertheless have gone a few steps further. In placing children on equal footing with a woman's output and bemoaning the lost libraries or museums of creative works that overburdened mothers were never able to produce, writers such as Phillips end up presenting a message that is less conflicted than what they might seem to have in mind. In an either-or choice, women's creative works should always win.

Phillips's book aims to celebrate the award-winning artists and writers who chose ultimately to put their artistic production first, ahead of their children. Contrary to the author's intent, however, the book reads instead as a sobering catalog of human sacrifices. In each case it is the child or children who are sacrificed. There is painter Alice Neel, who abandoned her daughter with her first husband in Cuba to move back to New York City and begin her career as an artist. That daughter struggled with coming to terms with that

---

[2]Erika Bachiochi, *The Rights of Women: Reclaiming a Lost Vision* (Notre Dame, IN: Notre Dame University Press, 2021), 155-64.

abandonment her entire life, eventually committing suicide in her fifties. Novelist Doris Lessing likewise left behind two children and a first husband—in this case in then-Rhodesia—to move to London and begin her writing career. Novelist Alice Walker's only daughter, Rebecca, felt lonely and ignored by her mother when a child. At fourteen, Rebecca got pregnant and had an abortion—actions she herself attributed to maternal neglect.[3] While mother and daughter were always close, Rebecca always knew she came second to her mother's art.

These are all stories of mothers sacrificing their children on the altar of their craft. Or, to use another metaphor, one no less apt, these are tales of mothers devouring their young to grow and flourish as artists. Instead of nurturing their children, these mothers grew from their children's diminishment. It seems, even as some of these mothers abandoned or neglected their children, these children's mere existence nevertheless transformed their creative mothers' work into something more profound than before—a topic about which Walker was particularly outspoken.

Phillips concludes that every one of her subjects made the right choices. The proof lies in the widely recognized—and, let's face it, widely sold—brilliance of their artistic output. And to ensure this artistic output, the creative mother needs two key ingredients, Phillips notes: time and self. Both require a degree of selfishness.[4] It may seem unfortunate, but that is just a fact of life. Some sacrifices, therefore, are simply necessary. Of course, this recipe for artistic success presumes that we belong wholly to ourselves—an anthropological stance that is decidedly atheistic. In this view, the children who were sacrificed were autonomous beings, just like their creative mothers. If they felt neglected, perhaps it was their own fault for not recognizing and embracing their own autonomy and for relying too much on their mothers.

But discussions of creative work are not the only ones where such assumptions come up. In a provocative piece titled "Designing Woman," Leah

---

[3] Julie Phillips, *The Baby on the Fire Escape: Creativity, Motherhood, and the Mind-Baby Problem* (New York: Norton, 2022), 234.
[4] Phillips, *Baby on the Fire Escape*, 273-74.

Libresco Sargeant provides a Barthes-worthy social commentary on the use of the breast pump in the contemporary workplace to enable—or is it to force?—women to get back to work as quickly as possible after giving birth.[5] The pump is a powerful machine, as it allows a mother to be away from her baby while still continuing to provide her baby with necessary nourishment. Hooked up to a machine at regular intervals even while miles away from her baby, the mother will simply pump milk while continuing to work at her desk. Her maternal functions, therefore, need not disrupt her (paid) work productivity.

And yet, Libresco Sargeant notes, this technologically assisted ideal denies nature in powerful ways. Children will always disrupt our lives, she notes, because that is their purpose. And mothers' bodies do not operate quite as straightforwardly as the machine presupposes, because our bodies are not machines. A nursing mother's body is closely attuned to her baby, responding to that baby's (or, really, any baby's!) cry by letting down milk. The denial of adequate maternity leave, which forces so many women back to work as little as three weeks after giving birth, fights against this natural created order, by which a mother truly is a mother to her baby, first and foremost. The breast pump's technology has decidedly transhumanist aims, as it attempts to improve on nature by "designing woman" for the modern workplace, writing a baby out of its mother's arms and writing motherhood out of existence, creating instead just a worker, hooked up to a strange machine but working nevertheless.

Sure, one might object, wet-nurses existed in previous periods of world history, offering a similar path to freedom for a mother at the cost of denying nature. But we should note that relatively few women could afford these wet-nurses, whereas in our society the pump is now viewed as an essential item to put on every baby registry, if the mother has any inclination toward breastfeeding. But, the question arises, in this world in which technological enhancements facilitate the separation of mother and baby, allowing the

---

[5]Leah Libresco Sargeant, "Designing Woman," *Comment*, September 15, 2022, https://comment.org /designing-woman/.

mother to be a worker first and a generally fully autonomous person, what is the difference between a mother and a surrogate these days? The line, it appears, has become blurred, as some women give birth to children with whom they share no genetic material, while others outsource all child-rearing of the children to whom they have given birth. A variety of modern advances, set to optimize human experience through machinery, have now conspired to undo the motherhood of the past. Or, rather, the machines or inventions do no such conspiring of their own. All they can do is reflect the values of those who promote their use.

POSTMODERN SURROGACY AND THE UNDOING OF MOTHERHOOD

In a recent satirical essay, a fictional mother nonchalantly walks the reader through a typical day of juggling the unrealistic demands of her child's pre-school and her high-profile job: "I am a freelance neurosurgeon, the only job that is both well-paying enough to afford $30,000 in tuition and flexible enough to deal with all the school holidays."[6] This mother, the essay makes clear in humorous detail that leaves the reader wanting to weep as well as laugh, wants to be involved in her preschool-aged son's life—although, the essay's conclusion jokingly notes, she does not yet care about her infant daughter, who is too young for school. The mother's contributions largely consist of helping with projects that others have thought up for her pre-schooler and chauffeuring him to his expensive school and activities.

The essay is undoubtedly funny. Yet, this mother and the very real and not really funny phenomenon she represents in our society is the quintessential postmodern surrogate. Indeed, while this mother is fictional, her description of her day's routine bears uncanny resemblance to the routine of an over-worked lawyer-mother whom legal scholar Ivana Greco describes in an ar-ticle advocating for better family policy.[7] The mother in both cases may

---

[6]Ruyi Wen, "A Parent's Typical Day, as Envisioned by My Child's Preschool," McSweeney's, Decem-ber 30, 2022, www.mcsweeneys.net/articles/a-parents-typical-day-as-envisioned-by-my-childs-preschool/.

[7]Ivana Greco, "A Home Security System," *American Compass*, September 21, 2022, https://american compass.org/a-home-security-system/.

technically parent her children, but she is not fully their mother in a traditional formational sense. Societal expectations and her work conspire to prevent her from spending time with her children. Greco's work in advocating for better support and recognition of the value of homemakers is historically rooted and reminds us, yet again, that the way things are is not the only way they can be.

Once upon a time, not so long ago, a woman who gave birth to a child was that child's mother. This reality, so simple and so basic in its biological and theological senses, had repercussions and expectations for the woman in question.[8] First and foremost, of course, she conceived and carried that child for nine months until birth, ideally growing in necessary maternal virtues in the process. Next, she hoped, if all went well, *Deo volente*—if no childhood diseases or accidents intervened, which was a big if, to be fair—to care for this child and raise the child to adulthood, not only contributing her genetic material to the making of this child at the cellular level but also forming this child's environment, morality, and education. Maintaining a close relationship with that child, ideally through a complete family unit that included that child's father and perhaps siblings, the mother expected to participate actively in everything that would result in raising a whole person, ready to launch into life.

Yet, as science became king of the modern world, some began to dream that perhaps this process could be perfected, like everything else around. Locomotion of people and goods was greatly sped up by such inventions as the steam engine, the railroad, and finally air travel. Likewise, agricultural yields were multiplied exponentially through modern practices and mechanization. As Isaac Asimov's futuristic novels predicted already in the 1950s, food could be manufactured entirely from yeast-like products in state-of-the-art labs—a reality we now see manifest in lab-grown meat, even if the concept remains deservedly controversial.[9] If all else is up for optimization

---

[8]As we saw, for example, in Agnes Howard, *Showing: What Pregnancy Tells Us About Being Human* (Grand Rapids, MI: Eerdmans, 2020).

[9]Elizabeth Wainwright, "Will Lab-Grown Meat Save Us?," *Plough*, October 17, 2022, www.plough .com/en/topics/justice/environment/will-labgrown-meat-save-us.

through modern technology, why not improve somehow on this messy business of person making at some or all stages of the process? How about some lab-optimized humans to go along with that lab-grown meat and genetically enhanced grain seeds?

In his essay "Humanae Vitae and the Brave New World," Catholic theologian John Cavadini analyzes the repercussions of such an approach to the making of image bearers through Aldous Huxley's dystopian novel *Brave New World*, a novel I have mentioned a few times.[10] When, as in this novel, humans are manufactured entirely in labs and grown in artificial wombs, the word *mother* becomes a dirty insult that makes people blush. As for family, the entire concept has, of course, been abolished through that technology. Freed from responsibilities to care for others, each member of such a scientifically advanced society can live in blissful, sexually liberated hedonism until government-mandated death by euthanasia at a certain point in late middle age, just before the body fails so much as to make the person a burden on others.

As it happens, through the modern technology of surrogacy, Huxley's vision has now become a partial reality. An embryo created in a petri dish can, following rigorous inspection to ensure genetic perfection, be medically implanted in the womb of a woman who is of no biological relation but (usually out of financial desperation) is willing to work as a gestational surrogate to carry this child. The result is a brave new world of our own making, and much messier in some ways than even Huxley could have foreseen.

Feminist scholar Sophie Lewis has been particularly critical of this practice of modern surrogacy, "womb rental," whereby it is generally wealthy couples who take advantage of this expensive technology, usually hiring a woman of a much lower socioeconomic status to carry their child to term.[11] Lewis rightly highlights the ethical tragedies manifested by the children borne by surrogates. These women, after all, are treated merely as objects,

---

[10]John Cavadini, "Humanae Vitae and the Brave New World," Church Life Journal, October 21, 2022, https://churchlifejournal.nd.edu/articles/humanae-vitae-and-the-brave-new-world/.

[11]Sophie Lewis, *Full Surrogacy Now: Feminism Against Family* (Brooklyn, NY: Verso, 2019).

vessels, walking wombs, who then give up to the biological parents the children whom their bodies nourished intimately and caringly through the nine months of pregnancy. Their bodies pay the price—as all bodies who have undergone the ordeal of pregnancy and childbirth do—but reap no reward of a child of their own to raise and nurture. And while they are paid for their services, the fee ends up being laughably low.

To be clear, at the same time, I am not saying that better pay for surrogates would suddenly remove any ethical concerns from this practice or that, say, the realization of Huxley's ideal of a fully nonhuman gestation in a baby hatchery would be the optimal solution here. We might also acknowledge here the existence of concubines in various societies in antiquity and beyond, whose purpose was largely reproductive—and whose position therefore was exploitative. Indeed, few evils are as horrifying as breeding slaves. Yet, there is something nefariously new in the plot twists that modern science has brought forth in the realm of surrogacy.

Can a woman ever forget a child to whom she has given birth, asks Isaiah 49:15? But then, is a child genetically unrelated to a surrogate but implanted in an artificial medical setting truly the child of her womb? Would such a mother, carrying a child without any genetic connection to her, not be better off simply forgetting this child? Except the scars and memories borne of an intimate nine-month relationship make it rather difficult to forget a bond this indescribably powerful. Early on, there were occasions of surrogates going to court to claim custody of the child they had carried. Subverting nature in so unnatural a way, it appears, takes a heavy toll on the psyche. Lewis's controversial conclusion, ironically, is that the best or only solution to these dilemmas of surrogacy is the abolition of gender and of family as we know it altogether.[12] In resolving the crisis of unnatural actions, the only path forward may appear to be yet more unnatural solutions.

But even as Lewis and others have rightly criticized the ethical dilemmas of gestational surrogacy, made possible by modern science, there is a worse surrogacy afoot that remains unexamined and perhaps was never predicted

---

[12]Sophie Lewis, *Abolish the Family: A Manifesto for Care and Liberation* (Brooklyn, NY: Verso, 2022).

until it gradually materialized in our world. Let us now turn to the mother at the center of the satirical essay with which I opened this section. Our fictional freelance neurosurgeon exemplifies the phenomenon that has quietly yet no less perniciously invaded our world. We are only beginning to see its repercussions on family relationships and society at large. Our society's demands on parents have created a curious creature: the post-modern surrogate. These are mothers who are mere vessels, carrying their own children to birth but then treating them as objects to be shaped into something spectacular through exceptional education by others.

Gestational surrogates are hired to grow a child in the womb, surren-dering the baby to the biological parents after birth. But what about these unintended surrogates—the mothers unable to shape or raise their children but who must give them up to "professionals" who will take care of them and educate them from birth in the most scientific way possible? We saw some of this in the previous chapter's analysis of the assembly-line life of the ideal child. But as we consider the mother's side of this story, we see the stripping away of choices, all in the name of creating workers who are societally conditioned to place their work—creative or merely corporate—ahead of their children.

Ultimately, in considering our society's double lie that work is more im-portant than children and that motherhood should always come second to work, including such creative work as writing, we would do well to reflect on the close theological connection between creating words and creating life. God's earliest words, as presented in Genesis 1, had creative, generative power in speaking creation into being. Furthermore, the first craft project in the world involved God shaping the first man, Adam, out of dirt and breathing life into him. In our own writing, in the use of words for the purpose of creating something new, God's words of delight in us continue to enthrall and call us as his creations.

Reflecting on language and words as God's generative creations should call us back to the central place of humanity in God's vision of creation whenever we forget well-ordered priorities. Thinkers such as Barthes demand that we write children and motherhood out of women's lives in order to privilege their other creations, but we have to remember, this lie can only exist in a worldview that has no God.

Sometimes we forget that the way the world is right now is not how it has to be. Let us consider two glimpses of a better balance, of a more theologically well-ordered anthropology. I turn to two stories of very different creative mothers from the ones Phillips celebrates. Their stories show that while the tension between obligations to one's art and one's children is real, it does not always have to conclude the way that the most recent iteration of feminism generally suggests. These two creative women's experiences furthermore challenge the idea that in order to create, a mother must belong wholly to herself. It is, rather, in the giving away of self to love others that these two mothers create beautiful stories that continue to move and inspire readers centuries later.

> Sometimes we forget that the way the world is right now is not how it has to be.

THE ACCIDENTAL WRITERS: A STORY OF TWO MOTHERS' JOURNALS

In a gloomy prison about 1,820 years ago, a young nursing mother, desperately missing her baby, concludes the journal that she has been writing over the previous few weeks. Tomorrow she will die. She has never written anything like this journal before. But then, she has never faced a challenge like this one before either. Raised in a sheltered home before her marriage, her life seemed so ordinary, so unexceptional for her place and time. Until she met Jesus.

This is the story of Perpetua, a noblewoman who was martyred in Carthage in AD 203 along with her enslaved woman, Felicity, and several men who were also convicted of the same crime—acceptance of Christ and the rejection of Roman religion. After her death, someone from the local church lovingly edited her journal, added an introduction with more background and a conclusion with the description of the actual execution, and published it under the title *The Passion of the Saints Perpetua and Felicity*.[13]

Journals, perhaps more than most other types of writing, reveal their author's personality, but as with anything written, they also reveal something about the writer qua writer. In Perpetua's case, her journal reveals that she was not merely literate. An elegant writer, she tells her story with emotion, expertly bringing the reader into her experiences while deliberately structuring it into three narrative episodes punctuated by three intervening visions. Such tripartite division was a favorite Roman rhetorical technique. There is, in other words, much art and aesthetic awareness in her journal, as one would expect of someone well-read, well-educated, and thoughtful about the act of writing. Even the act of writing a journal is one through which she subtly connects her work to a specific genre of Roman literature: the *commentarii*.

It is important to keep in mind the rather different nature of the genre of personal journals in Perpetua's world compared to our own. Today, the idea of someone keeping a journal is perfectly normal and acceptable—my husband has crates of notebooks of his old childhood journals, for instance, which he started writing at the age of six. Details about family trips abound, as do observations about day-to-day activities. Our eight-year-old has been keeping his own journal for the past year or so as well. Neither of these collections of documents are intended for public consumption. They are, rather, personal mementos, reflecting a desire to process and remember events important to no one other than the writer for the most part.

By contrast, in the Roman world, all writing was inherently public facing. Just think of all the letters that survive from the Roman world, including those in the New Testament. Far from what we think of when we write letters or emails—personal correspondence—these were all written as public documents to be disseminated widely, even if they did have a specific addressee

---

[13]For a translation, see W. H. Shewring, trans., *The Passion of Perpetua and Felicity* (London, 1931), available at Medieval Sourcebook, https://sourcebooks.fordham.edu/source/perpetua.asp.

(or group of addressees) to begin with. It was the most important individuals in society who kept what may be the closest relative to Perpetua's journal: military commanders, who kept their own journals on campaign with the goal of publishing them after.

Perhaps the most famous representative of the genre is Caesar's *Gallic War*, the carefully crafted campaign log from his campaigns against Rome's much-feared neighbors in the 50s BC. We will get to the devaluing of human life that pervades Caesar's journal in chapter six. Right now, however, we can consider another aspect of the typical Roman worldview that comes through in this journal: cultural heroes.

In the Roman world, cultural heroes—those individuals whom everyone wanted not only to imitate but also emulate—were the great generals and politicians. The two roles, after all, went hand in hand. It was through political victories that a leader could gain a high enough office to allow him (always a "him"!) to command an army in a foreign war. Through distinguished victories in foreign wars, he gained more political capital, allowing him to win additional electoral victories at home. The cycle continued throughout each successful politician's life.

Caesar used his journals from the Gallic campaigns to court political favor back at Rome by publishing reports of his successes against the Gauls, Rome's most fearsome enemy, while still on campaign. This meant that although he was far away from the city for nearly a decade, his political star and popular appeal were ascendant nevertheless. His later biographers, Suetonius and Plutarch, emphasize his popularity among the people just as they note fellow Roman senators' fear of that very popularity.

Caesar's writings already in antiquity were a mainstay of Roman education, right along with Cicero and Vergil. Thus it would not be surprising if Perpetua was familiar with Caesar's journal from the education that she likely received from a tutor at home. She likely thought of the genre of military commanders' *commentarii* as her own role model in keeping a journal of her spiritual campaigns as they unfolded. Spiritual warfare is, appropriately and likely not coincidentally, a major theme running through her journal. Her visions show the battle of Christ and the forces of evil over the souls of believers. In her final vision, strikingly, she sees herself transformed into a man for a duel with an Egyptian warrior. Writing in a man's genre in a man's world, Perpetua the mother uses this genre to show her artistic brilliance alongside her love for her child and most of all her love for Christ.

But I am getting ahead of myself in telling the story. With this important background in mind, let us get back to her story as we can imagine it unfolding. What is she thinking and feeling as she is still in the prison on that final night? She wonders over the previous days, as her body, used to nourishing her infant son and so attuned to his needs, feels the physical pain of his absence. While he was able to be with her in her prison for some of her time there, it was not right for him to stay there with her until the end. At this point, she is at peace with his absence and with her fate. But she is not alone in this prison. Together with her is an enslaved pregnant woman, Felicity, guilty of the same crime: professing belief in Jesus in a world where this is an offense. As a result, she is subject to the same sentence: death in the arena. But pregnant women cannot be executed according to Roman law, so the unresolved question looms over the narrative: Will the two women die together tomorrow, or will one of them have to wait a bit longer, until she delivers her baby?

Suddenly, Felicity wonders at the unexpected sensation coursing through her body. Could this be labor? An hour later, there is no doubt. The contractions grow stronger, longer, and the spaces between them shorten. As her baby finally makes its appearance toward dawn, she is exhausted from this sleepless night, her last one on earth. But she is also grateful that she will now be able to face her execution together with the others with whom she had been arrested.

It is not that Felicity does not love her newborn baby. She feels an extraordinary sensation of overwhelming love, looking at this tiny creature whom she had felt in her body for so many months and who is now, for these brief hours, in her arms. Originally enslaved in the house of the young mother and writer with whom she is now imprisoned as an equal in crime, she also knows that she is not afraid of death, if it means an eternity with God. For the two women, the noblewoman and her enslaved fellow believer, their faith has become the great equalizer, so extraordinary for their society, which views this faith as a threat to order in the empire. It will be through Perpetua's *commentarii* that these heroic feats will achieve glory in the Christian community equal to the most famous Roman military commanders.

Over a millennium and a half later, in a cold New England farmhouse, a hassled wife, mother, and midwife makes the unusual decision for a woman of her place and time to begin keeping a journal. She will continue writing it, logging her deliveries but also more mundane details such as the annual planting of cabbages, until her death twenty-seven years later. This is the story of Martha Ballard, a midwife in rural Maine, who faithfully kept her journal from 1785, when her midwifery practice began to ramp up, until her death at the age of seventy-seven in 1812. While her journal is now safely ensconced in the Maine state library archives, it is best known through the Pulitzer Prize–winning book about it by historian Laurel Thatcher Ulrich.[14]

In introducing the midwife and her diary, Ulrich notes her almost poetic language at times as she mentions divine providence in her life: "Here the religious sentiments become a kind of refrain, punctuating and accentuating each stage in the narrative. Such a passage reveals a storyteller, if not a writer, at work."[15] Far from simply throwing words on a page, it seems, we are looking at a woman who often (albeit not always) instinctively felt and thought about beauty, something we know also from her affinity for the aesthetics of clothing and home decorations, modest as they always were in her life.

While Ballard's diary is not quite as one-of-a-kind as that of Perpetua was for her respective time period, it is still sufficiently unusual for a woman. In other words, just like Perpetua, through the mere decision to write it, Ballard decided to take on an art form generally and most commonly associated

---

[14]Laurel Thatcher Ulrich, *A Midwife's Tale: The Life of Martha Ballard, Based on Her Diary, 1785–1812* (New York: Vintage, 1991).
[15]Ulrich, *Midwife's Tale*, 8.

with men in her time period—we might name George Washington's diaries, for instance—and adopt it for her own purposes. This meant keeping the form of the genre, logging key daily events, while writing about vastly different subject matter: delivering babies. Let us get just a few more glimpses of these stories that Martha Ballard so carefully and artfully—but not too artfully—inscribed in her twenty-seven-plus years of writing.

It is a cold winter's night, and the snowfall, which began as just a gentle shower, has increased to a full-blown storm. But babies come when they come, as the midwife knows. She is therefore not surprised to get a summons in the middle of the night. Quickly getting bundled up, she resolutely gets on a horse and crosses the frozen Kennebec River to get to the laboring woman on the other side. Labors are challenging because they are so unpredictable. Sometimes she has been awakened out of bed and rushed to assist only to discover that a false labor was afoot. Other times, she arrived too late—a problem because missing a birth meant also missing her fee. But most of the time she arrived just in time to assist, as is the case this night. Her work combines the tasks of what a modern-day doula or labor coach would do, coaching a woman through the physically and mentally grueling hours of contractions and pushing, with the work of an informally trained medical professional, which she was. She takes pride in her extraordinary success rates. Unlike the doctors of her day, who had only recently begun challenging midwives' competence and competing with them for their work, she has hardly ever lost a mother or child.

It is midday, and the exhausted midwife, who has not slept all night, is riding home across the frozen, snow-covered river. She successfully delivered the baby a couple of hours ago, and after making sure that all is well, she has just now left the mother and baby resting together with the rest of their family. Her work is done, although she might check on the new mother in a few days just to make sure that she and the baby are continuing to do well. Later in the day, she will add an entry to her journal about her nighttime adventure. She has delivered some babies before, but only recently, now that her own children are all out of infancy and early childhood, has she made midwifery into a bona fide career. She enjoys the task of helping other women and feels confident in her craft. Her faith, gentle yet strong, comes across clearly in her journal, manifest in her regular expressions of gratitude to God for keeping her and the women whose babies she delivers safe in their most vulnerable moments.

Ballard was a mother herself, nine times over, and she knew from personal experience what it felt like to give birth. But she had a quiet pride in her work, as her writings show. Last but not least, her habit of writing about this work, and in a way that makes this journal much more than just a matter-of-fact log of deliveries and payments, continually shows her identity and instincts as a creative writer.

Not all creative mothers have historically thought of themselves as writers first. Both Perpetua and Martha Ballard are examples of writing mothers who most likely never thought of themselves as writers first. If asked about their identity or primary occupation, their writing would never have come up in response. But write they did, led instinctively to tell a powerful story of which they were an anchoring part, even as they had no idea who—if anyone—would ever read their journals. It is through their writing alone that we know them and their stories. Challenging Barthes's recommendation of the great divorce of identities, their motherhood, writing, faith, and faithful service to those around them interlaced in ways that cannot be easily disentangled.

CONCLUSION: DIAGNOSING THE SICK BODY

In the sanctuary of the pagan god Asclepius in the city of Epidaurus in Greece, thousands of tiny and full-scale stone ears, arms, hands, feet, breasts, and other body parts have been found, some carved of stone and others made of clay. The sick who flocked to the sanctuary for pilgrimage came in search of a miracle of healing that they hoped to get via incubation, as they were admitted into the sanctuary to sleep there for the night. Sick for years, in some cases, their desperate hope was that Asclepius, son of the god Apollo and a god of healing in his own right, would visit them in a dream and would reveal a cure or perhaps even heal them in the night outright. Those healed eventually dedicated a model of the formerly ailing body part as a token of their gratitude.

The dream to be healed is powerful. But knowing that healing is needed requires first recognizing that the body is sick. In this first part of the book, I considered just a few symptoms that are so common in everyday modern life that no one even recognizes them as symptoms of widespread disease. Ultimately, the symptom that ties all others together is that of absence: the absence of the dream of becoming a mother and having children who will disrupt one's otherwise perfectly ordinary, modern workaholic life. It is difficult to dream of something one does not see idealized or actualized. And it is difficult to be countercultural in choosing to dream of something that is actively under attack and is being written out of existence. How can we say that the sickness is the devaluing of motherhood and of human life more generally when doctors in our society label people as the cancer on the face of the sick planet?[16]

While thoroughly modern, this notion of a body politic that is desperately sick yet refuses to see the sickness in its reality is one that should also seem familiar to us as Christians. Jesus (and later on Augustine) turned to the analogy of sickness regularly in teaching people about their desperate need for God, a need that so many did not seem to recognize. Jesus' comment that it is not the healthy but the sick who need a physician presents a direct connection between sin and healing: "Those who are well have no need of a physician, but those who are sick. I came not to call the righteous, but sinners" (Mk 2:17 ESV).

The sickness we have discussed so far is one that does not lead to physical death—although it certainly does lead to spiritual death. Yet, the devaluing of one kind of life is a canary in the coal mine predicting a devaluing of another kind of life. For years, pro-life advocates had predicted that the

---

[16]W. M. Hern, "Has the Human Species Become a Cancer on the Planet? A Theoretical View of Population Growth as a Sign of Pathology," *Current World Leaders* 36, no. 6 (December 1993): 1089-1124, https://pubmed.ncbi.nlm.nih.gov/12291996/.

devaluing of fetal life in America would result in the devaluing of the lives of the elderly and infirm. In Canada now, as euthanasia has become the sixth-leading cause of death, as MAID (medical assistance in dying) has made this nightmare come true.[17] Originally intended as an extreme measure to assist the elderly—a statement from the outset that correlated a reduced value of human life with advancing age—the measure has rapidly expanded to become a last resort for the sick and the poor of any age. In his heartbreaking article on this topic, Anglican priest Benjamin Crosby takes churches to task for not doing enough to fight this development, passively choosing instead to go along with the culture of devaluing human life.

There is nothing new, however, in this devaluing of life to the point of actively encouraging the death of those considered less valuable in society. As we turn to the second part of this book, we will see that this practice of ranking people in society by worth and value was common to the pre-Christian Roman world. In a world without the recognition of the *imago Dei* in every human being, violence of all kinds against the weak was rampant and seen as perfectly justified by the strong. It is to a closer examination of this world, and the difference that the rise of Christianity made in it, that we turn next.

---

[17]Benjamin Crosby, "Where Are the Churches in Canada's Euthanasia Experiment?," *Plough*, February 27, 2023, www.plough.com/en/topics/justice/culture-of-life/where-are-the-churches-in-canadas-euthanasia-experiment?fbclid=IwAR1cBV0p6PtN2OkAtcQGHfB9amChydDq_TMDtoh4HGL-_ZgdMEEYhHN2t8M.

PART 2

VIEWS OF
PERSONHOOD
IN THE ANCIENT
MEDITERRANEAN
BEFORE
AND AFTER
CHRISTIANITY

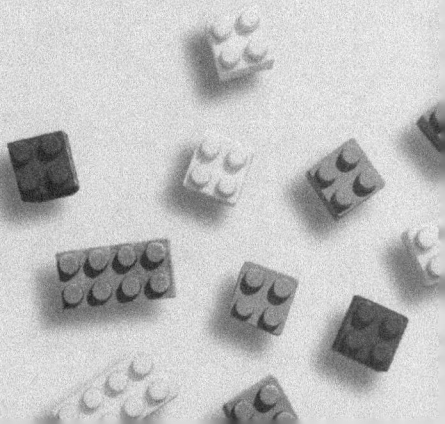

5

WORTHLESS

The Devaluing of Women, Children, and Human Beings in the Pre-Christian Mediterranean

ONCE UPON A TIME, man lived alone. But the gods—yes, in this story, it is the plural *gods*, as it usually was in the ancient Mediterranean—decided to collaborate on a group project to shame all group projects. They made a woman for the man out of earth and water, and each god or goddess endowed her with a special gift—charming smile, fancy dress, great jewelry and accessories, the works. Even her very name reflected her origin as a special gift—Pandora, the gift of all the Olympian gods.

But, as the adage goes, some gifts just keep on giving, and not in a good way. This particular gift in the end turned out to be a terrible curse. In fact, it was meant to be a curse all along, for it was made as punishment for humankind for a terrible deceit that made mockery of the gods. But before we look at the nature of the curse, let us go back to the beginning and consider why the gods wanted to punish humanity so harshly. This particular story, leading to the creation of the first woman, has much to tell us about the polytheistic Greeks' anthropology—their view of human beings—and especially their view of women in the world.

It all started with a ruse, writes ancient Greek poet Hesiod, who lived sometime in the eighth or seventh century BC. Or, even more accurately, it started with a squabble between different generations of gods, with humans as the losers caught in the middle, as is too often their fate in Greek mythology.

In the first-ever ceremony of sacrifice to the gods, the crafty Prometheus, a Titan (i.e., an older-generation god), decided to trick the younger king of the gods, Zeus. He invited Zeus to the ceremony in his honor and asked him to choose one of the two piles of meat as his. Prometheus divided the meat from the sacrificial animal into two piles, making one of them look very attractive. But it was all a trompe l'oeil: the attractive pile, with glistening fat on top, largely consisted of bones and inedible parts of the animal underneath. The less attractive pile, on the other hand, had most of the meat.

Ancient pagan gods were not omniscient. Zeus fell for the trick. But once he realized the truth, he took revenge on humans, for whom Prometheus had been a steady protector: Zeus hid fire, that essential element for basic comfort in human life. Not to be outdone, Prometheus the trickster revealed the secret of how to obtain fire to humans. Once again learning the truth after the fact, Zeus decided on the worst revenge yet. "The price for the stolen fire will be a gift of evil / to charm the hearts of all men as they hug their own doom," says Hesiod in his epic *Works and Days*, a poem about the agricultural life cycle and the hard work that it requires of human beings in a world filled with adversarial gods and unjust human rulers.[1]

Here follows the story of the creation of Pandora, the first woman, whom Zeus ordered to be made (as Hesiod puts it) "with the mind of a bitch." This beautiful woman became the prototype accursed gift for all men thereafter. The gift came with a special accessory, a twisted dowry of sorts: a large *pithos*, or storage jar, filled with all kinds of evils (no, it wasn't a box!). Of course, Pandora knew the rule: she was never supposed to open the jar. Infinitely curious nevertheless, one day she opened the jar, unleashing disease and

---

[1] Apostolos N. Athanassakis, *Hesiod: Theogony, Works and Days, Shield* (Baltimore: Johns Hopkins University Press, 2004), 66.

misery on the world. Only hope remained sealed in the jar, for Pandora slammed the lid back on to trap it there.

This story, from one of the earliest surviving works of Greek literature, provides essential information about the Greeks' view of anthropology. First, as in the Judeo-Christian tradition, men and women were created separately. The differences between these two stories tell us much more than the similarities, however. In Genesis, God's creation of woman is a beautiful gift and blessing—even if, along with Adam, she soon falls into sin. She is made from Adam's very rib and meant to complete Adam, for whom (as God declared) it was not good to be alone.

By contrast, the life of humans in Greek mythology, already not easy before the creation of woman, only gets much worse once Pandora arrives on the scene and unleashes curses and diseases on the earth. In addition, we see that the first woman was not even made from the same substance as men. She is, one could say, less human as a result. Indeed, as Adrienne Mayor notes in her analysis of Pandora as an ancient automaton, depictions of this myth in Athenian vase paintings emphasize Pandora's doll-like and artificial-looking appearance. She is repeatedly depicted standing stiff as a statue but with that devastatingly charming yet destructive smile that Hesiod mentions as well.[2] She is, one can only conclude, not fully human. Or, more precisely, she is less than human.

Women were certainly treated as less than human in the Greek world. At the very least, they were seen as less valuable than men and less complete than men, who were seen as the default standard for humanity at its best. As for marriage, Hesiod himself notes that it is simply a necessary evil, required for procreation. Yet, as we will see, even in the case of procreation, there was ambivalence about just how much work women really did in this area.

But now let us consider a different tale, one more historical and from another Mediterranean civilization. In the mid-fifth century BC, the newly expanding city of Rome, having only recently sloughed off the monarchy in favor of a republic, adopted its first official law code. The Twelve Tables, so

---

[2] Adrienne Mayor, *God and Robots: Myths, Machines, and Ancient Dreams of Technology* (Princeton, NJ: Princeton University Press, 2018), 162-66.

creatively named for obvious reasons, dealt largely with property law. But property for a freeborn male in the Roman world included not only his inanimate possessions but all souls under his roof—free and enslaved, women and children. Some laws are particularly telling concerning the father's power over the children. Table IV, which presents several laws on the father's *patria potestas*, his official power over all beings and possessions under his roof, opens with an ominous dictum: "A notably deformed child shall be killed immediately."[3]

The ancient world was not friendly to disability or ill health. Exposure of unwanted infants, even healthy ones, was practiced regularly throughout the Mediterranean. The injunction to the father in the Twelve Tables, however, is phrased as an order rather than merely a statement about the extent of his power over his household. In other words, the father does not just have the option to cull the weak from Roman society. Rather, it is his duty to the state to do so.

There is no mercy or compassion in the Twelve Tables, only plain economics. In the premodern agricultural world, caring for a child with severe physical disabilities would have been an inconceivable burden, and the state was certainly not going to help with it. One might even imagine someone in the Roman world explaining, as some pro-choice advocates have done when recommending aborting all children with Down syndrome, for instance, that a life with such disabilities is just not worth living. Indeed, the United Kingdom allows the abortion of children with Down syndrome up until birth and has repeatedly upheld appeals challenging this law.[4]

As these two glimpses demonstrate already, the ancient world had an attitude toward human life, and especially the lives of women and children,

---

[3]For a translation of the Twelve Tables, see Allan Chester Johnson, Paul Robinson Coleman-Norton, Frank Card Bourne, trans., *Ancient Roman Statutes: Translation, with Introduction, Commentary, Glossary, and Index* (Austin: University of Texas Press, 1961), available at https://avalon.law.yale.edu /ancient/twelve_tables.asp.

[4]See, for example, "Legislation Which Allows Abortion of Babies with Down's Syndrome up until Birth Upheld by Court of Appeal," Sky News, November 25, 2022, https://news.sky.com/story /legislation-which-allows-abortion-of-babies-with-downs-syndrome-up-until-birth-upheld-by -court-of-appeal-12755187.

that could perhaps be described as utilitarian. But utilitarianism does not fully describe it, either, for not all abuses in this world were for the benefit of others. It seems, rather, that we are looking at a world that saw no problem with the casually devastating cruelty of the strong toward the weak, as articulated perhaps most famously in the Melian dialogue in Thucydides's *History of the Peloponnesian War.*

When a small island state, Melos, asked Athens to allow it to remain neutral in the war, not joining either the Athenians or the Spartans as an active ally, the Athenians gave the Melians an ultimatum, arguing that the laws of the universe allowed the strong to do as they will, while the weak had no choice but to submit: "You know as well as we do that, when these matters are discussed by practical people, the standard of justice depends on the equality of power to compel and that in fact the strong do what they have the power to do and the weak accept what they have to accept."[5]

The Melians, either overly honorable or just plain foolish, refused to join Athens in the war effort. The Athenians took their city by force, killed all the men, sold all the women and children into slavery, and resettled the city with Athenian colonists. Standard procedure in ancient warfare, and yet so harrowing that even Thucydides the Athenian general was bothered. But then, if the strong can do what they want while the weak simply have to accept what comes their way, what else might we expect but these kinds of atrocities and many more?

In the three chapters that form this second part of the book, I will examine in greater depth this world that seems so far away, both geographically and culturally, and yet is in a strange way a mirror image of our own world. We live in an increasingly post-Christian society, one in which the weight of culture, as I noted in part one, is shifting away from Christian values that treasure human beings. In her book *Humanly Possible*, Sarah Bakewell attempts to demonstrate the value of human beings and equality of all human

---

[5]Thucydides, *History of the Peloponnesian War* 5.84-116. For a translation of the dialogue, see "The Melian Dialogue," trans. Rex Warner, http://fs2.american.edu/dfagel/www/Class%20Readings /Thucydides/Melian%20Dialogues.pdf.

life apart from Christian thought.[6] But the result of such attempts feels forced, resting on no firm premises apart from a desperate hope in some intangible goodness. Much as we, modern creatures, might not like the black-and-white declarations of Christianity, Bakewell's formidable tour of humanist thought only further highlights the inability of secular ideas to prove what the doctrine of the *imago Dei* declares incontrovertible.

In light of the post-Christian devaluing of human preciousness, this mirror image of the pre-Christian Mediterranean is helpful in shedding light on some foundational questions: What is a human life worth if the doctrine of the *imago Dei*, the acceptance of the preciousness of every human life, is taken out of the picture? On this tour of the ancient Mediterranean, we will see the fate of Melos—the systemic abuse of the weak by the strong—repeated on small and large scale in war and in peace. Furthermore, we will see active attempts to justify such abuses by establishing a hierarchy of worth in which women and children intrinsically ranked lower than able-bodied freeborn men. Mythology, as the myth of Pandora already showed, is an excellent source of information in this area, for myths reflect the values, beliefs, and popular explanations for why things in a society are the way they are.

In this chapter I provide a survey of the attitudes toward women and children in the Greco-Roman world, based on an admittedly select but representative sample of sources from Greek and Roman literature, mythology and religion, history, and law. The stories from these diverse sources from the pre-Christian Greco-Roman world show clearly that, in the socially and

---

[6]Sarah Bakewell, *Humanly Possible: Seven Hundred Years of Humanist Freethinking, Inquiry, and Hope* (New York: Penguin, 2023).

economically stratified communities of the ancient Mediterranean, misogyny was an ingrained part of the worldview and general anthropology, women were seen as subhuman, and (as the Twelve Tables already suggested) children's value depended on their status and perceived health. We begin with a shocking question to which you might have thought the answer was obvious: Are mothers even parents?

ARE MOTHERS PARENTS?

Agamemnon, the supreme commander of the Greek forces at Troy, was really looking forward to a hot bath that evening. He had every reason to rejoice. After ten long years, the Trojan War was finally over, and he had just arrived back home to Argos to a loving welcome from his wife, Clytemnestra. Red carpet included.[7]

Sure, perhaps someone smarter would have foreseen trouble in paradise. After all, Agamemnon had to sacrifice his own daughter with Clytemnestra to the goddess Artemis before the goddess granted him the favorable winds needed for his fleet to depart for Troy. Maybe he should have known that his wife had still not forgiven him something as major as the loss of their child a decade later. And maybe, just maybe, he should not have paraded his newly conquered Trojan concubine, the princess and prophetess Cassandra, in front of his wife upon his arrival home. But then, Agamemnon was a Greek man, and he was a king. If anyone thought in terms of might makes right, he certainly did. As it turns out, he miscalculated.

Minutes after Agamemnon's return home, his wife, with the aid of the lover she had taken on in Agamemnon's absence, murders him in that hot bath that she had prepared for him, ostensibly to welcome him home properly. But the story does not end there.

In addition to the daughter whom Agamemnon had sacrificed ten years earlier, Agamemnon and Clytemnestra also have another daughter and, most important, a son, Orestes. Determined to avenge his father's murder

---

[7]An earlier version of parts of this section was published as "Erasing Motherhood: Scientific Misogyny, Ancient and Modern," *Fairer Disputations*, May 19, 2023, https://fairerdisputations.org /erasing-motherhood-scientific-misogyny-ancient-and-modern/.

and furthermore expressly ordered to do so by no less authority than Apollo, the god of prophecy, Orestes promptly returns to Argos from exile and kills his mother. But kin bloodshed in Greek religion was a terrible offense. Out of Clytemnestra's blood arise the Furies, also known as Eumenides, or the Kind Ones, primordial goddesses of revenge, whose job it becomes to pursue Orestes the mother killer until death from insanity, all in the name of justice.

In Aeschylus's trilogy, *The Oresteia*, which is our best source for these myths, the goddess Athena, the patron goddess of Athens, proposes an alternative solution: she invites Orestes and the Furies to come to Athens to get a fair trial. Athena then summons a jury of Athenian citizens and presides over the proceedings herself. Apollo meanwhile undertakes the duties of a defense attorney, while the Furies, of course, are the prosecutors.

In this strange trial of Orestes for the murder of his mother, there is no doubt in anyone's mind that Orestes killed Clytemnestra. But what comes under attack at the trial is the question of their kinship. Yes, of course, justice has to be served, and anyone who has killed a close blood relative has to be punished. But is Clytemnestra, the mother who gave birth to Orestes, his blood relative? In his winning argument at this trial, Apollo argues, in a nutshell: no.

> Then learn the truth, the one named mother
> is not the child's true parent but the nurturer
> of the newly sown seed. Man mounts to create life,
> whereas woman is a stranger fostering a stranger,
> nourishing the young, unless a god blights the birth.[8]

Apollo's argument, while not representing the most common of Greek medical views on pregnancy, nevertheless represents a strand. In that strand, which proves so effective in this particular courtroom trial, mothers are not parents. Therefore, by killing Clytemnestra, Orestes did exactly what he must: he avenged the murder of his father by killing the stranger (to him) who was the murderer.

---

[8]Aeschylus, *The Furies* 657-661, in Aeschylus, *Oresteia*, trans. Peter Meineck (Indianapolis: Hackett, 1998).

Apollo's argument is striking for our consideration of the extent of the devaluing of women in pre-Christian antiquity. The language used here to describe the mother of a child as nothing but the vessel that stores and nurtures the child until birth, otherwise simply "a stranger fostering a stranger," echoes the modern language used to describe commercially contracted gestational surrogates. Genetically strangers to the children they foster, they carry them until birth and then hand these children over to their biological parents, whose genetic material the children possess.

Modern surrogates most often have no genetic connection to the children they carry. Therefore, it is a more extreme claim that the mother who conceived, carried, birthed, and raised a child is also nothing but a surrogate, rather than a true blood relation. By this claim, all of the important work of creating a child is done by the father, the only true parent. The mother's work is rendered, by contrast, completely passive and replaceable. After all, anyone else with a womb could do likewise. But then, did we not see Pandora, the first woman, created as an artificial automaton, a being not fully human?

Apollo's explanation does not stop there, however. Following proper legal procedures that require proofs in court, he then produces Athena as the witness and proof of his argument—for in Greek mythology, Athena was born fully formed from Zeus's head (and yes, in case you are wondering, the king of the gods did have a headache that day). As one of the most powerful goddesses in the Greek pantheon and one whose creation did not require a mother or a typical process of gestation, Athena is indeed powerful proof of how this parenting ideal works.

Indeed, as the original audiences of Aeschylus's plays would have known, Athena's birth was technically not the only time Zeus gestated and birthed his own child. In another myth, that of the birth of the god of wine, Dionysus, Zeus rescued a baby from his incinerated pregnant mother and sewed the baby into his thigh for the remainder of the gestation period. The Greeks would also have remembered a parallel story to the birth of Athena—that of Zeus's wife, Hera, who decided to show him that he was not the only one who could create a child alone. She too bore a child all by herself—the god Hephaestus.

But while Zeus's solo creation, Athena, was perfect in every way, Hera's fatherless effort, Hephaestus, was lame in one foot and so ugly (Homer says) that he was the laughingstock of all the gods.[9] Hera's efforts, in other words, only prove the superiority of the male creation of children. Without a father's assistance, the birth of Hephaestus reminds us, even a goddess cannot create a perfect product.

Thus, the myth of Pandora offers hints about the early Greeks' view of women as subhuman, while the *Oresteia* challenges the necessity of mothers for procreation, in a strange way forestalling such futuristic scenarios as the dreams of artificial wombs and incubators, à la Aldous Huxley's *Brave New World*. But how did the Greeks think about women in other contexts? What were their views on women in everyday life settings, such as in marriage? One of the earliest pieces of evidence on this subject is a biting invective poem by Semonides of Amorgos, a rough contemporary of Hesiod. In Semonides's poem, we learn that all women can be classified into ten categories, correlating to specific animals with their attendant characteristics.

THE SCIENTIFIC CLASSIFICATION OF WIVES
IN THE GREEK POPULAR IMAGINATION

"From the start, the gods made women different," says Semonides by way of introduction.[10] Of course, we already knew this much from Hesiod, but from Semonides we learn that there is more. From this first premise about the different nature of women from men, we proceed to the ten types of wives (which for Semonides really also means all women), corresponding to different animals or forces of nature whose characteristics they exemplify.[11]

---

[9]For example, the concluding scene of book 1 of Homer's *Iliad* is a feast on Mount Olympus, where the gods, stressed from following the events of the Trojan War, unwind by laughing at Hephaestus limping around their banqueting room, serving drinks to the rest.

[10]For the complete translation, see "Women, by Semonides of Amorgos (Poem 7)," trans. Diane Arnson Svarlien, 1995, https://diotima-doctafemina.org/translations/greek/women-by-semonides -of-amorgos-poem-7/.

[11]The word *gynē* in Greek means both "woman" and "wife," whereas the word *anēr* means both "man" and "husband." In a society where singleness was not a real possibility, the conflation of categories in the vocabulary reflects this worldview.

The sow is fat, lazy, and filthy. This last characteristic also pervades her home. The fox is cunning and ever scheming. The dog is overly curious, all bark. Her yapping never stops, Semonides notes matter-of-factly, and her husband "can't stop her barking; not with threats / not (when he's had enough) by knocking out / her teeth with a stone, and not with sweet talk either."

Next is the earth woman—a reference to Pandora, it seems, as Semonides adds that this was the type of woman that the Olympian gods had made as a gift for men. This type, he notes, does not know good from bad and has no useful skills at all. Mirroring her is the sea woman, whose moods are as changeable and unpredictable as the ocean. She can seem to be the best wife on some days and the worst on others.

Switching back to animals for the remaining five types, Semonides next describes the donkey. This type of woman is stubborn and (Semonides emphasizes) requires much beating to get her to do what her husband needs her to do. She works hard but will eat her family out of house and home. To top things off, she is sexually voracious and promiscuous—a vice she shares also with the next type, the crafty weasel, who does not share the donkey's work ethic, alas. Next, the woman born from a horse is beautiful to look at, but she is all looks and no substance. A high-maintenance gal par excellence, she cares only about her beauty, refuses to do any work, and does not let her husband touch her. Then there is the ape. This type is ugly, shameless, and cruel to all her loved ones.

For the grand finale on his list, Semonides saves the one rare type of wife who is a treasure: the bee. A hard worker, she is a loving wife and mother who will reap the reward of growing gracefully into old age, surrounded by loving and accomplished children. She is the only good type of woman that Zeus created. Why? Because this was the punishment the king of gods decreed: "by the grim contrivances of Zeus / all these other types are here to stay / side by side with man forever. Yes, / Zeus made this the greatest pain of all: / Woman."

Three underlying assumptions are clear throughout the list. First, men (unlike women) are all rather similar to each other. There is no need to classify husbands into different categories. Second, this division between the different types of men and women sets up each home and marriage as an agonistic contest. The husband must always struggle to subdue his wife and make her do his will. Beating, even to the point of knocking out teeth, is perfectly acceptable in particularly dire circumstances, Semonides seems to suggest. Understanding the scientific classification of wives should help husbands, of course, in the peculiar way that one should always seek to better understand the evil in one's life. If one knows what kind of wife one has, one might understand her kind better and maybe know better how to cope. But the overall tone is hopeless—because, third and last, this is a curse that all men share because of Zeus's punishment.

It is to this comprehensive, all-devouring nature of the curse that is a wife that Semonides devotes the final portion of his poem. A wife, he warns, consumes her husband's material resources, including food. She also consumes any peace or leisure he ever might have hoped to have. What does he get in return, one might wonder upon concluding the poem? What advantage is there to marrying? Why do it? Semonides remains silent on this question. Indeed, the sole mention of children resulting from a marriage is when he describes the one good type of wife, the bee. As for sex, that benefit of marriage that Christianity has emphasized from its beginnings in limiting sex exclusively to marriage, Semonides does not even mention it as something that men might be thinking about when marrying. Rather, the only mentions of sex in the poem are in describing the types of wives who are particularly promiscuous and will bring grief to their husbands through their uncontrolled desire. In Greek thought, women, rather than men, are habitually portrayed as unable to control their sexual desire and therefore need to be watched closely by their male guardians.

In considering Semonides, we would be remiss not to recognize that no society is homogeneous in its views on any subject. The same periods of Greek literature that produced the openly misogynistic myths and poems that we have considered so far, from Semonides's poem to the stories of Pandora, have also documented such happy marriages as that of Hector and

Andromache in Homer's *Iliad*, and such self-sacrificial mythical wives as Alcestis, who offered to die in her husband's place. To be fair, even Semonides, in his misogynistic list of the ten different types of wives, includes one exemplary type. Still, we see the overall weight of cultural opinion skewed toward devaluing women and indeed expressly presenting them as a curse on men.

We now turn to investigate the broader science of misogyny, as seen in Greek and Roman philosophical, literary, and medical writings. Over time, the Greeks and Romans developed a more robust and profoundly scientific misogyny, going far beyond the classification system offered by Semonides originally perhaps at least partly tongue-in-cheek.

THE DEVELOPMENT OF SCIENTIFIC MISOGYNY IN ANCIENT GREECE

Sometime in the second quarter of the fourth century BC, Plato wrote what became one of his most famous works, *The Symposium*. The story of an aristocratic drinking party that purportedly took place in 416 BC, *The Symposium* tells of an evening during which the guests, including Socrates and the crème de la crème of Athenian intellectual elite, decided that since they all had had too much to drink the night before, they should substitute the drinking with speeches on a theme that night. This wise plan eventually gets derailed by the arrival of a party crasher, but not before the original guests have had the chance to deliver elaborate speeches on their agreed-on theme—love.

The prize for the most bizarre speech perhaps ought to go to Aristophanes, famed comic playwright and guest at the party. He tells a different myth of the origin of men and women, one likely of his own making—or, more likely, of Plato's. In this myth, human beings used to be fused creatures, two who were literally one, with four arms and legs each. They threatened the gods, however, and so Zeus—yet again intervening to harm humanity, as he did in the myth of Pandora—cut them apart. The newly separated humans now spend their lives pining for the other half that would complete them sexually and emotionally. Some men find this satisfaction in women. But the men who find the greatest satisfaction and feeling of completion, per Aristophanes, are those who find it with other men. Why? Because only men have the virtues—such as bravery—that men intrinsically desire in their partners.

The entirety of *The Symposium*, with its emphasis on homoerotic love, makes it clear that in the eyes of the conversationalists, true love cannot exist between husbands and wives or between men and women. Even Socrates, whose speech in the dialogue hinges on the testimony of a wise woman, Diotima, assumes that the ideal love is between two male bodies. But then, of course, the very nature of symposia was misogynistic. Respectable women were excluded from the festivities. Only flute girls were allowed to be present. Treated as disposable, they usually did more than just play the flute.

Around the same time when Plato imagined Aristophanes making a speech ruling out women as partners in romantic relationships, Aristophanes was parodying other Athenians' misogyny in real life. In 411 BC, five years after Plato's imagined symposium took place, Aristophanes staged to great acclaim his comedy *Thesmophoriazusae* or *Women at the Thesmophoria*. Thesmophoria was an annual fertility festival in honor of Demeter, the goddess of crops, and it celebrated all kinds of fertility, including that of women. The festival was known as specifically a women's celebration, and men were banned.

This festival Aristophanes chose as the setting for his fictional parody. The plot of the comedy goes as follows. The famed Athenian tragedian of the day, Euripides, is alarmed to discover that the women of the city are plotting to kill him for misogyny. The women, it appears, have taken the plots of his tragedies, which habitually show women in poor light, to be harmful to the reputation of their entire gender. One example the women in this comedy note as particularly offensive is Euripides's *Medea*, a tragedy about Jason (of Jason and the Argonauts fame) and the common-law barbarian wife he brings back to Greece from his travels. Offered the opportunity to marry the daughter of the king of Corinth, Jason promptly ditches Medea. Not one to take offense lightly, she kills her two children with Jason, along with Jason's betrothed and the king, before dramatically escaping to safety in a dragon-drawn chariot. Medea, unlike anyone else in Greek tragedy, is her own *dea ex machina*.

Literary critics today find in *Medea* genuine compassion for the jilted woman. Jason, by contrast, comes across as an insensitive opportunist. But in Aristophanes's imagination, the play is yet another example of the irrational potential of women to destroy all around when their wishes are unmet. Furthermore, he suggests, whether in earnest or entirely tongue-in-cheek, that Athenian women saw this both as evidence of misogyny and as unmasking their true nature. At any rate, Euripides, familiar with women's murderous impulses from his plays, comes up with a brilliant plan: he convinces a relative to disguise himself as a woman, infiltrate the women's festival, and warn Euripides of the danger to his life before it is too late. Of course, in reality, things go awry when the false woman is unmasked, and chaos ensues. This is, after all, comedy.

Most likely women did not attend Athenian comedic performances. It was therefore a male-only audience who got to laugh at this plot and to observe a comedy parodying the city's women. Even the chorus of women in plays was played, as were all other parts in Athenian drama, by men in drag. We see, in other words, public entertainment that is predicated on everyone's awareness of Euripides's perceived misogyny. But instead of considering it a matter of any concern, it becomes the funniest joke in town. It is a joke that is specific to men, reinforcing further the idea of women's enmity with men since their creation by Zeus.

We cannot take comedy at exact face value. Humor is, after all, humor. But just as with Semonides's list of the ten types of wives (and, more generally, women), humor reveals the innermost sentiments and assumptions of a society in a way that is unfiltered and extreme because there is a free pass of sorts for expressing the most shocking of ideas in jest. Within a generation of Aristophanes, the foremost Greek scientific writer of his day formulated a theory that justified women's subhumanity more decisively than ever before.

Born in northern Greece in 384 BC, Aristotle spent twenty years first as a student and then a teacher in Plato's Academy in Athens before moving on to greener pastures closer to home, including a stint as the personal tutor of teenage Alexander the Great. Over the course of his forty-year writing career, he produced treatises on topics as varied as history and grammar, astronomy and meteorology, logic and philosophy, politics and government, literature and poetry, music and aesthetics. But of paramount interest here are Aristotle's writings on science and medicine, especially those that pertain to the nature of women.

What is woman, and how is she different from man? The question occupied Aristotle a great deal. The answer, he surmised, would have significant implications not only for medicine but for philosophies of government and the ordering of a well-run society. To find answers, he combined observations from the natural world with conclusions about men and women, to the point that in some parts of *The History of Animals* the reader must pay attention closely to see whether the animal under discussion in any given moment is human or not.

Aristotle found overall that the female of each species, including human, is usually smaller, softer, and requires less food than the male (alas, having observed the effects of large meals on my husband as opposed to myself, I can confirm). Also, the female is generally less brave and requires the protection of the male. This is true, he notes, even of mollusks. In drawing conclusions specifically about men and women, Aristotle summarizes:

> The fact is, the nature of man is the most rounded off and complete, and consequently in man the qualities or capacities above referred to are found in their perfection. Hence woman is more compassionate than man, more easily moved to tears, at the same time is more jealous, more querulous, more apt to scold and to strike. She is furthermore, more prone to despondency and less hopeful than the man, more void of shame or self-respect, more false of speech, more deceptive, and of more retentive memory. She is also more wakeful, more shrinking, more difficult to rouse to action, and requires a smaller quantity of nutriment. (*The History of Animals* 9)[12]

---

[12]The differences between men and women, as well as between the male and female in other animal species, occupy the early part of *The History of Animals* 9. For a translation of this section, see Aristotle, *The History of Animals*, trans. D'Arcy Wentworth Thompson, https://penelope.uchicago.edu/aristotle/histanimals9.html.

Aristotle's findings here echo many of the observations that we already found in Hesiod and Semonides. Women's proneness to deception is a reminder of the deliberate creation of Pandora. The various emotional qualities of women, at the same time, echo Semonides's various types of wives. It seems that we have in fact come full circle. While Semonides used animals to designate the ten different types of wives as a poetic organizational principle, Aristotle now presents similar conclusions from his study of actual animals.

Ultimately, Aristotle decides that woman is, at the most basic level, a mutilated or imperfect man—a conclusion he spells out most explicitly in *On the Generation of Animals*, his study of animal reproduction.[13] As we have noted already, this view of the fundamental nature of women built on the legacy of previous Greek thought from the myth of Pandora on. Still, Aristotle's work now cloaked such mythological theories in a solidly respectable veneer of science that continued to dominate scientific thought well into the Middle Ages.

Furthermore, just as Aristotle's erroneous ideas about other scientific concepts, such as blood circulation and the role of the heart in the process, resisted challenges for millennia because of the high regard that all his work held, so did his pseudoscience on the nature of women continue to be authoritative.[14] Like his predecessors, Aristotle did not find women's ability to bear children particularly impressive. Rather, the ability to get pregnant was for him yet another example of women's physiological imperfection. Like Aeschylus, he was convinced that it was the male who was the real (and perfect) parent of each child. Admittedly, unlike Aeschylus, Aristotle thought that the female's contribution to the creation of the child was needed—the male parent contributed the seed, while the female parent contributed the menstrual blood, and the two essential ingredients then worked

---

[13]For a good translation with helpful notes, see C. D. C. Reeve, *Aristotle, Generation of Animals & History of Animals I and Parts of Animals I* (Indianapolis: Hackett, 2019).

[14]For the story of how Aristotle's and Galen's erroneous theories of blood circulation resisted challenges and revisions until the early modern period, see Dhun Sethna, *The Wine-Dark Sea Within: A Turbulent History of Blood* (New York: Basic Books, 2022). For an overview of the book's argument, see my review: *Bryn Mawr Classical Review*, January 5, 2023, https://bmcr.brynmawr.edu/2023/2023.01.05/.

together—but his admission of some contribution of women to the process is scarcely an advance for the recognition of women's worth.

It is important to remember that Aristotle's findings about the inferior, mutilated nature of women encompass conclusions on both the physiological and emotional differences between the two sexes. It is not just that women are smaller in size, for instance. More significant for justifying their role in society, most notably their exclusion from government and full citizenship, are their emotional characteristics. The same qualities, in other words, that Hesiod, Semonides, and Aristophanes singled out as dangerous to men and to stable society now were scientifically justified to explain women's inadequate, subhuman nature. Forever incomplete by her very nature, woman could never be what man was in Greek society.

SCIENTIFIC MISOGYNY IN THE ROMAN WORLD

A century before Aristotle developed his scientific theories about the nature of woman as imperfect or mutilated man, the earliest Roman law code, the Twelve Tables, which I mentioned in this chapter's introduction, spelled out Rome's earliest laws on the guardianship of women. Table V, which deals with laws of inheritance and guardianship, focuses on ensuring that women at all stages of life are managed by a male relative. There is an intriguing phrase included to explain this regulation: women need a male relative "because of their levity of mind."

This phrase may be a later interpolation, coming from a much later Roman law code. Yet, even if it is a later addition, it reflects a concept that was foundational to Roman law and society: women were mentally incapable of governing themselves or their affairs. As a result, of course, they were not fit to participate in government or politics.

Overall in the Roman world it was legal thinkers, rather than scientists, who took on the work of theorizing misogyny. While Emperor Augustus, in an effort to encourage higher birthrates among the Roman aristocracy, offered to remove the requirement of guardianship for women who had born three or more children, even then no further political perks were forthcoming.

Instead, it is striking that during the age of Augustus we encounter Rome's most scandalous scientific guide to picking up women. This guide, the brain-child of the elegiac poet Ovid, gives us a tantalizing window into the Roman side of systematic misogyny.

In *The Art of Love*, a manual in three books (or scrolls), Ovid provides his tested and guaranteed science of picking up women. It is truly a science. All it takes is knowing where to go—and since it is Rome, the options are many and varied, from the races and the theater to the beach and parks and more. Then, once you identify your target—a process similar to that used by hunters, Ovid readily admits—you just move in. No need to take no for an answer. Some women take more work than others, but seduction eventually is just about guaranteed. The manual is shocking in many ways, and to our post-#MeToo eyes it appears more clearly as the abusive and misogynistic how-to rape manual that it really is, a document displaying zero respect for women's dignity as human beings.[15] An instant bestseller in Rome, it clearly struck the right nerve with audiences. It seems that far from shocking (male) readers, Ovid's advice seemed at the very least entertaining, if not downright appealing.

The Art of Love appeared in AD 2. Just six years later, Emperor Augustus exiled Ovid from Rome to one of the least desirable and backwater places possible for the urbane Rome-loving poet—the city of Tomis in the Roman province of Moesia, modern-day Romania. Ovid spent the rest of his life writing mournful poems to Augustus, appealing for a recall to Rome, but to no avail. In one of these he mentions the reason for his exile: it was a poem and a deed. Many have since theorized that the poem in question was none other than *The Art of Love*.

We might ask, what about the poem upset Augustus? Certainly not its misogyny. Augustus had no problem with Ovid's low view of women and their chastity. He did, however, have a problem with the immoral behavior

---

[15]I offer more in-depth detail analysis of Ovid's work in *Cultural Christians in the Early Church: A Historical and Practical Introduction to Christians in the Greco-Roman World* (Grand Rapids, MI: Zondervan Academic, 2023), 40-44.

that he feared Ovid's writings would encourage and which his own marriage legislations worked so hard to discourage. As I mentioned above, eager to encourage a higher birthrate among the Roman aristocracy, Augustus went so far as to remove the requirement for guardianship for women who bore three children. But, of course, the only children who counted for the tally were those born legitimately, that is, in the context of a Roman marriage.

The misogyny that Ovid's writings represent continued alive and well in the pagan world, even as Christianity was slowly growing over the three centuries after his death and presenting its own dramatically counter-cultural vision of valuing women as fellow image bearers right along with men. But we have yet to consider children, whose lives too were objectified and devalued.

CHILDREN AS OBJECTS IN THE ANCIENT MEDITERRANEAN

A century after Ovid poetically suffered his exile, a much more respectable Roman citizen, Gaius Plinius Secundus, best known to us now simply as Pliny the Younger, partially retraced Ovid's steps as he set forth from Rome to a site on the side of the Black Sea littoral that lay farther south from Ovid's former exile, the Roman province of Bithynia. But while for Ovid his exile was the worst punishment of his life, for Pliny this sending out was the best reward of his distinguished political career. To cap off his lengthy period of senatorial activity and service in Rome, he was sent to Bithynia for a term as governor of the province. A prolific letter writer, Pliny is one of our best sources for provincial government in the Roman Empire—all because, assured of his own importance, Pliny painstakingly collected his correspondence for publication. One entire book (scroll) of this lengthy collection is devoted to Pliny's correspondence with the emperor during his term as governor.

Risk averse and skittishly afraid to make any misstep that might offend Emperor Trajan, any time Pliny came across any kind of difficult situation—ranging from the need to manage fire safety in the province capital, to questions about the cost of repair of public buildings, to how to deal with Christians in the province (spoiler alert—this one got messy!)—he sent a detailed

missive to the emperor, explaining the situation and his own stopgap solution. Having sent off his letter via the literal pony express to Trajan, Pliny
would settle back for the next several months to await the emperor's answer.

The letter of relevance to our story here has to do with abandoned infants
in the province. The problem apparently was common enough to give the
erstwhile governor a real headache. But the concern that he had was not
perhaps one that we would have. Pliny did not wonder why so many people
in his province were abandoning their newborns, leaving them to die or be
picked up to be raised by others. Rather, being the serious Roman jurist that
he was, his prime concern had to do with these children's status as adults:
Should abandoned children who have been rescued by someone and raised
in that person's household be considered free or enslaved?[16]

The Roman world operated on status as determining someone's value in
society and really more generally. Some people, put simply, were more important and more valuable than others. Citizens, especially aristocratic ones,
were particularly valuable. But the distinction between free birth and enslaved status was paramount. An enslaved person was at the bottom of the
social pyramid, and while acquiring freedom and social advancement was
possible, it was far from guaranteed. By abandoning their unwanted infants,
the people of the province showed not only a lack of concern whether these
children of theirs lived or died but also a lack of concern for their future fate
if they survived.

As I noted at the beginning of this chapter, the ancient world was not
tolerant of disabilities. We can safely assume that abandoned children who
were rescued by passersby and raised in their homes were healthy. In fact,
they were healthy enough to defy the odds of infant and child mortality that
plagued the ancient world and live to adulthood. That is when their queries
came to the governor. Some of these formerly abandoned children, it seems,
raised the question upon reaching adulthood: If no one can prove that I was

---

[16]For a translation of Pliny's letter, see "LXXI. To the Emperor Trajan," in Pliny the Younger, *Letters*,
The Harvard Classics (New Haven, CT: Harvard University Press, 1909–1914), available at www
.bartleby.com/9/4/2071.html.

born enslaved, should I not have my freedom? At the end, showing compassion, Trajan concurred and advised Pliny to allow any of them who claimed freeborn status to be free, but on the condition of repaying to their benefactors the cost of their upbringing.[17] For the unfortunates who started their lives with abandonment and rescue by families who then raised them as enslaved members of their household, perhaps this was the best possible outcome.

We may well ask whether there was something specific to Bithynia that caused this practice of infant abandonment, but we have enough evidence to know that this is the wrong question to ask. Across the empire, in Egypt, we have evidence that a practice existed throughout antiquity of exposing unwanted infants on village dung heaps. There were two reasons for the popularity of this location for this purpose. First, the dung heap stayed warm, thus keeping the child warm for as long as possible, allowing the greatest possibility of rescue by someone else. Second, this was a communal place where villagers would come on a regular basis for fertilizer. In a sense, we might imagine this practice as akin to modern-day recycling centers, where one can bring unwanted furniture or other household goods to be left to be potentially collected by someone else. Except in this case, we are not dealing with furniture but with real, live infants.

The practice of exposure of infants in the ancient Mediterranean emphasizes a utilitarian commodification of infants and children as things. Just like defective models are not tolerated in the modern world, as we see in the common practice of aborting children with Down syndrome, they were not tolerated in antiquity. But it is particularly striking and indicative of the low value of children's lives that sometimes even perfectly good "products" were discarded or recycled, just like we might give away an extra kitchen gadget when we do not need a duplicate.[18]

---

[17]For Trajan's response, see "LXXII. Trajan to Pliny," in Pliny the Younger, *Letters*.

[18]For a broader overview of the life and death of children, especially in the context of families in the late Roman Empire, see Christian Laes, Kathariina Mustakallio, and Ville Vuolanto, eds., *Children and Family in Late Antiquity* (Leuven: Peeters, 2015), and Maria E. Doerfler, *Jephthah's Daughter, Sarah's Son: The Death of Children in Late Antiquity* (Berkeley: University of California Press, 2019).

CONCLUSION

The overview of evidence in this chapter is, by necessity of space, cursory and incomplete. Yet, taken as a body of evidence, these snapshots provide a representative picture that should make us uneasy. What is a human life worth in a world where there is no assurance of the preciousness of every human being? The development of scientific misogyny in the Greco-Roman world shows that a stratified system was the default view: men were clearly worth much more than women. Women's role in producing children, furthermore, was minimized, as we saw in the emphasis in Aeschylus on the father alone as the true parent. Minimizing women's roles as mothers was part and parcel of the discourse of scientific misogyny and the devaluing of women as human beings. But perhaps surprisingly, considering the emphasis that the ancient world placed on heirs, children's lives as well were seen as disposable.

There remains another piece of the puzzle to consider as we try to understand the systematic devaluing of women's and children's lives and preciousness as human beings in the pre-Christian Mediterranean world. This story involves another system of valuing some individuals over others: military service. In the next chapter, I explore the ways in which war in the ancient world further emphasized the value of some individuals and their lives (i.e., men who were able to fight in the military) over others (i.e., everyone else). Some people had a greater value for their state, while others could be more valuable dead than alive.

6

THE USELESS ONES

Devaluing Civilians in War and Peace

SOMETIME DURING THE REIGN OF BYZANTINE emperor Justinian (AD 527–565), a retired military engineer by the name of Syrianos decided to spend his golden years writing a comprehensive treatise on defensive and offensive strategy. Maybe not a typical retirement project, but a clear case of "write what you know." Syrianos was no literary master, as far as writing prowess goes. But his research—the fruit of decades in the military profession—was on point. His aim in writing this manual on military arts appears to have been to educate the ordinary civilian and armchair warrior about the minutia of how armies, past and present, operate.[1] Just what did it take to win consistent victories of the sort Justinian's military was aiming for in that last great age of Byzantine imperial expansion? In a nutshell, a lot.

THE USELESS AND THE USEFUL

Our engineer took his task seriously, providing background information on such basics as the structure of the state and the types of citizens, professions, and leaders—from tax collectors to those managing trade and public

---

[1]George T. Dennis, ed., *The Anonymous Byzantine Treatise on Strategy*, in *Three Byzantine Military Treatises* (Washington DC: Dumbarton Oaks Research Library and Collection, 1985), 3-4.

building projects. After all, understanding these civilian structures in time of peace has always been key for mobilizing them expediently for success in wartime. So far, so good. But toward the end of this list, we suddenly get a curious category that does not fit in with the rest: the *achrestoi*—literally, "the useless ones." Who were they?

Syrianos explains: "The unproductive are those who are unfit for any kind of work, private or public, because of old age, bodily infirmity, insanity, or some other excusing cause."[2] Syrianos expressly names the elderly and the sick in this list. He does not name women and children, but they are implied by the general umbrella terms in the list—especially the reference to "bodily infirmity," although perhaps "insanity" too.

We can quibble that women and children in antiquity, just as today, carried out plenty of private and public work of different sorts, from fetching water and cooking to taking care of the home—including caring for the elderly and the sick—to engaging in support work on a farm (if living outside a city) or small-scale trade (if living in a city). For women, keeping a house running and taking care of children is not exactly a walk in the park, as many of us know. Furthermore, pregnancy and childbirth themselves are a labor, physical to an extreme degree. Surely raising future citizens is an important private and public work.

We are free to think this way, but Syrianos does not have this framework in mind. The definition of work for him does not include these kinds of invisible (to him) labors. For Syrianos, work in both peace and war is the kind of effort that can directly contribute to military success. Nothing else matters. And—this is key—people's worth for society is determined accordingly. At least he speaks compassionately about caring for these people, whose worth for the state in wartime was not positive and not even neutral. Their very presence in the state at war was a drag on the state's resources: as he explains, someone must be appointed to take care of them, and for such caretakers, this work of mercy is their contribution to the war effort.

---

[2]Dennis, *Anonymous Byzantine Treatise on Strategy*, 19.

Even as Syrianos speaks kindly about "the useless ones," his thought process reminds us that in the Christian Byzantine world, just as in earlier Greco-Roman antiquity, people in any state could be clearly divided into two groups. The worth of each of these categories has, since the earliest days of ancient city-states, been defined by their military value or lack thereof. This vestige of the pagan way of thinking about the value of different people refused to die, it appears. The categories of useful and useless were ultimately military ones. Syrianos was far from an original thinker in presenting these categories. He was merely parroting what had been the default system for valuing and devaluing people throughout antiquity, reverting in this case to the pre-Christian perspective on the matter.

On the one hand, there were the potential soldiers—those males who had the bodily strength and (oftentimes) necessary financial resources to fight in time of war, even if they were not professional military personnel. On the other hand, there were those who did not have any use for the military— women, children, slaves, foreigners, the elderly, the sick, and those too poor to afford armor (in those ancient militaries where supplying your own armor was required). They were the multitudes who could not win your victory for you. Rather, keeping them contained was key for not suffering a military loss, as one mythological king, Eteocles, found to his chagrin in Aeschylus's tragedy *Seven Against Thebes* (467 BC). Tragedies, while telling mythological stories, reflect real social anxieties about particular scenarios that could occur. *Seven Against Thebes* is no exception.

Seven Against Thebes is a tragedy about the two sons of Oedipus fighting over the kingship of Thebes after their father's abdication. One of the brothers, Polynices, rallies an army that he leads with six other heroes to besiege Thebes, presently under the control of his brother, Eteocles. It is bad enough to have to manage life under siege conditions. Making matters worse for Eteocles is the widespread panic in the city, as the women descend into utter despair and hysteria, fearing capture—with good reason.

Eteocles repeatedly berates them harshly for distracting him from his more important immediate tasks in leading the war efforts, but his screaming at the terrified civilians has a rather predictable result: they are only more afraid and unmanageable. Eteocles is an unlikeable character, but his difficulties in managing civilians in crisis reflect a challenge that all commanders could face in wartime. No one wants panicked women running amok around the city while trying to coordinate its strategic defense.

A few ancient authors do suggest emergency situations for utilizing those who would fall under Syrianos's "useless folk" category in wartime, instead of merely sidelining them. Another retired military professional, Aeneas the Tactician, wrote a military treatise titled *How to Survive Under Siege* in the mid-fourth century BC, in which he provides survival hacks for a besieged city filled primarily with civilians. For instance, if you get your cows drunk, put some bells on them, and drive them out of the city gates into the enemy camp at night, the enemy just might give up in terror and go home. Another of Aeneas's memorable gems involves the idea of dressing up women in pots and pans and parading them on the city walls. From afar, Aeneas assures his readers, they look just like real soldiers, so the enemy will think your army is much larger than it really is. This might make the enemy think twice before attacking. But, Aeneas notes grimly, do not give away the trick by letting these fake soldiers throw anything at the enemy. They will throw like girls.

But such instructions were for absolute emergencies where outright survival was at stake. Overall, as far as leaders were concerned, a firm division persisted in the ancient world between the two categories that Syrianos outlined. Furthermore, we consistently see a clear connection between the value of people for the state in war and in peace. Full citizenship from the earliest days of the Greek city-states in the eighth or seventh century BC was the privilege of those who fought for the state in times of war.

The "useless folk," by contrast, while certainly much more useful for the state in peace than in war, were also likely to be targeted and victimized by the enemy in various ways in war. Systematic rape of women and girls, in particular, has been a methodical strategy in war since earliest documented conflicts. It is no accident that Homer's *Iliad*, the earliest literary work from the Greek world, opens with the desperate attempts of a father to get back his daughter, who had been kidnapped by attackers and made into a sex slave of the Greek commander-in-chief, Agamemnon.

In this chapter we continue our investigation of the devaluing of human life in pre-Christian antiquity by looking specifically at the devaluing and outright abuse of civilians, especially women but also children, in wartime. Our Byzantine engineer could dub them useless, but at least he displays a care for this group, since the useless people he is talking about are those of his own state. For his earlier pagan counterparts, there was less sympathy. Targeting civilians on the enemy side, it seems, was simply an accepted fact of war, although civilians at home suffered much too. What does a world without the Judeo-Christian theology of personhood look like? The horrific and systematic mistreatment of civilians in ancient warfare is in some ways the best gateway into answering this important question that we forget to ask, living as we do in a modern world permeated through and through with Judeo-Christian values.

Historians do not deal in counterfactuals, with the question of what might have happened if something important had not occurred. Yet, the past sometimes offers the strongest evidence of such a counterfactual, allowing us to ask this key question: What is the value of any individual human life without God's love and powerful declaration that each one of us is a beloved son or daughter? The clearest answer comes to us directly from the pen of one of Rome's (and history's) most famous military commanders and writers: Julius Caesar. Like Syrianos, Caesar wrote what he knew. And what Caesar knew was war.

GENOCIDE AND THE *IMAGO DEI*

For centuries since antiquity, many an intermediate Latin student's experience with prose began with the same sentence: *Gallia est omnis divisa in partes tres* ("Gaul as a whole is divided into three parts"). This matter-of-fact opening of Julius Caesar's *Gallic Wars*, a journal-style documentation of his nearly decadelong campaigns in Gaul (58–50 BC), sets the stage for a blow-by-blow narrative of a brutal war.[3] In the process, Caesar highlights in often graphic detail his army's indiscriminate slaughter of Rome's enemies and unloved next-door neighbors.[4] Here is one example.

In 55 BC, two nomadic Germanic tribespeople, the Tencteri and the Usipetes, driven by another tribe from their previous region, had the misfortune of coming across Caesar in a region located at the intersection of two rivers, the Waal and Meuse, in modern-day Netherlands. They asked Caesar for asylum, and Caesar's account suggests that he did not consider them a real threat. Yet, he next unapologetically tells of his deliberate annihilation of this group of defenseless families. Men of military age were among these migrants, but, as Caesar casually notes without trying to hide this fact, most were women and children. Even the men were not war-ready. Here they are, the useless ones, as far as military worth or threat goes. For the events that unfold, they indeed turn out to be useless in military terms—most of all to themselves.

Clinically narrating the massacre with no trace of emotion, Caesar says that at first, the Roman soldiers attacked the men in the camp, catching them by surprise. As the terrified women and children began to flee in panic, Caesar sent the cavalry after them in hot pursuit. Horrific slaughter ensued both on land and in the river, into which some jumped in a vain attempt to escape.[5] At the end, Caesar adds triumphantly, the Romans suffered no losses, and only a few men were wounded, even though the enemy numbered 430,000. A resounding success, as far as Caesar was concerned.

There are two ways to read this account. Caesar, of course, meant to frame this as a brilliant victory that showcases both his own leadership and the

---

[3]For studies of Caesar's narrative technique, see Andrew Riggsby, *Caesar in Gaul and Rome: War in Words* (Austin: University of Texas Press, 2006). For a highly readable yet comprehensive biography of Caesar that includes coverage of his near-decade in Gaul, see Adrian Goldsworthy, *Caesar, Life of a Colossus* (New Haven, CT: Yale University Press, 2006).

[4]Parts of this section were previously published in "Genocide and the Imago Dei," Church Life Journal, November 14, 2022, https://churchlifejournal.nd.edu/articles/genocide-and-the-imago-dei/, and "How We Learned to Hate Genocide," *Christianity Today*, February 14, 2024, www.christianitytoday.com /ct/2024/february-web-only/how-we-learned-to-hate-genocide-christian-history-violence-.html/.

[5]Caesar, *Gallic Wars* 4.14-15. For a translation of this passage see C. Julius Caesar, *Caesar's Gallic War*, trans. W. A. McDevitte and W. S. Bohn (New York. Harper, 1869), available at www.perseus.tufts .edu/hopper/text?doc=Perseus%3Atext%3A1999.02.0001%3Abook%3D4%3Achapter%3D14.

competence of his troops in the best light possible. The trope of the heroic army of just a few facing a vicious and dangerous enemy that outnumbers it is common enough in ancient military writings. Just think of the three hundred Spartans who for a time held off the hundreds of thousands of Persians at Thermopylae. Sure, the three hundred were killed tragically, but their self-sacrifice bought the rest of the Greeks precious time to mobilize. But in the story Caesar tells us, there is something even better: there is no tragic death of the few Romans. Rather, they prevail against the numerical odds. This is all, of course, credit to the excellent Roman leadership.

Caesar's intended reading, heroizing the Romans (most of all himself!), is not the only way to read this episode. We have two millennia of distance and a different view of the preciousness of human life. Furthermore, unlike Caesar's Roman audiences, we are not blinded by an unequivocal hatred of the Gauls—and for all intended purposes, we can include these tribespeople in that broader umbrella. The Gauls are the only enemy against whom one must fight for survival rather than merely for glory, said Caesar's contemporary and friend, politician and historian Sallust (*Jugurthine War* 114.2). Unlike Caesar and Sallust, we can look at this account and note logically that the ease with which Caesar's men slaughtered so many people in this case readily suggests a different interpretation, one that is more ominous. How might a Gallic or Germanic eyewitness have narrated these events?

The refugees were weary. Fleeing from a dangerous situation in their previous home, they had arrived at their encampment looking for one thing first and foremost: rest. Well, a second thing, too: safety, however temporary. After many weeks of travel, they were exhausted, hungry, discouraged. The women, children, and the elderly in particular were worn out by the rapid marching. The pregnant women—not mentioned, but surely there were some!—in the camp felt particularly vulnerable. At last, this multitude of families set up camp, hoping to rest for a while in this isolated place. But their hopes were swiftly dashed when Caesar ordered an attack on them— something they had not expected, since they were clearly more akin to ghosts than a threatening army at this point.

Disoriented, the men could hardly resist the attack and lacked proper armor to face the professional Roman army anyway. The cavalry attack on defenseless women and children was stunning in its brutality. The cavalry were the heavy guns of ancient warfare, so why send them unprovoked against the weakest and nonmilitary folk? The forest air rang with the screams and cries of the attacked and, later, with the groans of the dying. As bodies piled up on the blood-soaked ground or washed ashore from the river, the survivors could feel nothing but sheer terror.

A century and a half after Caesar, another Roman historian, Tacitus, famously put a condemning speech in the mouth of another barbarian and enemy of Rome, a British tribesman, about the Romans' treatment of local populations in areas they conquered:

> There are no tribes beyond us, nothing indeed but waves and rocks, and the yet more terrible Romans, from whose oppression escape is vainly sought by obedience and submission. Robbers of the world, having by their universal plunder exhausted the land, they rifle the deep. If the enemy be rich, they are rapacious; if he be poor, they lust for dominion; neither the east nor the west has been able to satisfy them. Alone among men they covet with equal eagerness poverty and riches. To robbery, slaughter, plunder, they give the lying name of empire; they make a solitude and call it peace. (Tacitus, *Agricola* 30)[6]

There are hints in Caesar's own account to support this narrative of rapacious slaughter, transforming a populated camp into a city of the dead. If the tribespeople he attacked really were dangerous and ready for war, we should expect that the Romans would have suffered at least some casualties, however minimal. But, as Caesar emphasizes, the Romans did not suffer a single loss in this "battle." Even the number of the wounded among his troops, he brags, was minimal.

Clearly the account we are reading here is not of a true battle. This is a brutal massacre of mostly unarmed people, many of them women and

---

[6]For a translation, see Tacitus, *Life of Cnaeus Julius Agricola*, trans. Alfred John Church and William Jackson Brodribb, Ancient History Sourcebook, https://sourcebooks.fordham.edu/ancient/tacitus-agricola.asp.

children. Just how many of these 430,000 defenseless refugees did Caesar's men kill? Ancient military writers' number reports are notoriously untrustworthy, but in this case, we have archaeological evidence confirming the truly horrifying loss of life that occurred.[7] The remains found suggest that the Romans killed approximately 150,000 people on this occasion. To be clear, this is only one occasion out of a number of massacres that Caesar describes over the course of his journals.

While Caesar published these journals in order to win popular approval in Rome—and it largely worked!—many readers today are rightly horrified by Caesar's casual and deliberate cruelty toward the Gauls, whose main crime seems to have been resistance to the Romans' efforts of conquest. Or, as our chosen example shows, sometimes the Gauls' main crime simply amounted to being in the same space as Caesar at the wrong time. Going a step beyond mere horror and disapproval over such massacres, scholars such as Michael Kulikowski and Kurt Raaflaub label Caesar's efforts in Gaul an outright genocide, showing yet more clearly our different perspective on this war in contrast to its positive perception by the original audiences of Caesar's scrolls.[8] There used to be some resistance to using the modern term *genocide* to describe events in antiquity. The new three-volume *Cambridge World History of Genocide*, however, dedicates the first of its three volumes to genocide in the ancient and medieval world, reminding us that there is value in distinguishing genocide from other types of mass violence.[9]

To be clear, I fully agree that Caesar's actions constitute genocide and we are right to condemn them. Yet, this relatively recent and darker view of Caesar also feeds into this intriguing question: Why might we today think

---

[7]Liz Leafloor, "150,000 Fled for Their Lives, but Were Slaughtered by Julius Caesar Army, Bones Reveal," Ancient Origins, December 14, 2015, www.ancient-origins.net/news-history-archaeology/150000-fled-their-lives-were-slaughtered-julius-caesar-army-bones-reveal-020659.

[8]Michael Kulikowski, "A Very Bad Man," *London Review of Books*, June 18, 2020, www.lrb.co.uk/the-paper/v42/n12/michael-kulikowski/a-very-bad-man; and Kurt Raaflaub, "Caesar and Genocide: Confronting the Dark Side of Caesar's Gallic Wars," *New England Classical Journal* 48 (2021): 54-80, https://crossworks.holycross.edu/cgi/viewcontent.cgi?article=1350&context=necj.

[9]Ben Kiernan, T. M. Lemos, and Tristan S. Taylor, *The Cambridge World History of Genocide*, vol. 1, *Genocide in the Ancient, Medieval and Premodern Worlds* (New York: Cambridge University Press, 2023).

that his actions—including both this particular genocide and any genocide more broadly—are wrong, whereas the Romans did not? Considering this question and the divergent answers to it tells us something both about the Romans and about our society's deeply seated vestiges of Christian value of human life, which are being eroded in the post-Christian worldview.[10]

It is because of two millennia of Christian valuing of human life that we believe that murder and other deliberate harm against other people is wrong. Unlike the Greco-Roman pagans, who had no such framework for seeing the preciousness of human life, we do not delight in the suffering of the weak. Rather, we do not want to see such suffering—it troubles us, stirs deep emotions in us. Jesus wept. We too, as a result, instinctively desire to weep with those who weep. But, as Caesar's writings show, this was not the case outside the Judeo-Christian worldview. The pre-Christian residents of the ancient Mediterranean world were not like this.

Let us come back to our big question for this chapter: What is the worth of a human life in a world where the *imago Dei* does not exist? Caesar's actions provide a clear answer applicable to much of the ancient Mediterranean: it depends; let each man (most of the time) or woman (sometimes) be the judge. Without a firm and unwavering commitment to the doctrine of the *imago Dei*, we are all Caesar in our own eyes and Gauls in the eyes of others. Of course, all others around may be potential Gauls in our view as well. A declaration of war could be forthcoming at any moment.

To be fair to Caesar, we should note that any other Roman military commander would have acted in the same way in the same situations. The period of the late Roman Republic was a pressure cooker that drove aristocratic politicians with consular aspirations to ever greater searches for wars to win abroad so they could parlay these achievements into political victories at home.[11] The Gauls simply got caught in the middle of this unfortunate

---

[10]Louise Perry provides a striking summary of this erosion in progress in our society in her essay, "We Are Repaganizing," *First Things*, October 1, 2023, www.firstthings.com/article/2023/10/we-are-repaganizing.

[11]One short and sweet overview of the volatile political mess that was the late Roman Republic is Harriet Flower, *Roman Republics* (Princeton, NJ: Princeton University Press, 2010).

calculus. Caesar, a product of his time and space, acted in accordance with his society's values. If we wanted to get a little cheeky, we could even note Caesar's well-known reputation for *clementia*, clemency, compared to some other contemporary generals. The Gauls would demur.

At any rate, the massacres that Caesar casually highlights in his journals would not have been out of place in most other military narratives from the Greco-Roman world since the Homeric epics. Military glory—the highest form of undying, epic glory, to which every Greek and Roman man aspired in his heart of hearts—was predicated on kill rates and human trophies. In some cases, we could say, the Gauls were valuable for Caesar, but they were worth more to him dead than alive. As for civilians, these "worthless ones" in wartime, captive women especially could acquire a value for their conquerors as visible portable trophies. Their value, in other words, yet again lay in the abuse they suffered and the glory that this abuse acquired for their conquerors.

WORTH MORE DEAD THAN ALIVE

It is fitting that the most often quoted, albeit perhaps apocryphal, saying of Soviet dictator Joseph Stalin has to do with death: "The death of one man is a tragedy. The death of a million is a statistic." Caesar would disagree: documenting the number of deaths is important; but unless we are dealing with the deaths of Roman soldiers, none of them is a tragedy. Syrianos made a distinction in valuing the worth of people in terms of ability to contribute to the war effort: you were either useful or useless. For Caesar, by contrast, everyone was useful. But some were more useful dead than alive.

In his descriptions of massacres, Caesar displays repeatedly an interest in documenting kill rates and numbers of enemies. As we saw in our earlier discussion of a massacre of the Germanic tribespeople, Caesar notes that his troops had attacked 430,000 people, and while he does not provide the number of those killed, he implies that it was very high—and, indeed, archaeological evidence confirms this. Why did he include these numbers? High numbers are impressive, so certainly featuring them to dazzle his Roman readers with his army's heroic feats was part of the reason. But there is another, specifically political reason why Caesar wanted to keep a record of the number of enemies he faced in the field and especially the number of the enemies he had killed.

As I mentioned earlier, the political world of the Roman Republic was a pressure cooker. Politicians were all after the same great prize—the triumph—but the road to it was not easy. In the Roman world, political power and military commands and victories kept feeding each other in a deadly loop. The Roman *cursus honorum*, the order of elected offices, demonstrates this clearly.

An aspiring Roman politician began his preparation for a potential political career at age eighteen by—what else—securing a military appointment for the next decade. A scion of a respectable family did not, of course, enlist as a simple legionary. Rather, one would expect friends and relatives to pull strings to place the precocious youth as an assistant of sorts, likely at a post of military tribune, helping a senior politician with a military command. Upon turning thirty (for those of patrician rank) or thirty-two (if plebeian), the aspiring politician began the process of seeking election to offices that were arranged as a ladder or even a pyramid.

The lowest elected office—that of the quaestor—allowed those who had held it lifelong membership in the Roman Senate. Election to subsequent positions, as the pyramid narrowed, was not guaranteed. At the top of the pyramid was the grand prize, the office of the consul. Just two were elected each year. It was only consuls or former consuls who could, after acquiring a distinguished military command and winning a significant victory, petition the Senate to be granted the highest honor to which any Roman could aspire: the triumph.

So, what exactly was the triumph? It was a celebration parade of a victorious general with his army. But it was much more than just that. For a day, the general being honored got to play god—and everyone knew it. It began with appearances. He would dress up as Jupiter, the king of the gods, including possibly painting his face with red paint to look like the terra cotta cult statue of Jupiter Optimus Maximus (Jupiter the Best and the Greatest). The general rode slowly in a chariot on the designated triumphal route to the adoration of all Romans, with just one more companion in the chariot—a slave, who would whisper in his ear, "Memento mori"—remember that you are still mortal, even on this day when you dress up like a god, look like a god, act like a god.

The honorand's soldiers marched behind him on foot and were required, as part of the festivities, to sing bawdy songs about their general. Perhaps these served the same purpose as the slave in the chariot—they reminded the general, on the best day of his life, that he was still imperfect and mortal. Perhaps they also had an apotropaic function, swaying away the gods' jealousy from the man who played god for a day. There is, after all, a fine line between propriety and hubris. The biographer Suetonius includes one of these soldiers' songs from Caesar's quadruple triumph, confirming our belief that these ditties were definitely of the no-holds-barred variety: "Men of Rome, protect your wives; we are bringing in the bald adulterer. You fornicated away in Gaul the gold you borrowed here in Rome" (*The Deified Julius* 51).[12]

Closing the procession were captives in chains—kings and queens in-cluded, if possible—and floats displaying particularly impressive spoils of war. One of the reasons attributed to Cleopatra VII's suicide is in fact her desire to avoid the humiliation of marching in Octavian's triumph in 30 BC.[13] In AD 70—much later than the days of Caesar, of course—celebrating his victory over the Jews, the emperor Vespasian famously paraded for public display the iconic menorah and ritual vessels taken from the Second Temple in Jerusalem.[14]

Historian Mary Beard emphasizes that all these customs that we think we know about the triumph are conjectures, often based on much later evidence. We have no way to confirm or deny, but her more skeptical argument does not affect the most important point: the triumph was the pinnacle of any

---

[12]Suetonius, *Lives of the Caesars*, vol. 1, *Julius. Augustus. Tiberius. Gaius Caligula*, trans. J. C. Rolfe, Loeb Classical Library 31 (Cambridge, MA: Harvard University Press, 1914). I substituted a less offensive *f*-word for the verb involved. Caesar's soldiers were not a gently spoken crowd.

[13]Duane Roller, *Cleopatra: A Biography* (New York: Oxford University Press, 2010), 146-47.

[14]These images are displayed in the representation of the triumphal procession of Vespasian and Titus on the Arch of Titus. For images from the arch, see "Arch of Titus," Roman Monuments, https://penelope.uchicago.edu/~grout/encyclopaedia_romana/romanurbs/archtitus.html.

Roman's existence.[15] Descendants of those who had once celebrated a triumph continued to brag about this accomplishment, as it became folded into the family's lore.[16] This military achievement, then, for both the winner of this honor and for his descendants became a further bargaining chip for accumulating greater political power—more elections to the rank of consul, allowing the winners the chance to win further triumphs.

How does all this relate to our main point here—that for Caesar the Gauls and, really, any foreign enemy were worth more dead than alive? Very directly. The request for a triumph required the applicant for the honor to demonstrate to the Senate that he had killed a minimum of five thousand enemies. Military and political honor in the Roman Republic, in other words, was directly measured by the cost of enemy life, dividing the world clearly into those whose lives were more valuable as spoils versus those who conquered.

This idea that some bodies were worth more dead than alive was not new to the Roman military and political ethos. We see the same idea ingrained into the essence of ancient Greek warfare from the earliest times. In the *Iliad*, the earliest surviving work of Greek literature, composed and recited orally for centuries before there even was a Greek alphabet for writing it all down, several stock episodes of *aristeia* appear. The term *aristos* simply means "the best."

Every warrior wanted to be the best of all, and the *aristeia* episodes are epic action sequences documenting the impressive accomplishments of one particular warrior in action. Often they involve divine inspiration—literally—as in book 5 of the *Iliad*, where the Greek hero Diomedes, temporarily strengthened by the goddess Athena, goes on an epic slaughter rampage on the battlefield, felling enemies like flies. Blood flows in rivers, and bodies and body parts fly in all directions around the Homeric battlefield. This is glorification of violence and killing to an extreme degree. Diomedes's greatness as a warrior is firmly established in the minds of the

[15]Mary Beard, *The Roman Triumph* (Cambridge, MA: Belknap, 2007).
[16]Harriet Flower, *Ancestor Masks and Aristocratic Power in Roman Culture* (Oxford: Clarendon, 1996), 101-2.

listeners, all at the cost of the dead warriors whom he had slaughtered. There is no other way to become *aristos*. Someone always has to pay the price for another's martial glory.

While the arrival of hoplite warfare changed how the Greeks fought starting in the Archaic period (ca. 800–490 BC), the notion of some bodies being worth more dead than alive continued in a new form. The hoplite phalanx allowed the soldiers of each city-state to fight strictly in formation, the many acting as one body. But the new, unofficial laws of war added a new value to the bodies of those killed on the battlefield.[17] One of the most poignant events demonstrating this new value of the dead occurred during the Peloponnesian War (431–404 BC), the vicious internecine war between Athens and Sparta and their respective allies for control over the Greek-speaking world.

In 424 BC, the Athenians fought the Boeotians, allied with Sparta, at the Battle of Delium. The battle turned out to be a costly defeat for the Athenians.[18] Our concern, however, lies in what happened after the battle proper. Hoplite battles, especially ones this bitter, left bodies on the battlefield, and it was up to the losing side to formally petition the winners to allow them to collect the bodies of their dead for burial. Indeed, in his summary of the laws of hoplite warfare, historian Peter Krentz argues that this petition amounted to de facto admission of defeat. At times, Krentz notes, if the winner of a battle had vacated the battlefield prematurely without picking up the dead and then had to petition the technically losing side for the right to collect the dead, this amounted to reversing roles. The winner, in such a case, could become the loser.[19]

In Greek religion, proper burial of a body was supremely important for assuring a restful afterlife for the soul.[20] Normally, the winners of a battle,

---

[17]For the debate over laws or rules that may have governed hoplite warfare, see Josiah Ober, "The Rules of War in Classical Greece," in *The Athenian Revolution: Essays on Ancient Greek Democracy and Political Theory* (Princeton, NJ: Princeton University Press, 1996), 53-71; Peter Krentz, "Fighting by the Rules: The Invention of the Hoplite Agon," *Hesperia* 71 (2002): 23-39; and Adriaan Lanni, "The Laws of War in Ancient Greece," *Law and History Review* 26 (2008): 269-89.

[18]The philosopher Socrates and his young protégé Alcibiades both fought heroically at this engagement—Socrates as a hoplite and Alcibiades in the cavalry.

[19]Krentz, "Fighting by the Rules," 2002.

[20]See, for example, Sophocles, *Antigone*, whose plot revolves around the importance of giving a proper burial to the dead. Antigone considers this duty so important that she is willing to sacrifice her own life to carry it out.

however bitter, did not dispute the return of the bodies of the losing side. In the case of the Battle of Delium, however, they did. The Boeotians chose to use the bodies of the Athenian dead on the battlefield, amounting to about one thousand hoplites, as pawns to force the Athenians to cede additional territory to them. They finally allowed the Athenians to collect their dead seventeen days later (Thucydides, *History of the Peloponnesian War* 4.97-101).

This abuse of the bodies of the dead as bitter pawns in war became the subject of Athenian playwright Euripides's tragedy *Suppliant Women*, produced the following year. Tragedies often used mythological subjects with contemporary application, and the case here is especially obvious. In this tragedy, mothers of defeated warriors from Argos come to Athens to ask for help: their sons lie unburied near Thebes, where they had lost a war to the Thebans. The mothers, mourning their dead sons, ask the Athenians to intercede in getting the bodies back for burial. It takes the intervention of Athena, the patron goddess of Athens, appearing at the end of the play as the *dea ex machina*, to make justice possible.

Historically, Thebes was the chief city-state in Boeotia and an enemy of Athens during the fifth century BC, including in the Peloponnesian War. One need not page Dr. Freud to understand the omnipresent obsession in Athenian tragedy with the Thebans as immoral villains. Athenian playwrights kept coming back to horrific mythological injustices that happened in Thebes.[21] By contrast, most restorations of justice in Athenian drama happen in Athens—the Athenians (or their patron goddess, Athena) are frequently the rescuers of the other Greeks, whether they are helping the exiled Oedipus, the refugee Medea, Orestes in search of divine justice, or Euripides's mourning mothers looking to bury their sons.[22]

The Delium affair, along with similar stories in Athenian tragedies, highlights the use of bodies of the dead as valuable pawns in political struggles even after a war or battle was over. But while some enemies in Greek and

---

[21]Examples include Aeschylus, *Seven Against Thebes*; Sophocles, *Oedipus King* and *Antigone*; and Euripides, *Bacchae*.

[22]These are the plots of the following Athenian tragedies respectively: Sophocles, *Oedipus at Colonus*; Euripides, *Medea*; Aeschylus, *Eumenides*; and Euripides, *Suppliant Women*.

Roman warfare had more value dead than alive, others could have an excellent value—symbolic and monetary—while alive.

HUMAN TROPHIES

My completely unscientific polling of nonclassicist friends and students over the years suggests that most people think the main subject of the *Iliad* is the Trojan War. They might also mention heroes and demigods, and maybe even mention Helen as the cause of the war. These answers are not entirely wrong: the epic does take place during the Trojan War, and Greek and Trojan heroes and the legendary beauty Helen, whose kidnapping started the war, are all characters in the poem. Yet, the epic is about something both more complicated and more mundane: one hero's grudge. Or, to be more respectfully poetic about it, the epic is about the wrath of one hero over losing his human trophy of war. It is a story, in part, about beautiful women who were very valuable if captured alive. No, this does not make it a romantic story about love—the only true love involved here is a hero's love of his own glory.

Early in Homer's *Iliad*, a complicated quarrel unfolds that will ultimately drive the action of the epic. Indeed, the epic opens with the word *wrath*, and that wrath will not end until the conclusion of the poem. Whose wrath? That of the hero Achilles. What is Achilles so extraordinarily angry about? In a nutshell, a special trophy that was his until another commander took it away. Trophies matter, we learn, for a warrior's personal prestige and honor. But what seems unusual at first glance is that this particular trophy looked nothing like those soccer trophies my elementary school players receive at the end of each season. Let us take a few steps back and explain.

As the *Iliad* opens, we are dropped into the story mid-action. For nine years already, the Greeks have been besieging Troy. In addition, they have also been launching periodic sorties against neighboring towns, capturing provisions and other goods. Some of these goods, it turns out, are human. The father of one such captive, Chryses, is a priest of the god Apollo. At the beginning of the epic, he asks the Greek army's commander-in-chief, Agamemnon, to allow him to ransom back his daughter, Chryseis, whom

Agamemnon had taken as his concubine. Agamemnon refuses. This is a foolish decision. Apollo was the god of, among other things, plagues. When Chryses prays in desperation for Apollo's help and revenge, the god is happy to oblige, promptly raining down plague arrows on the Greek camp.

The Greeks, in their own desperation, do the only thing that one could do in such a desperate situation. They consult a seer, who promptly fingers Agamemnon as the culprit for the plague. Achilles forces Agamemnon to do the right thing and give back Chryseis to her father. None of this, to be clear, has to do with any of the warriors' concern for the aged priest father of the innocent young woman who had been kidnapped from her home and forcibly made a sex slave. The warriors do, however, all want the plague to stop, so if this is what it takes, so be it. Agamemnon, in his anger and arrogance, retaliates by taking away Achilles's own concubine, Briseis. This insult is the source of Achilles's wrath, which will lead him to withdraw from the fighting, setting into motion the rest of the events of the epic.

Why are Agamemnon and Achilles so angry about losing their respective concubines? The epic helps us out by making the women's status clear: Chryseis and Briseis were not just normal concubines or captive sex slaves. Rather, each of them was designated as *geras* (to use the epic term), a portable special trophy, for the man to whom she had been given. This means that they were not easily replaceable. The only replacement for *geras* could be another *geras*.

After each raid, spoils (human and material) were divided into two categories: the regular stuff and the extra-special goods. All warriors got a portion of the regular spoils. Then the most distinguished warriors got a special additional prize from the second category—effectively a trophy whose role it was to designate its recipient's superior status. As particularly beautiful female captives, both Chryseis and Briseis served as that special trophy of excellence for Agamemnon and Achilles respectively. And since prestige in Homeric society was visibly displayed, the loss of a trophy amounted to a real decline in one's prestige and honor. Agamemnon's demand makes sense in this regard: by requisitioning Achilles's trophy, he ensures that his own prestige remains intact after losing his original prize.

The matter-of-fact manner in which these events and transactions in human flesh unfold in the epic is a reminder of how accepted this reality of devaluing human dignity, especially of women, in wartime was in the early Greek world. One of the most emotional scenes in all of the *Iliad* is the moment Hector and Andromache say goodbye to each other for—as it will turn out—the last time. Hector, the Trojan hero, is about to go back into the fighting, while his loving wife is afraid for his life and for the consequences of the capture of Troy for her and her baby boy. She is right to be afraid, audiences knew. While the plot of the *Iliad* concludes shortly before the sack of Troy, later sources for Greek myths, including Athenian tragedy, clue us in to the fate of Andromache and her baby, which is exactly as she had thought. Andromache and Hector's baby son, Astyanax, is sentenced to execution by the Greeks. He is thrown down from the walls of Troy. Andromache, as befits a beautiful young woman, is promptly enslaved as a concubine for one of the Greeks.

Epic poetry is art, but it is art that reflects real life, rendering the horrors of war in beautiful hexameters that keep marching across the Trojan plain in much more organized formation than the warriors ever did. Descriptions of the sack of ancient cities in all periods of Greek and Roman history repeatedly confirm the horrifying truth: upon capture, males of fighting age were summarily executed, while women and children were sold into slavery.[23] We might name select representative examples that contemporaries already viewed as particularly vicious: the Athenian destruction and sack of Melos in 416 BC during the Peloponnesian War; the Roman sack of Carthage in 149 BC, Corinth in 146 BC, and Jerusalem in AD 70; and the Visigothic sack of Rome in AD 410.[24] But as the stories of Chryseis and Briseis remind us, plenty of terrorizing of local populations, including mass rape and kidnapping of women, was going on even before a stronghold was taken.

---

[23]Joel Christensen's work on Odysseus and posttraumatic stress disorder reminds us, though, that the warriors themselves were not well either. See *The Many-Minded Man: The Odyssey, Psychology, and the Therapy of Epic* (Ithaca, NY: Cornell University Press, 2020).

[24]For an overview of mass violence in ancient warfare, see Gabriel Bakes, *Spare No One: Mass Violence in Roman Warfare* (Lanham, MD: Rowman & Littlefield, 2021).

Historian Kathy Gaca has written extensively about the targeted mass rape of women and girls in ancient warfare as an organized military strategy.[25] After all, such abuse of the "useless ones" did not begin only at a war's end, with the capture of a city. Wars of the modern world show that this is not just ancient history. World War I and World War II, for examples, featured plenty of abuses of civilians, both indiscriminate slaughter and widespread rape. The Rape of Belgium during World War I is one particularly well-known example, but many others dot the twentieth century. In 1937, during the horrific Rape of Nanking, as this event was later dubbed, the Japanese purposefully targeted civilians in the Chinese city of Nanking. The events in question were so traumatic that Iris Chang, the journalist who wrote an award-winning book on the topic, suffered severe posttraumatic stress disorder by proxy and died by suicide.[26] More recently, similar systematic, widespread rape coupled with executions of civilians has been a terror tactic used by Russians in the brutal invasion of Ukraine.[27]

These modern examples, documented in much greater detail than our ancient sources offer, remind us that while the technology of war continues to evolve, the impact of war on civilians remains much the same in the age of air raids as it was in Homeric Troy. The "useless ones" may not wear military uniforms, but this does not mean that their bodies and their dignity are protected from the ravages of war. Their suffering echoes that of the defenseless tribes whom Caesar massacred so long ago. Whether they are worth more dead or alive to modern-day Caesars the world all over, civilians continue to be pawns in the deadly games of war and genocide. Abuse and

> Whether they are worth more dead or alive to modern-day Caesars the world all over, civilians continue to be pawns in the deadly games of war and genocide.

[25]See, in particular, Kathy Gaca, "The Andrapodizing of War Captives in Greek Historical Memory," *Transactions of the American Philological Association* 140 (2010): 117-61.

[26]Iris Chang, *The Rape of Nanking: The Forgotten Holocaust of World War II* (New York: Basic Books, 1997).

[27]Laurel Wamsley, "Rape Has Reportedly Become a Weapon in Ukraine. Finding Justice May Be Difficult," NPR, April 30, 2022, www.npr.org/2022/04/30/1093339262/ukraine-russia-rape-war-crimes.

devaluing of civilian lives in war are often accompanied by the abuse of one other entity: their land.

RAVAGING THE LAND

In the spring of 431 BC, the Spartan army invaded Attica, the region of villages surrounding the city of Athens, with the aim of ravaging the land. They did so again in 430 BC and most other years down to 425 BC. The Athenians, frustrated and terrified, withdrew each time within the city walls, abandoning their farmland to the ruthless attackers. True, crops are surprisingly tough to destroy in the fields—wheat burns only during a short window before harvest, olive and other trees are extremely difficult to chop down, and both processes simply take a long time, which an army on the march generally does not possess.[28]

As it happens, the Spartans were not able to inflict significant direct damage on the crops. Still, the strategy of ravaging the land was a common one in ancient warfare. It reminds us of a key truth: people's well-being and flourishing has historically been connected to their land in obvious physical ways. In agricultural societies, it was the land that fed those who farmed and protected it. But beyond that, communities tied to the land historically fostered ties of people to each other through the land they all loved, promoting networks of care. It was these networks, as much as the fruits of agricultural labor, that attacking armies at war usually tried to destroy.

There is one more key point here. If the pro-death and pro-destruction position involves the ravaging of a land to which people and communities are connected, the opposite applies as well: being pro-life and supporting human flourishing means supporting local communities and encouraging people to maintain roots. This is a point that seemed obvious for most people throughout world history, who did not go far from their village or city of birth. It was rather in wartime that uprooting most commonly happened— sacking of ancient cities and territories, as I have noted, was accompanied

---

[28]So argues Victor Davis Hanson, farmer and historian, who conducted experiments himself on various crops to test their destructibility: See *Warfare and Agriculture in Classical Greece* (Berkeley: University of California Press, 1998).

by the ravaging of both the people and their land, selling the people into slavery while often destroying their cities and farms before resettling these territories with other people. This is the story of the ancient Israelites, for instance, in the Old Testament—the Assyrian exile and the Babylonian exile. The forthcoming destruction of Jerusalem by the Romans in AD 70 is a tragedy to which Jesus refers multiple times in his ministry—after that moment, the Jews will be dispersed from their land for centuries. This is what a killing of a people, as opposed to mere individuals, looks like.

Human flourishing here on earth requires roots and communities, things the ancient world valued greatly, even as our modern society sometimes devalues them in our pursuit of promotions at the cost of staying close to family. The way of war in the ancient world, in its ruthless attacks on these entities, only highlights more clearly their importance for promoting a culture of life.

CONCLUSION: THE REDEMPTION OF USELESS PEOPLE

A few years ago, Amy Julia Becker, an author and theologian whose oldest daughter, Penny, was born with Down syndrome, wrote an article with a striking title for *Christianity Today*: "Why We Need 'Useless' People."[29] While Becker's argument focuses specifically on the redemption of people with Down, her point about how the world too often sees them as useless is notable: "Most people in our world still see Down syndrome as something both monolithic and negative—a condition to be eradicated rather than a group of individuals to be welcomed and loved."

Becker's article reminds us that labeling any group of people "useless," based on any criteria, whether military or health or ability-related, adds up to presenting a worldview in which the value of each individual's life is relative and subject to someone else's arbitrary judgment. Such a reality should terrify us, because any one of us could fail the usefulness test. Indeed, Canada's medical assistance in dying (MAID) experiment reminds us that at

---

[29]Amy Julia Becker, "Why We Need 'Useless' People," *Christianity Today*, March 21, 2017, www
.christianitytoday.com/ct/2017/march-web-only/why-we-need-useless-people.html/.

some point in our lives, each of us will fail the usefulness test, whether through sickness or simply by virtue of aging.[30] The church has historically led the way in resisting the view that our worth in God's eyes depends on our physical or intellectual perfection, or that any of us are better off dead than alive. God's love for us is not conditional on such qualifications. Neither should we have such criteria for determining the preciousness of the lives of others. Put simply, all lives are priceless.

In commemorating his victory over the Gauls later on, after the no less bloody civil war that he fought right after, Caesar minted a series of coins presenting the conquered bodies of his foreign enemies, often staged around a battlefield trophy—a tree decorated with the armor of killed and despoiled Gauls.[31] Used to pay the troops in his employ, these coins are a tangible reminder of the cost calculations involved in war. War is expensive, as the coins tangibly display, but for those who have gone to war—whether the Caesars of antiquity or the ones of our own age, who wage war on a different sort of useless people, at home or abroad—the cost-benefit calculus shows these wars to be profitable.

> **Human lives, whether in antiquity or today, continue to be held as a necessary cost whenever there is no philosophical or theological framework for valuing them.**

Human lives, whether in antiquity or today, continue to be held as a necessary cost whenever there is no philosophical or theological framework for valuing them. In light of such accepted cruelty and abuse of human life, it is difficult to overemphasize just how revolutionary the idea of the *imago Dei* was in antiquity and continues to be within all philosophical systems of world history. The idea that every single human, regardless of life stage, age, status, health, or physical or intellectual (dis-)ability level, is priceless and precious and

---

[30]Benjamin Crosby, "Where Are the Churches in Canada's Euthanasia Experiment?," *Plough*, February 27, 2023, www.plough.com/en/topics/justice/culture-of-life/where-are-the-churches-in-canadas-euthanasia-experiment.

[31]For images of some of these coins, see "The Gallic Wars (58–51BC)," Macquarie University, 2014, www.humanities.mq.edu.au/acans/caesar/GallicWars.htm.

unspeakably loved in God's eyes should seem unfathomable to us because of its uniqueness.

Too often we too live as though we do not fully believe it, hence the inconsistencies in our own behavior and policymaking. But the case of Caesar and the Gauls, just one example that displays the casual cruelty and disregard for human life on which the ancient pagan world was constructed, reminds us what a world without the knowledge of the *imago Dei* would look like. It would be a world of dystopia like Huxley's *Brave New World*, a world filled with self-creating misery and endless sorrow without hope. Thankfully, as the early Christians began telling a world filled with suffering, it is not the truth. It is to their work of redeeming "useless people" that we now turn.

7

THE REDEMPTION
OF USELESS PEOPLE

In 205 BC, over a decade into the Second Punic War, the vicious military conflict of Rome and Carthage, the Romans experienced a series of omens and prodigies that were severe enough to merit the worst-case-scenario recourse: consulting the Sibylline books. These were books of prophecy that were notoriously obscure and difficult to understand.[1] Perhaps this is why they were saved for the types of emergencies where no one could figure out what to do anyway. What was there to lose?

Clearly matters were dire indeed, because instead of the usual solutions, such as an amped-up sacrifice regimen or the construction of a new temple to a Roman deity, the books recommended instead importing a very strange foreign divinity—the Phrygian goddess Cybele, also known as Magna Mater (the Great Mother). Just how bizarre was Cybele and her cult in the eyes of the Romans? Well, for starters, her priests had to castrate themselves as part of their initiation ritual, which made this particular cult a more niche, self-selected group than most. The few surviving details about her cult emphasize just how desperate

---

[1]Mary Beard, John North, and Simon Price, *Religions of Rome*, vol. 1, *A History* (New York: Cambridge University Press, 1998), 62-63.

the Romans had to have been to import this goddess into Rome with much fanfare.[2]

As fascinating as problems and solutions in Roman religion can be (just what does the omen of the self-defenestrating donkey on another occasion mean anyway?), what is most relevant for our story at hand is what happened to the cult statue of Cybele when she arrived in Rome. The ship dramatically got stuck in the Tiber, just offshore—a reminder of how shallow and unfriendly to navigation the river was—and, in a miraculous feat, a young Roman woman drew the ship safely into the harbor singlehandedly, barely touching the rope to do so. The young woman's name was Claudia Quinta. As her name tells us, she was the fifth daughter in her family (Livy, *Ab urbe condita* 29.14).

THE COST OF DAUGHTERS

Daughters were an expensive luxury in societies, such as ancient Rome, where a family had to provide a dowry for them. A family with five daughters therefore would have been an anomaly, an unusual public statement reflecting the family's wealth and prosperity. In other words, sumptuously showy consumption could take the form of keeping that fifth daughter around. We do not hear of many others. A poorer family would have perhaps exposed one or more of these daughters instead of investing precious resources in raising them. At least for aristocratic families, marrying these daughters off was an opportunity to secure new alliances and connections, advancing the family's status.[3]

It was not only the individual families themselves who had to weigh the cost of daughters in deciding whether each was worth keeping alive. In the eyes of the Roman government, women were valuable primarily as the birthers of the next generation of Romans—cue the Emperor Augustus's policy, providing ample carrot-and-stick measures for aristocratic women

---

[2]Beard, North, and Price, *Religions of Rome*, 164-65.
[3]A good example of this use of daughters as political pawns is the life and marital career of Clodia Metelli. See Marilyn B. Skinner, *Clodia Metelli: The Tribune's Sister* (New York: Oxford University Press, 2011).

to bear at least three children.[4] These policies failed to produce the desired result, by the way.

We could also think back to an earlier time, in the days of the Peloponnesian War in the late fifth century BC. In his famous funeral oration, which he delivered to the Athenians to commemorate those killed in the first year of the war, Pericles, the leading democratic statesman of his day, encouraged the women of Athens to do the only good thing they could do for their state in wartime: have more babies (Thucydides, *History of the Peloponnesian War* 2.44).

In the midst of the robust tradition of scientific misogyny that we traced in chapter four, such valuing of women's contributions to society as baby growers (even while questioning whether they even qualified as the parents of these babies) rightly seems anemic or downright insulting to us. It leaves out all sense of personhood, reducing people to only the goods that they could produce. But as we have seen, the pre-Christian world unapologetically divided people into two categories: those who could actively contribute to the state's military efforts and those who could not. By encouraging Athenian women of childbearing age to have more babies, Pericles was at least offering them an indirect way to contribute to the war effort.

This leads us to an uncomfortable question: Is there any value to women qua women? Of course, this is a form of the larger umbrella question: How do we justify the value of any human being? The pre-Christian utilitarian approach I have just outlined has ramifications for answering this question for women, as it also involves the devaluing of individuals who did not marry. Since unmarried women could not produce legally born children who might grow to contribute to the war effort (and only the children of legally wed parents counted!), they had no value in the pre-Christian pagan worldview. The devaluing of women could also take the form of prioritizing baby boys over baby girls in an environment of scarcity, real or imagined.

---

[4]For an overview of Augustus's profamily policies and their failure, see Karl Galinsky, *Augustus: Introduction to the Life of an Emperor* (New York: Cambridge University Press, 2012), 96-99.

This is a reality that persists into the recent past. During China's thirty-six years under the one-child policy (1980–2016), it was mostly girls who were aborted or given away for adoption. If a family could have only one child, the priority was to have a boy, who might take care of his parents in their old age. As Pew Research Center notes, "China's one-child policy likely contributed to one of the most skewed sex ratios in the world. Today, there are about 116 boys born for every 100 girls born—a ratio much higher than the global one, 107 boys for every 100 girls."[5] In a horrifying article in *The Atlantic*, an American abortionist talks about killing a baby girl simply because she was a girl.[6] This is yet another pre-Christian policy reverberating in the modern world.

But even boys were never truly safe. In a world where the value of any individual life was subjectively determined, even being born as a perfectly healthy male of the highest social status was no guarantee of safety. Technically, gratuitous violence in the ancient world was reserved for specific categories of people, the useless ones, and generally in particular circumstances, such as war. Yet, the preciousness of any life could be declared null and void on a whim, if only the circumstances were right for such a declaration. One individual whose story demonstrates this in tragic detail is the mythical king Oedipus.

THE BABY ON A HILLSIDE

Once upon a time, the king and queen of a powerful city-state, Thebes, had a baby boy. He was healthy and hearty. This should have been an occasion to celebrate and rejoice. At last, here was a son and heir to the throne! But there was a problem. The royal couple had received a prophecy earlier that a son born to them would kill his father and marry his mother. So, the parents decided, the boy had to die to avoid such a horrific curse. Not willing

---

[5]Gretchen Livingston, "Without One-Child Policy, China Still Might Not See Baby Boom, Gender Balance," Pew Research Center, November 20, 2015, www.pewresearch.org/short-reads/2015/11/20 /will-the-end-of-chinas-one-child-policy-shift-its-boy-girl-ratio/.
[6]Elaine Godfrey, "The Abortion Absolutist," *The Atlantic*, May 12, 2023, www.theatlantic.com/politics /archive/2023/05/dr-warren-hern-abortion-post-roe/674000/.

to kill their son outright, the parents ordered that he be exposed on a hillside somewhere in the wild, outside the town.[7] His feet were pierced prior to exposure, mangling them in a way that perhaps would have made the baby especially undesirable for rescue and adoption, should anyone come across him. This horrific mutilation of their own perfectly healthy baby was the final act of cruelty and rejection of this child by his parents.

A night outside in the wild would have meant the death of the defenseless newborn, whether from the elements or from wild animals. His body was also bleeding from the cruel wounds inflicted on him by a palace lackey carrying out his orders. We can imagine the baby crying for a while in pain, until hunger and utter shock set in. Then he was silent, at which point a herdsman—a reality of many a seemingly isolated Greek hillside even today—found him. The herdsman did not keep the baby for himself, but through this rescue, involving a few additional steps, the baby was adopted by the childless king and queen of Corinth. For a while, Oedipus and his adoptive family lived happily. True, Oedipus's feet did not heal fully, leaving him lame-footed. But for a king's son who was not expected to do a day's work in his life, this was not as big a handicap as it might have been for someone else.[8]

In reading the myth of Oedipus as a mother, I am struck by a detail that scholars, ancient or modern, do not normally consider: the assumption by the baby's parents that the prophecy ruled supreme and that there was no other course of action that they could take. Had they held a different worldview—one in which their baby's life was unquestionably precious and trumped any prophecy about what he might do—they would not have treated him as a threat or an enemy. Instead, the only kindness his parents had given their newborn was not killing him outright but exposing him in the wild. But how much of a kindness was it, really? It was just a ruse to avoid shedding blood and therefore incurring religious pollution for their own baby's murder.

---

[7]One of the most extended narratives of these events comes from Sophocles's tragedy *Oedipus the King*.

[8]Daniel Ogden collects the stories of physically deformed babies who grew up to be kings and tyrants in *The Crooked Kings of Ancient Greece* (London: Bloomsbury Academic, 1997).

The tragic story of Oedipus illustrates that even the healthy infant son of a king in the ancient world could not assume that his life was indisputably precious and valuable. How much more precarious were the lives of others—the poor or enslaved, infant girls who were fourth or fifth daughters in a family eager for sons, physically or mentally disabled children or adults, the poor, single women or widows, and members of dishonorable professions? By insisting on the preciousness of all human beings in God's eyes, because all human beings are made in God's image, the early church dramatically rewrote traditional Greco-Roman societal expectations. This affected the early Christian community's view of all people, but especially of those whose lives were the most likely to be devalued in the pre-Christian worldview.[9]

In Christ, every human life is precious, not because of anything a person might do or because of a person's sociopolitical status or any other factor, but simply because a person exists. But how do we know that this is indeed what the early Christians both believed and practiced? Our best source, as it happens, is one that all early Christians knew, even if they did not always fully live out its values: the New Testament.

At the most obvious level, in the New Testament we see that instead of the traditional Greco-Roman division of people into the categories of "valuable" (and therefore somewhat more protected from cruelty) and "useless" (and therefore fair game for abuse), Christ and many (although not all) of his followers championed the unconditional preciousness of all people in God's eyes and the value of all people in God's kingdom, including the church here on earth.

When I was initially doing research for this chapter, the story I had assumed I would be telling would revolve around the church's display of care for families,

> In Christ, every human life is precious, not because of anything a person might do or because of a person's sociopolitical status or any other factor, but simply because a person exists.

---

[9]For an overview of the significance of the *imago Dei* in the creation narrative and the implications of this doctrine for human flourishing for us today, see Carmen Joy Imes, *Being God's Image: Why Creation Still Matters* (Downers Grove, IL: IVP Academic, 2023).

children, and the unborn.[10] But these actions, remarkable as they were in a world of death, were not the only manifestations of the church's revolutionary valuing of life. Instead, I found that the stories that predominate in the New Testament, especially in the ministry of Jesus, are those of redemption of several categories of people who were seen as the most useless of all in the ancient world, in war or in peace: unmarried single women, childless widows and orphans, the sick and the disabled—effectively, those seen as rejects in traditional Greco-Roman society. The prominent place of their stories throughout the New Testament is striking, especially in contrast to the Greco-Roman sources.

Historians look not only for what is present in the sources but also for what is missing. Absences are tricky to watch for but helpful in seeing what is important or not to the people we study. What is fascinating is the relative absence of unmarried people in ancient Greek and Roman sources, except for a few elite or elite-adjacent men. This absence does not mean that unmarried people, especially of poor and disadvantaged backgrounds, did not exist at all in ancient societies but rather that they did not matter enough to talk about. They were, yet again, the useless ones, invisible to most elite writers. In reading about them in the Christian sources, we find stories of redemption, spiritual and physical. These stories are a powerful witness of the church's mission to embrace a comprehensive ethic of life that reflected Jesus' buying back of sinful humanity in concrete action. This ethic meant seeing all people around as people and caring for the least fortunate in word, deed, and cash. Indeed, we hear stories like that of Macrina the Younger, who lived as a consecrated virgin in the fourth century AD rescuing exposed infants, among her many other good deeds.[11] Is this not redemption— sometimes in the most literal of senses, financial?

This focus in the New Testament more generally on the redemption of the useless ones, rather than the redemption of specifically mothers and children,

---

[10]An important book that tells the story of the church's revolutionary view of children is O. M. Bakke, *When Children Became People: The Birth of Childhood in Early Christianity* (Minneapolis: Fortress, 2005).

[11]Her brother, Gregory of Nyssa, wrote about her dedication to this work in his biography of her. See *The Life of Saint Macrina by Gregory of Nyssa*, trans. Kevin Corrigan (Eugene, OR: Wipf & Stock, 2005).

is not accidental. In contemporary discourse, the arguments against abortion have included for decades concerns that devaluing fetal life will lead to the devaluing of other lives—those of the elderly, the mentally infirm, the critically ill, and the poor. These fears are coming true.[12] It appears that just as the devaluing of fetal life and of motherhood in the modern world is the canary in the coal mine trying to call our attention to the larger problem of disregard for human life, so did the attention to and care for the lives of vulnerable unmarried people with no family attachments in the early church serve as a sign of a new culture of care—a culture that cherished the lives of all made in God's image.

SINGLE LADIES

In her 2008 Grammy Award–winning song of the year, "Single Ladies (Put a Ring On It)," postmodern American prophet Beyoncé expresses eloquently the gut-wrenching reality of the post-Christian dating culture and its effect on women. The single ladies of today are often, as their namesakes in this song, in a relationship. But it is one that is dysfunctional, likely prone to emotional abuse, and certainly not leading to marriage. "'Cause if you liked it then you should have put a ring on it," goes the catchy refrain. But the heartbreak that the song conveys lays bare a surprising truth: even in our society, with its culture of build-your-own-life in any way you want, being one of the "single ladies" too often feels like a rejection and a sort of inadequacy. Why? Because in a culture that does not recognize the personhood and the preciousness of each individual through the *imago Dei* that we each bear, we feel rejection more deeply than ever, even as we verbally continue to affirm and tout the value of the unmarried and the divorced in our midst.

Two thousand years ago, in the small Judean village of Bethany, a mere two miles from Jerusalem, there lived two single ladies. They were sisters.

---

[12]See, for example, Bill Gardner, "Death by Referral: When My Doctor Offered to Help Me End My Life," *Comment*, April 20, 2023, https://comment.org/death-by-referral/. Also, abortion now is strongly correlated with poverty. See Daniel K. Williams, "Abortion and the Class Divide," *Current*, July 30, 2021, https://currentpub.com/2021/07/30/abortion-and-the-class-divide/.

They lived alone in a small house along with their brother, who too was unmarried. In a society where most women married shortly after puberty and men sometime in their twenties, this trio was an anomaly. To be fair, we do not know their precise age and are left to reconstruct their story from the crumbs that the different Gospels drop for us to follow. Still, these three siblings are important enough to be mentioned, in varying degrees of detail, in all four Gospels. What is their story, and what does it show about Jesus' view of unmarried women and men in the church?

The first time we hear about Jesus' relationship with this unusual household, he is in Bethany—the only place on earth where he was never rejected, notes Frank Viola in his book on the significance of this little village for understanding Jesus' ministry.[13] Every time Jesus is in Bethany, he visits the home of Mary and Martha. It was Martha, in fact, who specifically invited him to visit and was eager to serve him:

> As Jesus and his disciples were on their way, he came to a village where a woman named Martha opened her home to him. She had a sister called Mary, who sat at the Lord's feet listening to what he said. But Martha was distracted by all the preparations that had to be made. She came to him and asked, "Lord, don't you care that my sister has left me to do the work by myself? Tell her to help me!"
>
> "Martha, Martha," the Lord answered, "you are worried and upset about many things, but few things are needed—or indeed only one. Mary has chosen what is better, and it will not be taken away from her." (Lk 10:38-42)

On this occasion, we hear nothing about Mary and Martha's brother, Lazarus. Jesus is there to visit the two sisters, and he seems fully engaged with them, talking with both and gently comforting the one who feels left out of the conversation at first. Where is Lazarus? Is he out of the house that day? Is he sick and sleeping in a corner somewhere? We just do not know.

Lazarus, however, will be at the center of the next visit of Jesus to this family—a visit that is left out of three of the four Gospels and only

---

[13]Frank Viola, *God's Favorite Place on Earth* (Colorado Springs: David C. Cook, 2013).

documented in John 11:1-44. This is the famous story of Jesus raising Lazarus from the dead after his illness. In that story, we hear of Jesus' deep love and compassion for all three members of the family. Jesus' reaction to the news of Lazarus's death makes it clear that he knew him well and loved him. We can fill in the timeline. Most likely, Jesus visited the family on a number of other occasions between the first visit with Mary and Martha and this one. Far from mere acquaintances, they were true friends.

Finally, all four Gospels include the story of a woman who anointed Jesus shortly before his death with an expensive perfume (Mt 26:6-13; Mk 14:3-9; Lk 7:36-50; Jn 12:1-8). While the other three do not name her, John does: it is Mary! Not all New Testament scholars agree that this Mary is indeed Martha's sister, but let us consider what it might mean if she is. John notes that Martha and Lazarus are with her on that occasion as well. While others rebuke Mary's waste of the expensive perfume, Jesus applauds her costly magnificence and prophetically notes that she has anointed him for burial. Alastair Roberts suggests that this story introduces a new economy of valuing life, as it shows Mary's self-giving, which prefigures that of Jesus for us. In the world that Christ ushers in, people are worth more than currency, monetary or liquid, like this costly perfume.[14]

Overall, it appears, every time Jesus came through Bethany, he made it a point to visit this family of three singles. These visits seem to punctuate his ministry from early on to mere days before his death, when Mary anoints him. But this summary of what the four Gospels expressly tell us about the siblings leaves many questions. While we cannot answer them with absolute certainty, we can fill out the story a bit more.

To start with, we know that people in Roman Judea lived with their extended family, often encompassing many generations under one roof.[15] The oldest male in the family would have functioned as head of the household.

---

[14]Alastair Roberts, "In Praise of Costly Magnificence," *Plough*, May 26, 2023, www.plough.com/en/topics/faith/bible-studies/in-praise-of-costly-magnificence.

[15]See Carolyn Osiek and David L. Balch, *Families in the New Testament World: Households and House Churches* (Louisville: Westminster John Knox, 1997), and Richard S. Hess and M. Daniel Carroll R., eds., *Family in the Bible: Exploring Customs, Culture, and Context* (Grand Rapids, MI: Baker Academic, 2003).

As I noted already, this was a society with no room for singles; everyone was expected to get married at some point in their life, and the exceptions were remarkably few—although we see a number of them in the New Testament, including Jesus and Paul. Therefore, we know that we see here a highly unusual household. It is safe to say that original readers would have wondered, What is wrong with these three? The original audience would have readily inferred that there must be brokenness behind the story of this family, which consists of three adults, all of them unmarried. What might their story have been? Let us start over.

Once upon a time, in a modest house in Bethany, there lived a family. They were deeply rooted in their community, as were others in this village. Life in ancient towns and villages was akin to living in a fishbowl. Everyone knew everyone else's business, guaranteed. While life was precarious and disease carried away some of the family's children in infancy, three children survived that perilous first decade of life. But then something happened—most likely, an outbreak of some sort of disease. The parents died, leaving Mary, Martha, and Lazarus orphans with no other close relatives. Furthermore, a childhood of sickness—so common in the ancient world—left Lazarus frail and always sickly. As the male in the household, he should have been leading the family and making such important decisions as arranging his sisters' marriages. But he simply could not. Without anyone else to help the trio, they were stuck in their status quo.

By the time Jesus met them, the two sisters seem to have an established status of sorts in the village—others respect them and seem largely resigned to their unmarried status. This suggests that they are a bit older, perhaps closer to thirty. But speaking of respectability, Luke mentions a hint of scandal regarding Mary, describing others' perception of her as a sinner. Was there perhaps some baggage in her past? Maybe a broken engagement that had set local tongues wagging? It did not (and still does not) take much for rumors to get started, and a woman's good reputation in the ancient world was always fragile.

As for Lazarus, he is too ill to work or do much. We hear of no occupation for him, which is unusual. The Gospels tell us the profession of most men we meet—fisherman, farmer, tax collector. As so often happens when one family member is frail, the two sisters are remarkably protective of Lazarus, taking care of everything in the house and keeping the family afloat. The stress of all that must be done must have been crippling. No wonder Martha complains about all she feels obligated to do. Indeed, Martha checks all the boxes for the stereotype of the dutiful and responsible firstborn.[16]

Financially, perhaps they were not the poorest of the poor—Mary, after all, breaks a flask of expensive perfume to anoint Jesus. Could this treasure, worth a year's wages, have been designated originally as her dowry? If so, it seems fitting that she, prefiguring medieval nuns, resigns herself to a marriage with God, showing her devotion to Jesus above all earthly ties. In weeping over Jesus as she was washing his feet and wiping them with her own hair, is Mary also weeping over her own unfulfilled dreams? Life here on earth has not been kind to her, and Jesus' promises of an eternity with him speak especially loudly to one like her.

Jesus' kindness to Mary and Martha extends to one of the most powerful miracles he performed during his earthly ministry: Lazarus's resurrection from the dead, three days after his burial. Jesus' sorrow over Lazarus's death gives us one of the most stunning verses in all of Scripture: "Jesus wept" (Jn 11:35). Prefiguring Jesus' own resurrection as redemption of all humanity, this moment is a poignant summary of the significance of this story, a beautiful reminder that Christ really did choose to befriend the single, the orphaned, the forsaken. Yes, he died for them first.

THE PLIGHT OF WIDOWS

In fourth century BC Athens, there was once a curious legal case involving an elderly immigrant woman who had been savagely beaten in an assault that took place at the home of a respectable citizen. Six days later, she died

---

[16]For an insightful overview of these birth-order stereotypes, see Frank Sulloway, *Born to Rebel: Birth Order, Family Dynamics, and Creative Lives* (New York: Vintage, 1997).

of her injuries. She was this citizen's former nurse, whom he had invited to live with his family after she had been widowed. What makes her case so curious is that no one could be held accountable for her death; in a city that prided itself on its legal system that protected its citizens, this woman turned out to be a legal loophole, a nonentity who could be murdered at will.[17]

What was it about this woman that made her life so worthless in the eyes of the law that her death could go unnoticed and unavenged? It was her lack of family protectors: she was a foreigner, rather than an Athenian; she had been widowed; and she appears to have had no other family (i.e., children) who could bring a lawsuit against her killers. In a democracy that valued citizens over noncitizens and considered the pursuit of justice to be the responsibility of the relatives and close friends of the injured party, a widow like her fell through the cracks of the legal system.

We can criticize the classical Athenian legal system all we want, but Jews, whether of the Old Testament or the New, did not treat widows much better. Just think how often the plight of widows comes up—or, rather, think how often people refuse to see the plight of widows. The entire story of Naomi and Ruth revolves around the precarious condition of childless widows. They are afraid that they will starve to death because no one cares enough to see them and help them. Their only recourse to staving off starvation is the practice of gleaning. This meant gathering leftover grain on the edges of the field during harvest—hardly a reliable source of food. This provision was originally proposed for this very purpose of providing for widows in Deuteronomy 24:17-19. Strikingly, in that provision Deuteronomy groups widows together with orphans and immigrants, reminding us of the similar difficulties of the "useless ones," people without protectors in society.

Ruth's story ends happily in marriage to Boaz, a redeeming kinsman. This story prefigures another redeemer, of course—Jesus. But the successful outcome she and Naomi achieved was the exception rather than the rule for childless widows in the ancient world. Naomi's fears throughout this story

---

[17]Rebecca Futo Kennedy considers this case, discussed in Demosthenes 47, in her *Immigrant Women in Athens: Gender, Ethnicity, and Citizenship in the Classical City* (New York: Routledge, 2014), 102-3.

are no mere paranoia, as we see just how many things could have gone wrong in this case. Indeed, we learn when Ruth asks Boaz to redeem her that there was another, closer kinsman who could have redeemed her. That kinsman, who must have known of Naomi and Ruth's difficulties, at no point was in contact with them since their return to Bethlehem. It was easy to ignore the destitute, even if they were relatives, even if they were living in the same small town.

We might add that Ruth was not only a childless widow but also an immigrant from Moab. No one kills or harms Ruth. Yet, Boaz twice offers cautions that gently hint at the lawless reality that loomed over anyone in her situation—someone could have easily assaulted her and would likely have gone unpunished.[18] These were the days of the judges, and we know how well this was going for Israel. More generally, unmarried or widowed women with no protector in the ancient world were always at risk of harm because, as the Athenians once reminded the Melians, the law of nature is that the strong do as they will, and the weak must submit.[19]

Widows feature prominently in the New Testament as well. Each time, there is an emphasis on the need to value them and care for them in a society where they were otherwise considered nonentities. For most people, they were invisible. As we consider what we see in the New Testament that other sources from the period prefer to ignore, widows are in this category as well. They appear repeatedly in the Gospels, where Jesus goes out of his way to notice them—at the temple, at the well, at a funeral for a widow's only son.

Beyond the Gospels, we see widows mentioned throughout the Epistles, in admonitions to churches to take care of them, especially those among them who are childless (see, in particular, Acts 6:1-6; 9:39; 1 Tim 5:3-16). These repeated reminders would not have been necessary had the communities involved been doing this already. Indeed, Acts 6:1-6 involves a repudiation of serving widows on the part of some leaders in the church and a recommendation instead to delegate this task, so lacking in prestige, to

---

[18]Boaz's concern in Ruth 2:8-9, 15-16 hints at this.
[19]I discussed Thucydides's Melian dialogue in chapter five.

others specially appointed for the purpose. We see even the church strug-gling to ensure that this important ministry of mercy was completed, despite the resistance of some.

The difference between the model of care that Christianity proposed for widows and the utter disregard for their lives in the pagan world is salient in Jesus' interactions with widows. The story of the Samaritan woman Jesus meets at the well in John 4:6-30 is particularly illuminating. In this incident, Jesus arrives with his disciples at Jacob's well in Samaria around noon. Herman Ridderbos notes the significance that Jesus took this road at all, as he could have avoided going through Samaria.[20] Tired, he decides to rest by the well at this time when it is abandoned—no one in their right mind, after all, would be out in the heat of the day. At that point, Jesus, the one able to provide bread at will, sends his disciples into town for food. Why? It is clearly a ruse. Indeed, when the disciples return later with the food that Jesus pre-sumably sent them to buy and offer him some, he tells them, "I have food to eat that you know nothing about" (Jn 4:32). He has orchestrated the whole thing just so he could spend time alone talking with . . . a disreputable Samaritan widow.

The woman arrives at the well at this time when no one else is getting water. We can easily read the situation between the lines, especially as we learn more about her: the community does not approve of her, so she is trying to avoid conflict and perhaps all-too-common words of abuse from others by getting water at a time when she was just about guaranteed not to be noticed. Except for Jesus. The woman is surprised, in fact, when he speaks to her and asks her to give him water. Again, the Son of God has no need of this well water, for (as he tells the woman right after) he can provide living water. But the ruse has a purpose, yet again: it breaks the proverbial ice.

In the modern office, we speak of the water cooler as the proverbial place where everyone can meet for brief conversations and socialization, even while meeting the basic human need to hydrate. Similarly, ancient fountains

---

[20]Herman Ridderbos, *The Gospel of John: A Theological Commentary* (Grand Rapids, MI: Eerdmans, 1997), 153.

and public wells served this function especially for women, whose task it was to fetch the water. In classical Athens, gatherings of women at the city fountains became a popular theme in decorating *hydriai*, the vessels that were designed for—you guessed it!—fetching water. Anyone excluded from such gatherings was, quite simply, not part of the community. This meant much more than exclusion from social fun. It meant not being part of a care network; it meant being designated as the person about whose suffering no one was concerned.

By talking to this woman kindly and compassionately, Jesus welcomes this stranger into his kingdom and acknowledges her as worthy of being in community with him. She is, in the eyes of all others, a stranger twice over. As a Samaritan, she mentions the disdain she and others like her have experienced from Jews, such as Jesus. At the same time, though, she has been ostracized by her own community and does not feel welcome to get water along with the other women of her city. It seems likely that this is connected to her difficult marital history—something over which she did not have much (if any) control but for which others judge her nevertheless. It appears she is a widow: "Jesus said to her, 'You are right when you say you have no husband. The fact is, you have had five husbands, and the man you now have is not your husband. What you have just said is quite true'" (Jn 4:17-18).

What is going on here? It seems likely that this woman has been repeatedly widowed, although perhaps also divorced at least once as well. We would not be remiss to see abuse as part of her story as well, Caryn Reeder suggests in her recent book.[21] Through it all, she does not have any children, or at least none that are mentioned here. A woman's inability to conceive was considered a legitimate reason for divorce in the ancient world, and after five husbands, whether ones who died or who divorced her, her infertility would have been well-known to all. Andreas Köstenberger notes two additional possible complications. First, the rabbis drew a limit at "three legal marriages at a lifetime, even in case of the death of previous husbands." Second, the

---

[21]Caryn Reeder, *The Samaritan Woman's Story: Reconsidering John 4 After #ChurchToo* (Downers Grove, IL: InterVarsity Press, 2022).

Greek word for *husband* is also generic for "man," so it is not entirely clear that we are speaking here of legal marriages.[22]

At any rate, after five husbands (some or all of whom may have been more akin to domestic partners) and no children, this woman was undoubtedly damaged goods in the eyes of all around. And in a world where a childless widow was defenseless if living alone, she appears to have chosen the option of cohabiting with someone who has no intention of marrying her, just to have some security. At least, she is not likely to starve to death while living with this man—but how long is this union of convenience going to last? This decision also does not protect her from social ostracism and the disdain of all, both locals and anyone passing through town.

As soon as Jesus' disciples return from town with the snacks they purchased, they are surprised to see Jesus talking to this woman. John has a poignant way of describing their reaction, cataloging their inner thoughts even as these thoughts remained unvoiced: "Just then his disciples returned and were surprised to find him talking with a woman. But no one asked, 'What do you want?' or 'Why are you talking with her?'" (Jn 4:27). Sure, no one asked these questions out loud, but they thought them loudly enough. Conditioned as they had been to see the world in categories, they pegged this woman accurately at first glance. No wonder that to be able to have a comfortable and comforting conversation with her, Jesus had to send the disciples away.

In their respective commentaries on this passage, F. F. Bruce and Andreas Köstenberger note that in Jewish tradition at the time, for any rabbi (or even a man in general) to speak with women, Samaritan or not, was considered a waste of time and, worse, improper.[23] This point is striking as we consider not only the time that Jesus literally went out of his way to spend with the Samaritan woman but also the time he had spent with Mary, Martha, and many more nameless women—widowed, single, physically sick, and

---

[22] Andreas Köstenberger, *John*, Baker Exegetical Commentary on the New Testament (Grand Rapids, MI: Baker Academic, 2004), 152-53.

[23] F. F. Bruce, *The Gospel and Epistles of John* (Grand Rapids, MI: Eerdmans, 1983), 112; Köstenberger, *John*, 148-49.

heartsick. So many of his day saw no purpose in any of them. Worse, they might have seen women like these as threats to their reputation and thus to be avoided. But the open secret of God's love for us is that we have all been made for God to delight in us. This purpose is enough.

Jesus' ability to see, acknowledge, and treasure the ones everyone else saw as useless or invisible is a consistent theme in his interactions with the single people, the widows, and the sick and disabled all around. The landscape was full of them, we realize as we read the Gospels, but only Jesus truly paid attention and saw them as valuable people, deserving of care, provision, and, most important, love. The stories of Jesus' care for and attention to such individuals as Mary, Martha, Lazarus, and the Samaritan woman at the well show that revolutionary valuing of all humanity begins with seeing the ones everyone else refuses to see—the dishonorably divorced or widowed, the infertile, the unwanted and uncherished of all ages, and, whether in a world of limited medical care (ancient) or a world of overly expensive medical care (modern), the sick and disabled.

CARING FOR THE SICK AND DISABLED

Sometime in the late fifth or early fourth century BC, a Greek physician wrote a treatise that became one of the most famous and influential in the Hippocratic corpus: *On Airs, Waters, Places*.[24] In this treatise he presents an analysis of the effect of location, weather, and the quality of water on the health of inhabitants of different regions. There are uncomfortable moments in the treatise that verge on scientific racism, but overall the point is that some people are sicker than others, and if you consider the characteristics of their habitats, you will see why.

The Hippocratic writers were indeed keen to identify various causes for disease, and for good reason: there was plenty of it around. As historian Kyle Harper shows, people in the ancient world were quite sickly.[25] Indeed, for those

---

[24]For a translation, see G. E. R. Lloyd, ed., *Hippocratic Writings* (London: Penguin Classics, 1983), 148-69.

[25]Kyle Harper, *The Fate of Rome: Climate, Disease, and the Fate of an Empire* (Princeton, NJ: Princeton University Press, 2017).

whose territories became absorbed into the Roman Empire, sickness only intensified after Roman conquest. Harper's most recent book continues the story of the impact of disease on world history from the dawn of humanity to the present, noting that for most of human history until just the past four generations or so, life was short and uncertain because of ever-looming disease.[26]

Many people died young, we know, and many people lived with chronic illnesses or disabilities. Jane Draycott's research documents attempts in the ancient world toward helping the disabled through such technologies as prosthetics, which we normally consider to be recent.[27] But just as is too often the case today, medical care correlated with wealth. Draycott's work makes it clear just how much anyone with disabilities depended on others to help them. Prosthetics and assistive technology could rarely replace the care of others, including often hired care. What happened to the many others who were sick and disabled who could not afford such care, or who invested much into treatment to achieve no results? Jesus repeatedly notices their plight, valuing their lives and their well-being in a world that saw them rather as cursed themselves and a curse on others.

In addition to Lazarus, whom Jesus raised from the dead, he also healed or raised from the dead five children. Other healings include the chronically ill—lepers, paralytics, a woman who had been mysteriously bleeding for twelve years, a blind man, and multiple demonically possessed people whose minds therefore were ill even if their bodies perhaps were well. What is common to all of these is their rejection from society as a result. Why? It seems that many Jews believed that the chronically ill did something to deserve their plight and therefore that their lives were not worth as much. This in turn exempted others from having to care for them.

We see Jesus pushing back against this attitude, saying instead that just as illness and death are the results of the fall, so is healing a foretaste of heaven. On one occasion, the disciples ask him, after seeing a blind man, whether it

---

[26]Kyle Harper, *Plagues upon the Earth: Disease and the Course of Human History* (Princeton, NJ: Princeton University Press, 2021).

[27]Jane Draycott, *Prosthetics and Assistive Technology in Ancient Greece and Rome* (New York: Cambridge University Press, 2022).

was this man himself who had sinned or his parents.[28] No other option seems possible to them to explain this. When Jesus says that neither is at fault but that this man's blindness had the purpose of showing God's glory, no one seems to understand. Jesus' subsequent healing of this man on a Sabbath leads to repeated questionings for the one miraculously healed from the Pharisees and to his eventual expulsion from the synagogue. Providing medical care for someone not seen as worthy of it has always been a subversive act. Treasuring a person as a priceless child of God nevertheless begins with recognizing that their suffering matters and that they are worthy of care and healing.

It is such recognition of a person's worth that takes center stage in Jesus' healing of the woman who had been bleeding for twelve years. Her story is included in a series of healings that take place in the span of just a single chapter, Luke 8. First, Jesus cures a demonically possessed man; next he is on his way at the request of Jairus, a synagogue leader, to cure his sick daughter. Before the chapter ends, the girl will die, but Jesus will raise her from the dead. But while he is on his way to do this, another healing takes place, one that seems almost passive for Jesus:

> And a woman was there who had been subject to bleeding for twelve years, but no one could heal her. She came up behind him and touched the edge of his cloak, and immediately her bleeding stopped.
>
> "Who touched me?" Jesus asked.
>
> When they all denied it, Peter said, "Master, the people are crowding and pressing against you."
>
> But Jesus said, "Someone touched me; I know that power has gone out from me."
>
> Then the woman, seeing that she could not go unnoticed, came trembling and fell at his feet. In the presence of all the people, she told why she had touched him and how she had been instantly healed. Then he said to her, "Daughter, your faith has healed you. Go in peace." (Lk 8:43-48)[29]

---

[28]This story takes up the entirety of Jn 9.
[29]This story is also told in Mk 5:25-34 and Mt 9:20-22.

What did it mean for this woman to have been bleeding for twelve years? Unclean by Jewish law, she could not get married, living instead in involuntary singleness, ostracized as impure by her community. In a society that viewed women as only potential wives and mothers, her uselessness was compounded. We hear of no relatives associated with her. Presumably she had family but all relatives had turned their backs on her long ago.

She was not in as dire straits as some could have been in this situation. In his telling of this episode, Mark notes that she had been going to doctor after doctor, but instead of healing her, the treatment only made her worse. This detail is significant regarding her socioeconomic status: she was wealthy enough to survive and even afford medical care.[30] But even her money could not help here, and it was running out. Commentators have noted that by forcing her to confess her healing in public in front of witnesses, Jesus guaranteed that it would be known and accepted in the community. After all, who would have believed her otherwise?

While Jesus' care for the sick and the disabled was an integral part of his earthly ministry, such countercultural valuing of people seen as worthless by society did not come naturally to Christians, just as it had not to Jews of Jesus' day or even to his own disciples. Indeed, Megan Henning's study of hell in early Christian apocalyptic literature shows vision after vision of hell filled with disabled people, many of them women. Their womanhood, illness, and disability, in the eyes of so many early believers who read and wrote this literature, showed their status as damned.[31] This had implications for how some early Christians thought that such people were to be treated in the here and now: if someone were damned, they deserved the fiery torments they were to receive in the next life and did not deserve assistance here on earth.

The apocalyptic visions of hell that Henning documents offer a reminder that Christianity has never been a magic wand that one could wave to fix

---

[30]John R. Donahue, SJ, and Daniel J. Harrington, SJ, *The Gospel of Mark*, Sacra Pagina (Collegeville, MN: Liturgical Press), 174.

[31]Megan Henning, *Hell Hath No Fury: Gender, Disability, and the Invention of Damned Bodies in Early Christian Literature* (New Haven, CT: Yale University Press, 2021).

everything in the sinful hearts of God's people. But in all periods, true believers live out the message of the Gospels. This is a sobering reminder that we need to test our version of Christianity against that presented in the New Testament, especially where issues of valuing the life and dignity of image bearers are concerned. This is also Jesus' point in repeatedly calling out the hypocrisy of the Pharisees. While the Jews of Jesus' day were not living it out consistently, the doctrine of *imago Dei* was not new. It is present in Genesis from the very beginning—God created all of us as priceless.

CONCLUSION: WHAT ANCIENT DIY MANUALS ARE TELLING US

Chances are, if you ever walk into that rare unicorn these days, the brick-and-mortar bookstore, you will find that there is one particular type of book that gets a particularly prominent place: the (self-)help or how-to-do-anything books. Indeed, the popular series of how-to books For Dummies includes such varied topics as English grammar, calculus, Italian, gluten-free living, cybersecurity, caring for curly hair, and ChatGPT.[32]

We the children of (post)modernity are not the first to appreciate this genre, however. As it happens, it was popular enough in the ancient world. Military manuals of different sorts have existed since at least the fourth century BC, ready to assist any curious reader on how to select the best possible warhorse, march in appropriate formation, carry out an effective siege, and conversely how to survive under siege. There were also manuals and treatises on other topics, from cooking to dream interpretation, farming, oratory, friendship, dating, and how to live well in old age.

But there is one topic on which no pagan writer ever wrote a how-to treatise: caring for others.[33] This absence speaks volumes. So does the rise of the new subgenre of treatises on pastoral care in the first few centuries of the church. We might name, for instance, Tertullian's and Cyprian's treatises in the third century AD on women's dress, which focused on ways the church

---

[32] A full list can be found at www.dummies.com.

[33] I discuss ideas in this section in my article, "The Opposite of Abuse Is Care," *Christianity Today*, November 1, 2023, www.christianitytoday.com/ct/2023/october-web-only/abuse-authority-pastoral-care-early-church-history.html.

could care and provide for women, whether single or married.[34] Then there was Cyprian's treatise *On Works and Alms*, focusing on the "white crown" that a Christian performing works of mercy for the poor might win in heaven.[35] The need for such exhortations of believers to works of mercy did not disappear after Christianity became accepted in the Roman Empire. In the fourth century AD, Ambrose, bishop of Milan, wrote a treatise about honoring consecrated virgins—women such as Macrina the Younger, whom I mentioned in the introduction to this chapter and who selected a life of singleness in Christ. Ambrose wrote another treatise, *Concerning Widows*, recognizing that their care was important, but this work was different from caring for consecrated virgins.[36]

In these works, we see repeatedly the teaching that the church is responsible for caring for the bodies and souls of the neglected and the abandoned at all ages and life stages, because their lives are priceless. The ones who need this care most often are single or widowed women—two categories of women who did not have a male protector and provider, and so the church took on that role instead. Through valuing these women, the church fathers present a comprehensive ethic that unconditionally values the life of every person in a cruel world.

The apocalyptic literature Henning surveys presents some lives as worthless, much as the pagan world had done. Pushing back against this view, treatises on pastoral care from early church fathers and bishops show that the early church saw the need for encouraging texts—these are writings that value life and speak this value to those even in the church who were tempted to turn away from suffering. But there is another important

---

[34]Tertullian's treatises on these topics include *To My Wife, On Head Coverings for Unmarried Women, On Women's Fashion*, and *On Modesty*. Cyprian, highly influenced by Tertullian, wrote *On the Dress of Virgins*.

[35]Geoffrey Dunn, "The White Crown of Works: Cyprian's Early Pastoral Ministry of Almsgiving in Carthage," *Church History* 73, no. 4 (2004): 715-40.

[36]For a translation of *Concerning Virginity*, see Ambrose, *Concerning Virginity*, trans. H. de Romestin, E. de Romestin, and H. T. F. Duckworth, *Nicene and Post-Nicene Fathers*, Second Series, ed. Philip Schaff and Henry Wace, vol. 10 (Buffalo, NY: Christian Literature, 1896), rev. and ed. for New Advent by Kevin Knight, available at www.newadvent.org/fathers/3407.htm. For a translation of *Concerning Widows*, see Ambrose, *Concerning Widows*, in Wace and Schaff, *Nicene and Post-Nicene Fathers* 10, available at www.newadvent.org/fathers/3407.htmwww.newadvent.org/fathers/3408.htm.

dimension to these texts, one that has to do with what it means to value life fully.

When we talk about valuing human life and dignity, most often the conversation revolves around, well, the sanctity of life at all stages. This is appropriate and good in a cosmic God-declared-it sort of way. But we saw that Jesus did not limit the valuing of human life to mere preservation of life but sometimes, as in his own willingness to die, the opposite. What Jesus' countercultural willingness to teach women shows, and what the later treatises from the church fathers pick up on, is the necessity of valuing people body, mind, and soul. Being truly pro-life means supporting and nourishing all three of these aspects of humanity, first and foremost because we need to glorify God with all three (Mt 22:37).

Treatises such as Cyprian's *On Works and Alms* provided healing words for a world that was sick, showing practical ways to display a countercultural care for human life. But treatises and how-to manuals have never been the only source of healing words. In the final portion of this book, I turn to three voices, two ancient and one modern. These three are very different from each other in some ways, but they have one important goal in common: to speak healing words into a sinful world that is all too often prone to choose death, whether actively or passively. In the process, they show the importance of valuing bodies, minds, and souls in caring for the lives of mothers, children, and all image bearers.

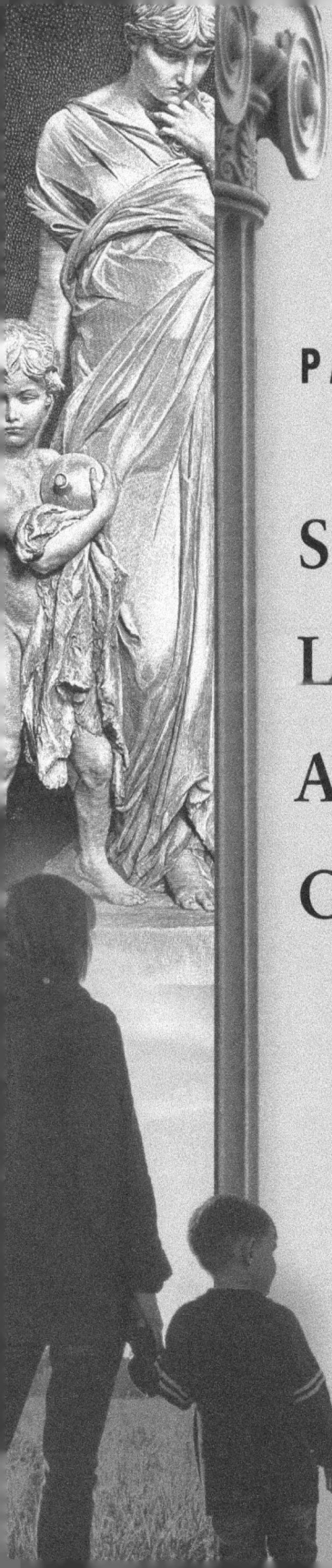

PART 3

SPEAKING LIFE INTO A CULTURE OF DEATH

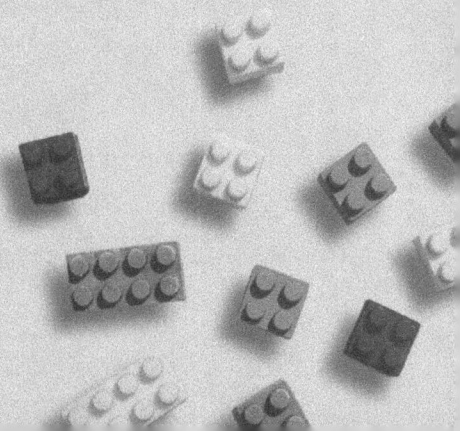

8

CONSOLATION FOR THE WEARY SUFFERER

IT WAS A TRAGEDY. On this everyone could agree. After all, this is not what happens to respectable families, in respectable cities, in this civilized age. True, his wife was a foreigner, and of the worst kind—a barbarian, one could (and did) say. Quietly and in their own homes, some even whispered that she was a sorceress. At any rate, she should have been grateful to be rescued from her previous life among the savages. He did remind his wife of this remarkable favor that he bestowed on her. But then, we use the term *wife* loosely. They never were legally wed, so she should have known that one of these days he would marry a respectable woman. It is just that it really is a shame about the children.

No one had expected, faced with the news that her common-law husband was getting married at last—and to the daughter of a king, no less—that she would react in such a drastic and horrific manner, orchestrating the highly gruesome death of the king and his daughter, then slaughtering her own two children in cold blood, all before escaping in a dragon-drawn chariot as her own *dea ex machina*. What kind of mother would do that? Perhaps every male audience member watching this tragedy—for this was the plot of a tragedy, Euripides's *Medea* (431 BC, produced a mere month before the

Peloponnesian War broke out)—wondered as he was walking home in a stupor from the play the night of the performance: Could this happen to me? Would my own wife and mother of my children ever do something like this?[1]

JUST ANOTHER TRAGEDY

Historians observe that the Athenian democracy was the quintessential "performance culture."[2] Attending dramatic performances, especially tragedy, was the most democratic and unifying behavior in Athenian democracy. Citizens could and often did skip civic duties, such as assemblies and voting, if they felt that they were needed elsewhere—say, at their farm during harvest. But no matter how busy, citizens somehow did prioritize the free entertainment that was their prerogative as Athenian citizens.[3] As a result, in reading Athenian drama, we get a glimpse of the subjects with which Athenians were confronted in their entertainment. These are stories, a shared literature, that they got to process collectively.[4] Entertainment generally reflects the concerns and anxieties of a society—otherwise, why would people come back to watch it time and time again?

But then again, this was a tragedy, a realm in which the story focused on distortions of all civilized norms. Everyone in the audience was an Athenian freeborn male over the age of eighteen. Each one of these men knew that the women in their lives were meant to know their purpose: bear children and bear their fate. As Thucydides, a contemporary Athenian historian and thinker, wrote in the Melian dialogue episode of his history of the Peloponnesian War, the natural order of things is effectively that might makes right.

---

[1] Medea continued to fascinate and horrify ancient readers in equal measure for the rest of classical antiquity. See James J. Clauss and Sarah Iles Johnston, eds., *Medea: Essays on Medea in Myth, Literature, Philosophy, and Art* (Princeton, NJ: Princeton University Press, 1997).

[2] For a range of ways in which this phenomenon manifested itself, see Simon Goldhill and Robin Osborne, eds., *Performance Culture and Athenian Democracy* (Cambridge: Cambridge University Press, 1999).

[3] Aristophanes's comedy *The Acharnians* has a field day with this idea: the protagonist of the play shows up on time to an assembly of citizens and is dismayed to find himself there alone. What makes the joke funny is, of course, a fictional citizen calling out such behavior in the play's real-life audiences.

[4] I reflected on this value of a shared literature for a democracy in "Democracies Need Shared Literature," Front Porch Republic, October 26, 2023, www.frontporchrepublic.com/2023/10/democracies-need-shared-literature/.

True, Thucydides's Athenian delegation that said this to the Melians was speaking to an enemy at war. But the principle generally applied elsewhere. Someone in Medea's position was supposed to admit that power was not on her side and act accordingly.

At the same time, Euripides pushed the envelope a bit by presenting Medea at least early on as the sympathetic victim, whereas Jason comes across as the villain of the story, the opportunist who ditched the woman who gave up everything for him out of her love. Yes, this is Jason—the hero you perhaps best knew as the leader of the Argonauts, the brave adventurers who sailed the ship *Argo* to the boundaries of the known world, Colchis on the Black Sea littoral, to steal the golden fleece from Medea's father.

Just how much did Medea sacrifice for her relationship with Jason? As part of orchestrating Jason's dramatic escape with the golden fleece from Colchis, Medea killed her own brother and kept throwing pieces of his body overboard the *Argo*. Since Medea's father kept interrupting his pursuit to pick up the body parts of his own son, Jason and the Argonauts were eventually able to get away. This is far from the only sacrifice Medea had made for Jason, however. In a striking speech in the play, Medea famously proclaims, "I would rather stand three times with a shield in battle than give birth once" (*Medea* 250).[5] Could these hints of Euripides's sympathy toward Medea have been the reason that Euripides placed third (and last) of the three tragedians competing in that year's Great Dionysia festival? The Athenian audiences, generally fans of Euripides's work, found this play difficult to stomach.

But everyone knew at the end of the play, if not long before, that the tragedy was Medea's own doing. Had she accepted her fate, everyone would still be alive at the end of the play, even if Medea would have been left with nothing—no home or homeland, no husband, no children. The latter were supposed to move with their father and his new bride into the royal house.

---

[5]For Medea's speech that culminates with this line, see David Kovacs, trans., *Euripides, with an English translation* (Cambridge, MA: Harvard University Press, 1994), available at www.perseus.tufts.edu/hopper/text?doc=Perseus:abo:tlg,0006,003:249#.

Sure, their illegitimate status would never have granted them royal privileges, but at least they would have been provided for. Jason's marriage and its attendant developments, had they proceeded as planned, would have made Medea the most useless of all the useless people. She was a woman belonging to no one in a world where women's status was determined through belonging. But this was of no consequence except for her alone.[6]

The shock of the tragedy for all observers was that Medea refused to play by the rules. Her actions in the process are revelatory. First, they lay open the inadequacy of a system that allowed no value for women, except as defined by their belonging to someone—a father, a husband, the city-state. A woman with no husband and no citizenship, as Medea found herself, was a nonperson. Her existence was a warning: someone desperate and disrespected could be a threat to the social order, as she had nothing to lose.

But second, Medea's refusal to submit to a system that did not see her worth and dignity as a human being shows a longing for something better. Medea, unlike everyone else, is sure that an alternative is possible. Lacking the aid of others, she creates her own. As so often happens, however, in a world without the knowledge of God, serving as one's own *dea ex machina* can only go so far. Medea's solution shows the limits of the system of self-rescuing and the longing that all of us carry within us for something better. It is no coincidence that we ultimately see this longing—and the tragedy of what happens when it is not fulfilled—through the story of a mistreated mother-turned-murderess in despair.

Medea's story leaves these longings unanswered. This is something that persists throughout Greek tragedy: the sense that the visible world is deeply broken rightly evokes a deep sorrow for this brokenness. Greek tragedy, and the Greek mythology that inspired it, has no further solution to offer, however. This brokenness just is a fact of life in an unfair system dominated by petty and unfair pagan gods. What could be the value of a mere woman,

---

[6]The best historical treatment of women like Medea in the Athenian democracy is Rebecca Futo Kennedy, *Immigrant Women in Athens: Gender, Ethnicity, and Citizenship in the Classical City* (London: Routledge, 2014).

a mother, in this context? Where could she find her value as a person, if forsaken by all the people to whom she was supposed to belong—and who therefore should have taken care of her and protected her in this hostile world? Seven hundred years after Euripides's tragedy, another mother who had felt these same longings and questions in her own life wrote the answers shortly before her martyrdom. This mother is none other than Perpetua, whose story we considered briefly in chapter five.

In the first two parts of this book, we looked at symptoms in both our modern society and in the pre-Christian pagan world that show the deeply rooted devaluing of human life that comes so instinctively to people in both antiquity and today. But in chapter seven, I showed some countercultural glimpses of another world, the world that Jesus wanted to bring about, beginning already here on earth. It is a world that was to embrace the "useless ones" in society, treasuring them simply and unconditionally for who they were as human beings—seeing the *imago Dei* latent in each and every person ever created, from Adam on.

Up until this point, the story has been largely historical. In this final part of the book, however, we get to build on this historical foundation and provide hopeful voices for going forward. After all, the history I have told so far has come full circle in a rather depressing way, showing how the modern culture of devaluing life too often bears mournful resemblance to the ancient one, despite the culture of life that early Christianity proposed. Thankfully, there is more to the story, and it involves all of us directly.

How might we encourage a comprehensively pro-life ethic of valuing children, motherhood, and ultimately all human beings as *good* in an absolute sense? The default, history shows, has been and continues to be the embrace of death. It is easier to foster the culture of devaluing life, and that is why this has been the default setting in many societies and time periods. Indeed, the best friend of this culture of death, as I have noted from the beginning of this book, is the tendency of people to rank other people: the idea that some people are more valuable than others. In such a ranking system, some people turn out to be useless or worthless. Taking care of them and devoting any resources to them is by this logic deemed unnecessary. But, as we see Jesus repeatedly proclaim, this is a lie. There is no person, no human being, who is worthless. So, we need voices that speak life into death in a way that is not only true and good but is also profoundly beautiful. This begins with the gospel, but it goes further. If we are that with which we fill our minds, then these voices and others like them are what we should be reading.

Over the final three chapters of this book, we will look at three different thinkers, two ancient and one modern, whose writings offer these much-needed hopeful voices. Each one, taken individually, provides a blueprint for embracing a comprehensive ethic of life from a slightly different angle, one that stems from the different personal place from which each of them writes. All three show that taking a consistently pro-life stance and speaking life into a culture of death means acknowledging the priceless nature not only of the body but also of the mind and soul. Unlike the Gnostics of the second and third centuries AD, orthodox Christians have always believed that our bodies matter; we are not just disembodied souls. At the same time, the modern temptation has been to focus on the life of the body, ignoring the holistic aspect of human flourishing. For Christians, respecting life should be about more than just keeping the body alive.

In the modern imagination, as I noted in part one, women's bodies and minds are respectively idealized for their beauty and productivity—but not the productivity of childbirth. This last type of productivity is the enemy of the workaholic culture of the modern world. In the ancient world, women and the "useless ones" as a military category were viewed almost as animals—nothing but a body to be used or slaughtered, if need be. In Christianity we see a clear valuing of human beings as body, mind, and soul, created to glorify God together. Acknowledging this essential and unique aspect of humanity means also acknowledging the broken nature of this world in all its dimensions, because our bodies, minds, and souls reside in this landscape, physical and increasingly digital. This means, finally, recognizing our rootedness in our communities as the places where we live and support others to choose life over death in every way, literal and figurative.

It is only by loving our immediate neighbors that we can see the priceless nature of human beings made in God's image. These last three chapters offer three voices of local application, reflections on what it means to see human beings as priceless in a world that contends ever more loudly that they are not. I could have chosen different voices to highlight, but there are reasons I chose these three. The first example offers us a rare glimpse of a mother's voice in the face of persecution. In the next chapter, Augustine's musings on this topic in the context of an officially Christian state serve as a sobering reminder that God's truth is under threat in this world even in states that officially claim Christian identity. This is in fact part of the argument of my first book, *Cultural Christians in the Early Church*.[7] Finally, we will conclude with the voice of a modern writer, Wendell Berry, who is a good representative of the same calls that Perpetua and Augustine offer but in the context of the modern, increasingly post-Christian environment.

FROM TRAGEDY TO *CONSOLATIO*

It was a tragedy, everyone who knew the family surely said. Making matters worse, it happened shortly after her baby boy was born. Married to another local noble around age twenty and now the mother of an heir, she knew she was well on track to fulfilling the duties expected of her as a Roman woman of a certain social standing.[8] But then came her conversion to Christianity, which changed everything. Never before had she done something that was utter disobedience not only to her father and husband but also the Roman state. The rejections followed: her husband divorced her; her father rejected

---

[7]Nadya Williams, *Cultural Christians in the Early Church: A Historical and Practical Introduction to Christians in the Greco-Roman World* (Grand Rapids, MI: Zondervan Academic, 2023).

[8]For an overview on Roman marriage, a topic for which we have abundant legal information, see Susan Treggiari, *Roman Marriage, Iusti Coniuges from the Time of Cicero to the Time of Ulpian* (Oxford: Clarendon, 1991).

her; the chief representative of the Roman state sentenced her to death in the arena. Born into privilege, she surrendered it all for her beliefs.

In some ways, Perpetua's story readily parallels Medea's. Here is yet another wife and mother who found the rug pulled out from underneath her when she disobeyed the life script that her society had for her and which the men in her family had attempted to enforce for her. Yet, Perpetua's reaction is different. Why? Because she knows that the one to whom she belongs is not an earthly father or husband. In her eyes, while her story ends with her own death in martyrdom, which she foresaw in a vision, the story is not a tragedy. Rather, the martyrdom account she wrote, which we looked at in some detail in chapter four, recalls another genre well-known in ancient literature: the *consolatio*. Such consolation is the antithesis of tragedy.

Let us go back to a dungeon, a prison dank and dark, much like the one where Perpetua spent the final weeks or months of her life. But this is not her prison. Instead, we are in the northern Italian town of Pavia, and the year is AD 523. In this prison we find a man. Much like Perpetua, he spends his final days before his execution on charges of treason keeping a journal. A lifelong distinguished politician, whose desire to broker peace at a politically fragile time proved to be his downfall, this is Boethius. His journal will become recognized as the final masterpiece of Roman literature on the cusp of the Middle Ages, *The Consolation of Philosophy*. Borders between time periods are always artificially imposed from hindsight—in this case by scholars over a thousand years removed. Boethius's longing for the consolation that philosophy, the love of wisdom, can offer indeed seems timeless, as apt in antiquity as it would have been to the intellectuals of the medieval world and indeed to Christians who strive to love the Lord with all their mind today.

What does a falsely imprisoned man most need as he awaits his execution? A consolation—words of comfort, peace, and hope. For Boethius, these words come from Philosophy personified. She visits him to converse, encourage, and console.[9] But her words are no empty hope. Instead, they are

---

[9]For a beautiful modern take on Boethius's dialogues, see Rick Kennedy, *The Winds of Santa Ana: Pilgrim Stories of the California Bight* (Eugene, OR: Wipf & Stock, 2022).

words of life rooted in deep theological principles—that virtue is each person's most treasured characteristic, that evil is an unfortunately common feature of this life, and that ultimately life in Christ defeats death.

Homeric heroes, who delighted in their version of virtue—*aretē*—saw it as an externally recognized characteristic. Everyone must recognize the hero as the best, or else it does not count. Philosophy encourages Boethius, by contrast, to think not of how people view other people—for his own unjust imprisonment shows the shortcomings of people's opinions—but rather of how God sees us all. Perpetua and other early Christian martyrs would have fully agreed. They, too, sought consolation in God's love and in the promises of eternity with God during those times when death threatens to overpower life—literally and figuratively. Indeed, another writer, one who lived in Perpetua's own home city and was probably born right around the time of her execution, thought of consolation in these terms even more overtly.

In the mid-third century AD, a time of high stress and political, economic, and environmental turmoil, a mysterious new disease began circulating around the Roman Empire. Historian Kyle Harper proposes, based on the description of symptoms that survived, that it was a filovirus, akin to Ebola.[10] Highly contagious and spread by bodily fluids, it was therefore particularly dangerous to those who took care of the sick and dying. Most of our knowledge of the symptoms and course of this disease comes from an unexpected source: a treatise that may have started its life as a sermon *On Mortality*, by Cyprian, bishop of Carthage, Perpetua's own town, from AD 248/9 CE to his martyrdom in AD 258.[11]

Cyprian was born right around the time of Perpetua's execution in a similarly well-to-do local family. He too came to Christ as an adult, in his case in middle age. Like Perpetua, he was eventually martyred for his faith. But unlike Perpetua, he first had a solid decade of leading the local church through some of its most difficult years of existence—for in

---

[10]Kyle Harper, *The Fate of Rome: Climate, Disease, and the End of an Empire* (Princeton, NJ: Princeton University Press, 2017), 137-44.

[11]For an overview of Cyprian's life and ministry in his historical context, see Allen Brent, *Cyprian and Roman Carthage* (New York: Cambridge University Press, 2010).

addition to all the other crises that the third century AD brought to the residents of the Roman Empire, the Christians also had to contend with the first-ever empire-wide persecutions. It is therefore no exaggeration to say that this is a time when the church and its people particularly needed words of consolation.

Cyprian provided these words. What kind of consolation to those under threat of death does he give? What words of life can bring comfort at such a time? For Cyprian, consolation means repeatedly reminding Christians: embrace life without clinging to this life alone, because you know how the story ends. Words of hope emphasize this knowledge:

> That in the meantime we die, we are passing over to immortality by death; nor can eternal life follow, unless it should befall us to depart from this life. That is not an ending, but a transit, and, this journey of time being traversed, a passage to eternity. Who would not hasten to better things? Who would not crave to be changed and renewed into the likeness of Christ, and to arrive more quickly to the dignity of heavenly glory. . . . He who is to attain to the throne of Christ, to the glory of the heavenly kingdoms, ought not to mourn nor lament, but rather, in accordance with the Lord's promise, in accordance with his faith in the truth, to rejoice in this his departure and translation. (*On Mortality* 22)[12]

The best words of consolation offer comfort in the present while reminding those who are suffering that this present evil is not all that there is; it will end, and it will end with something good. For Cyprian, embracing life as good meant remembering the best promise of all—eternity with Christ. Our bodies, we recall in the process, are inseparable from our souls. But while our bodies will die, our souls will not.

The point of consolation is to offer comfort to those who suffer. It is a call to life in a way that is transcendent, full, hopeful. To whom did Perpetua write her martyrdom account? We see, in the case of Boethius, that the first

---

[12]For a translation of the treatise, see Cyprian, "On the Mortality (or Plague)," in *The Ante-Nicene Fathers*, ed. Alexander Roberts and James Donaldson, vol. 5 (Repr., Peabody, MA: Hendrickson, 1994), available at www.ewtn.com/catholicism/library/on-the-mortality-or-plague-de-mortalitate-11412.

person one seeks to comfort is the self. Consolation is a remarkably autobiographical genre. Such preaching to oneself is undoubtedly part of Cyprian's motivations as well, even as he sought to comfort his grieving flock. But all of these writers had larger audiences in mind as well. A key audience for Perpetua was both the church more generally and other mothers specifically, as she showed in her consolation that motherhood is always a call to suffer, in ways big and small. All of us need such consolation, perhaps more than we realize.

> A key audience for Perpetua was both the church more generally and other mothers specifically, as she showed in her consolation that motherhood is always a call to suffer, in ways big and small. All of us need such consolation, perhaps more than we realize.

CONSOLATION IN DISCOMFORT

Perpetua's journal is focused on her own story and visions, so it is easy to forget that while she was imprisoned awaiting execution, she was not alone. Another woman, an enslaved member of Perpetua's own household, was there with her. As Perpetua writes words of consolation and imagines the garden that is heaven, we can imagine Felicity, who left no writing of her own and may very well have been illiterate, as her first audience. As the first audience of Perpetua's words, Felicity got to experience their consolation. No less important of a consolation was surely the friendship the two women shared during their final weeks, days, hours. After all, Perpetua likely helped to deliver Felicity's baby, born hours before the two women were martyred.

At the time of imprisonment, Perpetua was a nursing mother with an infant relying on her very body for his survival and nourishment. Felicity, on the other hand, was pregnant and feeling all the bodily discomforts that pregnancy brings in its final weeks, even while also knowing that she would be executed as soon as the baby arrived. But, it seems, Christ's and each other's consolation in discomfort kept both women from despair. The anonymous editor of their passion account added a graphic description of their martyrdom to Perpetua's own diary. He highlights in that account the joy he observed in both women, whose behavior during the execution seemed surprising to onlookers:

> They went forth from the prison into the amphitheatre as it were into heaven, cheerful and bright of countenance; if they trembled at all, it was for joy, not for fear. Perpetua followed behind, glorious of presence, as a true spouse of Christ and darling of God; at whose piercing look all cast down their eyes. Felicity likewise, rejoicing that she had borne a child in safety, that she might fight with the beasts, came now from blood to blood, from the midwife to the gladiator, to wash after her travail in a second baptism. (*Passion of Saints Perpetua and Felicity* 18)[13]

Perpetua and Felicity's martyrdom, just like Perpetua's diary before, emphasizes a love of life, but it does not make this earthly life an idol. Recognizing the preciousness of both body and soul at a time of persecution, their entire story is a prolonged consolation and a parable of God's provision for the weak and suffering. That provision ultimately might not look how we would like. We are sometimes—too often, we might and do say!—called to suffer. We are never, however, called to despair, even as this call is gaining strength in our own world. Indeed, in this book on valuing people, starting with mothers and children, we keep coming back also to the topic of euthanasia. There are good reasons for this, as will become apparent shortly.

On the website of the organization Dying with Dignity Canada, visitors are invited to share their story. After all, "Your personal story can inspire and inform others who are navigating end-of-life issues. Storytelling connects people through shared experience." So, visitors should "inspire and inform" and, ideally, "leave a legacy gift" to help inspire someone else to choose death.[14] Canada's medical assistance in dying has grown into a real industry

---

[13]W. H. Shewring, trans., *The Passion of Perpetua and Felicity* (London, 1931), available at https://sourcebooks.fordham.edu/source/perpetua.asp.

[14]See Dying with Dignity Canada, www.dyingwithdignity.ca.

since its legalization in 2016, preying on those who feel pain and despair. Does your life matter, the culture asks? If not, you can instead make your death the best it can be for you, the lies whisper.

As of March 2022, mental illness is sufficient reason to qualify for medical assistance in dying in Canada. This includes such conditions as the ubiquitous plague of the modern age: depression.[15] As one doctor interviewed by Reuters puts it, "Tired-of-life cases are happening." The same article quotes a woman with anorexia who was planning to seek medical assistance in dying. The statistics about the reasons people choose medical assistance in dying are jarring: 86.3 percent report "loss of ability to engage in meaningful activities"; 83.4 percent report "loss of ability to perform activities of daily living." Another 57.6 percent report "inadequate control of pain or concern"; 35.7 percent report "perceived burden on family, friends or caregivers"; and 17.3 percent report "isolation or loneliness."[16]

Consolation can be any pro-life relational action in a world that too actively encourages death as an immediate out because we are losing the ability to do things we once loved, are in pain, or feel deeply lonely and do not want to inconvenience other people. It is striking to note in reading these reasons why people choose their own death that all of these easily apply to mothers—especially mothers of very young children. This should give us pause and is worth examining in more detail.

"Loss of ability to engage in meaningful activities" that you used to be able to do before you had to focus on your baby all day and night? Check. "Loss of ability to perform activities of daily living," such as even taking a shower or making a meal for yourself and eating such a meal? If you have ever taken care of a newborn, you know that the answer to this is also, yes. Most especially, "isolation or loneliness"—so many new mothers report this, even as

---

[15] Anna Mehler Paperny, "Canada Prepares to Expand Assisted Death amid Debate," Reuters, December 12, 2022, www.reuters.com/world/americas/canada-prepares-expand-assisted-death-amid -debate-2022-12-11/.

[16] "Percentage of People Who Received a Medically Assisted Death Who Suffered from Select Conditions in Canada in 2022," Statista, 2023, www.statista.com/statistics/1189552/medically-assisted -death-recipients-nature-of-suffering-canada/.

churches and other organizations try to organize support groups for new mothers.[17]

Having a newborn is very isolating, many mothers report. This is especially so for first-time mothers. They face a terrifying responsibility for the well-being of a fragile creature that relies on them for every need while living into their own new identity. Many are loath to ask for help, conditioned by our modern life not to be a burden on others. The National Institute of Health has in recent years identified this "fear of dependency" as an issue that contributes to depression, especially in individuals of middle age and above—in other words, this is not just an issue for new mothers.[18] The awareness of postpartum depression and psychosis in our society is right and good, but it is difficult to deny that the modern life exacerbates these holistic crises of body, mind, and soul. Medical solutions to these crises are too little, too late.[19]

All the reasons for despair that lead some now to choose medical assistance in dying are often present in the lives of those who give birth to life—mothers. Indeed, some of these reasons for death-desiring despair apply already during pregnancy, as the responsibility for the new person growing within shuts us off increasingly more from previous activities, leading some to feel a sense of profound loss and significant physical discomfort and pain while expecting and nourishing a new life. Dying to self never feels easy.

To name just a few discomforts, we might note that many mothers spend the first trimester feeling nauseated or even violently sick. For the unlucky

---

[17]Rachel Gurevich, "Why You're Feeling Isolated as a New Mom," Verywell Family, May 5, 2020, www.verywellfamily.com/why-you-re-feeling-isolated-as-a-new-mom-and-what-to-do-4769084#:~:text=What%20you%20may%20not%20be,feelings%20of%20loneliness%20and%20disconnection.

[18]C. Adams-Price and M. Ralston, "The Impact of Fear of Dependency, Life-Space, and Health on Life Satisfaction in Mid-to-Late Life," *Innovative Aging* (November 2018), www.ncbi.nlm.nih.gov/pmc/articles/PMC6229735/#:~:text=Fear%20of%20dependency%20is%20a,as%20essential%20to%20well-being.

[19]For studies on postpartum psychosis, in particular, see Teresa M. Twomey, *Understanding Postpartum Psychosis: A Temporary Madness* (Westport, CT: Praeger, 2009). There are also a number of memoirs of women telling of their own battles with the condition. Of note is Jennifer H. Moyer, *A Mother's Climb Out of Darkness: A Story About Overcoming Postpartum Psychosis* (Amarillo, TX: Praeclarus, 2014).

few who suffer from hyperemesis gravidarum, this violent illness persists through delivery. For others, the second trimester is a bit of a respite from the challenges of the first one. Still, steady weight gain causes discomfort—one does not carry increasingly more pounds around for months and months without feeling the effects. Sleep disruptions are also typical, and for some, like me, who are prone to migraines, pregnancy is a time when these get worse. Except you cannot take the usual medications to stave off the pain. Finally, the third trimester is a time when virtually no woman is comfortable. Everything hurts, joints are creaky and loose, and it is impossible to sit, stand, walk, or lie down comfortably.

Once the baby arrives, it often takes months—and sometimes years—to get into a good sleep routine. A 2019 study by the University of Warwick researchers concluded that sleep disruptions for parents may continue for the first six years of a child's life.[20] My third child would wail mournfully if anyone tried to put her down at all during her first month outside the womb. My husband spent two hours each night pacing around the house with her as she mourned loudly and angrily the loss of her quieter and darker home. Meanwhile, I got my only uninterrupted sleep of the day. The rest of the night, I semislept while holding her. A friend once remarked that only after becoming a father did he understand why sleep deprivation is recognized by the Hague Convention as a torture method. Parents know. But, most important, so does the God who provides consolation and encouragement to embrace life—for mothers and for all who are suffering.

THE GOD WHO PROVIDES

This story, too, had all the makings of a tragedy. An enslaved woman was forced by her infertile mistress to conceive the son of her owner—indeed, let us not mince words here. We would not be wrong to call this rape, but in the ancient Near Eastern context, this kind of abuse was all too common and accepted—expected, even—for enslaved women, only further heightening

---

[20]"New Parents Face 6 Years of Disrupted Sleep," ScienceDaily, February 25, 2019, www.sciencedaily .com/releases/2019/02/190225192116.htm.

the many kinds of suffering they bore. In this case, once the woman became pregnant, things got worse. Her mistress, jealous of her fertility, abused her. Finally, the enslaved woman ran away. Alone, without any resources, she returned soon after. After the birth of her baby boy, the mistreatment continued. At last, driven away by her owners, the woman with her child went into the desert, expecting to die a painful death. Miraculously, God intervened and provided food, water, and safety for them both in the present, promising them safety in the future.

You have perhaps recognized the story already. This is the story of Hagar, Abraham's Egyptian slave.[21] Striking in her story is God's treatment of her. While Hagar knew nothing but abuse and suffering from Abraham and Sarah, God appeared and spoke to her twice—twice more than he appears to most people in the Bible. On both occasions when Hagar thought that she would soon die, God provided for her physically and spiritually, by speaking to this woman all others considered worthless. God's respect not only for her body but also for her soul provides an important reminder that a truly pro-life ethic means acknowledging that it is not only people's bodies that need nourishment to survive.

In a vision that Perpetua recorded in her journal shortly before her execution, she saw Jesus as a shepherd. Lovingly, he handed her a milk curd, providing with this one simple act both physical nourishment and spiritual encouragement. Perpetua was very much aware of her need for the latter. At the same time, she also reflects on earthly nourishment and the physicality of one's earthly body, especially in her frank discussion in her journal of the need that her breastfed infant has for her, and then her discomfort when her parents remove the baby from her, forcing her to go through the uncomfortable process of weaning.

Finally, God's provision for Perpetua includes a respect for her mind. The same deacons from the local church who ministered to her, providing for her body and soul, also brought her the writing implements she needed to write her journal. No one seemed to think it odd that she did this, even

---

[21]This two-part story is told in Gen 16; 21.

if, as I noted in chapter four, her decision to write her own story was highly unusual.

Two important conclusions from Perpetua's story here provide final comfort for us as well, whether as mothers or simply as people of God who must nevertheless live while on earth in the death-making industrial complex of secular modernity. First, the deacons who ministered to Perpetua remind us that as Christians, we are part of a community. Often God's provision and consolation looks like other people. Second, the deacons' provision of writing implements to Perpetua, respecting her mind and her writing, provides a beautiful contrast with modern feminist narratives of writing as an almost zero-sum game at the expense of children. For Perpetua, it was her identity as a mother that made her so vividly aware of the importance of life, even as her devotion to her God made her aware that this life here on earth was not the end goal.

CONCLUSION

Perpetua's journal convicts us as it reminds us of the importance of biblical anthropology. Such an anthropology looks like Perpetua and Felicity, who confidently knew their preciousness in God's eyes while living in a world that saw them—body, mind, and soul—as useless and worthless. This view contrasts sharply with the modern world's desire to predicate the value of anyone's life on some criteria on a sliding scale, one that is sliding, as we see in the unfolding story in Canada, to be ever more inclusive of reasons to allow euthanasia.

Covering this culture of death with the fig leaf of individual choice or autonomy only tries to hide the ugly truth: this, like so many other modern industrial complexes, is all about profit. Those profiting are not the dead or the suffering. The devaluing of life in our world is a lucrative business, even if it takes a different shape from executions in the arena or enslavement and mistreatment of the vulnerable. But God is the same today as two or three thousand years ago. And God still cares.

9

SEEKING THE CITY OF GOD

THERE WERE ONCE TWO CITIES. The where or when really does not matter for our story. What matters in this case is the different fates of the two. Residents of both cities knew for certain in which one they dwelt. One of these cities was a city at peace. Weddings, births, and sure, the occasional litigations or mediations of conflicts were a part of everyday life there. Such is life, and this was first and foremost a city of life. Not so the other city. War was underway. Armies surrounded it on the outside, while the people inside mourned their coming death.

A TALE OF TWO CITIES

What are these two cities, you might wonder? The description fits the episode featuring the shield of Achilles in book 18 of Homer's *Iliad*. This is the story with which the metalsmith god Hephaestus decorated the new shield he crafted for the Greek hero Achilles. A warning tale, we can imagine, of what war does to people and civilizations, to their bodies, minds, and souls. But this story is no mere myth. At the time of this writing, nearly two years into Russia's brutal invasion of Ukraine, the two cities may well be Ukrainian cities, such as Kyiv or Bakhmut or Mariupol, first as they were just two years ago—at peace, flourishing, with people walking on the streets on fair-weather evenings, enjoying city life, fine food, and outdoor music. Then I imagine these cities as they are today, gutted by ruthless bombing that continues to kill civilians daily. Bakhmut effectively does not exist anymore. Captured by Russia, it has been largely destroyed, and most of its residents have fled.

What a difference war makes. Ukrainian novelist and journalist Andrey Kurkov wrote about the Russian invasion of Ukraine in 2014 in his novel *Grey Bees.* In it, a middle-aged villager who has lived his entire life in the same house suddenly finds himself all alone in his village, with just one other neighbor. Except Sergeyich is not exactly all alone. Once a beekeeper, always a beekeeper. He lives to keep his bees alive and thriving, constantly concerned for their well-being first and foremost. At one point, he reflects to himself mournfully that bees just do not understand war. They do not know what all the shelling and destruction means, because war is not part of their nature. By implication, war is part of humanity's fallen nature. Unlike the bees, we know what war means: death.

Political theorists love to cite Augustine as the promulgator of just war theory: sometimes war is necessary if that is the only way to restore peace. I wonder what Augustine would say about the wars of our more recent times, including the war in Ukraine now. Indeed, regardless of what we might think about Augustine's views on just or unjust wars, Augustine's view of human life as priceless is without dispute. But Augustine also realized, as other residents of the Roman Empire knew just as well, that each individual's life was rooted in a particular place, even if that place was part of the larger whole, the empire.

Discussed in the abstract, national and international policies sometimes overlook that people are rooted in a particular place. This means that solutions and recommendations for valuing life in any crisis must begin locally. Complicating matters further, in this global age, international crises are always just a plane ride away. Yet for Augustine, even in the age of the donkey express, although Rome was far away from his sea of Hippo in North Africa, it did not feel so far away from what was arguably the greatest humanitarian crisis of his age: the vicious sack of Rome by the Goths in AD 410. The shocking and unexpected transformation of Rome into a city of death affected Augustine profoundly, just as it did the rest of his contemporaries all over the empire.

In this chapter we turn to Augustine as our second voice advocating for a culture of life, focusing on the message of *City of God*, which he wrote originally as a response to the brutal Gothic sack of Rome. In light of this horrific military disaster that shook Rome and his own community, Augustine encourages his readers to think about what it means to value human life as priceless when global empires all around rage in war.

War continues to be a life issue in the world today, even as we may feel that we Americans are doing fine. These are not our wars, one could say—indeed, many do say. It is easy to disengage and ignore conflicts like the one in Ukraine or Israel, since it is not here. Augustine's response to the sack of Rome shows how Christians can welcome refugees and love them at a time when they are shaken not only physically but spiritually. This begins, ironically, with listening to stories of death, and then speaking words of life in love to those who suffered.

> Augustine's response to the sack of Rome shows how Christians can welcome refugees and love them at a time when they are shaken not only physically but spiritually.

Much of Augustine's response, in response to the concerns of refugees that he heard, many of them firsthand, is rooted in retelling a theologically orthodox history of Rome and its empire.[1] Augustine too was writing a tale of two cities—the heavenly city of God and the earthly city of Rome.

HISTORY: TALES OF LIFE, TALES OF DEATH

It is no coincidence that Augustine turns to writing history in the wake of this tragedy that rocked the Roman Empire. An orthodox understanding of

---

[1] For a theological and historical overview of how Christians should think about empires, ancient and modern, see N. T. Wright and Michael Bird, *Jesus and the Powers: Christian Political Witness in an Age of Totalitarian Terror and Dysfunctional Democracies* (Grand Rapids, MI: Zondervan, 2024).

history and theology go hand in hand for Augustine. He retells Roman history from its beginnings to show his conviction that a proper understanding of history is essential for a theologically accurate valuing of human lives in all periods, including the present. God has always loved people, believers and nonbelievers, each one lovingly made in his image.

Augustine's readers, pagans and Christians alike, found the ground beneath their feet shaken and shifting as a result of the sack of Rome, a seismic event like no other in living memory. We have to remember that for Augustine's contemporaries, the Roman Empire was the anchor, the foundation of their world. They could not imagine a world without it. True, the city of Rome was no longer the capital of the empire—Constantine had moved the capital to a city he named after himself in AD 330, eighty years before the sack. Yet, Rome remained a powerful symbol of the empire's greatness. Its sack rocked the Romans' world like no other disaster they had ever imagined, perhaps because this one seemed unimaginable until it happened.

In retelling the history of Rome, and especially emphasizing previous disasters in that history, Augustine wants to dispel the perception of pagans that it is the pagan gods' wrath at the Christians' betrayal that caused this disaster. At the same time, he aims to comfort Christians who fear that God has abandoned them.[2] It seems a natural human impulse, when suffering, to feel that it is divine punishment. Yet, as the story of Job reminds us, sometimes suffering that defies our understanding has much more complicated reasons behind it. For anyone not ready to go overly deep into theological weeds, however, Augustine has more concrete historical facts to show that horrific suffering and death have always been part of Roman history.

Long before Christ was born, God cared for all people, including those, like the pagan Romans, who dwelled in darkness, worshiping gods who could not help them. Their life was full of death, Augustine notes, filled with

---

[2] I explain this in detail in chapter eight of *Cultural Christians in the Early Church: A Historical and Practical Introduction to Christians in the Greco-Roman World* (Grand Rapids, MI: Zondervan Academic, 2023).

"those evils which alone are dreaded by the heathen—famine, pestilence, war, pillage, captivity, massacre" (*City of God* 3.1).[3] These were all regular features of life in the Roman world before the birth of Christ. Ignorant men have given rise to such sayings as "Drought and Christianity go hand in hand," but they forget previous disasters in Roman history (2.3). Augustine documents such previous disasters over the course of book 2 of *City of God*, showing that the pagan gods never protected the Romans from disasters that altogether are not much milder than the present sack of the city by the Goths. He concludes the book with the confident statement that "Incomparably more glorious than Rome is that heavenly city in which for victory you have truth; for dignity, holiness; for peace, felicity; for life, eternity" (2.29).

Yet, in summarizing the previous historical disasters from which the Romans' pagan gods could not save them, Augustine is keenly aware that those suffering in the present need words of comfort. When reading book 1 of *City of God*, a striking realization should dawn on us. There is only one way that Augustine could have received such detailed information about what happened during the sack of Rome: he must have spoken with survivors at length.

This should not surprise us. After Rome was sacked, it was left destroyed and with no provisions. Famine set in quickly. Instead of staying behind to suffer and rebuild, many fled. One popular destination, as it happens, was Augustine's own Hippo Regius. As his intimate knowledge of the tortured innermost thoughts of both Christian and pagan survivors of the sack shows, Augustine ministered to them in person.

Augustine documents the suffering of these survivors and presents his own responses to them in book 1 of *City of God*. Their suffering was not inconsiderable. Many lost family and friends to the sword as the Goths rampaged through the city, slaughtering even civilians. The rape of women during the sack of the city was widespread, as it always was whenever an ancient city was breached. The Goths tortured some people to death to get them to reveal hiding places of treasures. They captured others and sold

---

[3] Quotations of this work follow Marcus Dods, trans., *City of God* (Peabody, MA: Hendrickson, 2011).

them into slavery. They refused to release the bodies of the dead to their loved ones for burial.

Still, even in this widespread suffering, God's care for all who suffer was manifest. Augustine emphasizes one miraculous provision: cruel as they were, the Goths spared those who chose to hide in Christian churches throughout Rome. This meant, Augustine poignantly notes, that some pagans were saved from harm and violence in this surprising way:

> But what was novel, was that savage barbarians showed themselves in so gentle a guise, that the largest churches were chosen and set apart for the purpose of being filled with the people to whom quarter was given, and that in them none were slain, from them none forcibly dragged; that into them many were led by their relenting enemies to be set at liberty, and that from them none were led into slavery by merciless foes. (1.7)

Emphasizing the same truth that God once showed to Hagar—God sees your suffering!—Augustine encourages those who survived to choose life. Indeed, this last concern was significant, as some survivors, especially women who had suffered rape, did die by suicide. Augustine finds this devaluing of one's own life in the midst of suffering deeply troubling and keeps coming back to this point on multiple occasions in book 1 of *City of God*, urging Christians to remember that the commandment against taking someone else's life applies also to preserving one's own life (1.20).

Augustine's response to the sack of Rome provides powerful tools for processing such modern traumas of devaluing human life as the two world wars, the Holocaust, and the current Russian invasion of Ukraine. In all of these, we want to ask: Where is God? Indeed, many have. In his novel *Night*, Holocaust survivor Elie Wiesel famously describes losing his own faith in God's existence as a result of his experiences. That is also the question that Augustine and residents of the Roman Empire of his day, pagans and Christians alike, asked. But if someone reproaches a Christian with the question "Where is your God?" Augustine says it is appropriate to throw the same question right back to the pagan, who suffers these same misfortunes, with the reminder that "the family of Christ is furnished with its reply: our God is everywhere present, wholly everywhere, not confined to any place" (1.29).

To hear of God's presence and knowledge of all suffering may not be the answer we want when we just want the pain to stop. But it is nevertheless an answer that gives comfort. God is everywhere, and God sees. In the meantime, as the subtext of Augustine's own writing suggests, God's awareness of suffering does not mean that we should leave the suffering of others to him alone. Rather, like Augustine, we are called to minister through speaking with those who suffer, including survivors and refugees from wars. This is not an easy task, and yet it is one that involves speaking life into death. It also involves listening as Augustine did and allowing survivors to bring their stories to light.

> To hear of God's presence and knowledge of all suffering may not be the answer we want when we just want the pain to stop. But it is nevertheless an answer that gives comfort. God is everywhere, and God sees.

WRITING MILITARY HISTORY AS AN ACT OF COMPASSION

Speaking life into a world bent on death does not mean ignoring suffering and death; it means recognizing them as an injustice that God hates and will destroy when he returns to destroy all sin and death. In the meantime, Augustine's graphic description of the sack of Rome gives us a model for writing military history as an act of compassion. This model, however, did not originate with Augustine. We could go back to Homer for such a model, or we could look to the Athenian tragedians, such as Aeschylus. Living in a world where war was endemic, they had good reason to think about ways to speak life into a world filled with violence.

Early in Aeschylus's tragedy *Agamemnon* (458 BC), a messenger arrives in Argos from Troy to let Queen Clytemnestra know that her not-much-beloved husband, Agamemnon, has finally won the Trojan War and is on his way home. The nameless messenger is a minor character, but what he has to say has implications far beyond the play. His story, as a veteran eager to tell of his experience from a perspective that challenges the official narrative, reminds us that writing (and reading) military history can be an act of profound and subversive compassion. But compassion for whom? And how might we arrive at it?[4]

Instead of taking a line or two to deliver his message and leaving the stage forever, as a proper messenger ought, this messenger launches into a mournful description of the Trojan War from the perspective of a common soldier. For ten long years, he and countless other Greek soldiers, who sailed to Troy with the much more famous, big-name heroes, lived in constant discomfort and distress—physical, emotional, spiritual. But, the soldier notes, "Who, unless he is a god, is free from suffering all his days?" (Aeschylus, *Agamemnon* 553).[5] At least the evil is over now, he says, so we need not speak of it further.

The anonymous soldier may have felt that he was done talking about war, but military history dominated the interests of ancient readers, whether in the form of war monographs, such as those of Herodotus, Thucydides, or Sallust; military manuals, such as those of Xenophon and Aeneas Tacticus; or epic poems, from the Homeric epics on. We are not so different today. Sales of books on military history show that this continues to be one of the most popular genres of historical writing for the general public. Publishing on the Civil War, in particular, has been so prolific, that according to Civil War historian Brian Holden Reid, if we were to add up all the books on the subject, we would find that one new book on the war has been published for each day since General Lee's surrender at Appomattox to the present.[6]

As Amazon's up-to-the-hour tracking shows, books on a wide range of military history topics just keep on selling. Both world wars have received at least as much attention as the American Civil War. Ancient military

---

[4]This section of the chapter is adapted from a previously published essay, "Can Writing (and Reading) Military History Be an Act of Compassion?," April 5, 2022, Current, https://currentpub.com /2022/04/05/can-writing-and-reading-military-history-be-an-act-of-compassion/.

[5]For translation, see Herbert Weir Smyth, trans., *Aeschylus*, Loeb Classical Library (Cambridge, MA. Harvard University Press, 1926), available at www.theoi.com/Text/AeschylusAgamemnon.html.

[6]Brian Holden Reid, "The Civil War, 1861–5," in *A Companion to American Military History*, ed. James C. Bradford (Malden, MA: Wiley-Blackwell, 2009), 99-122.

history has its fans as well. In fact, Sun Tzu's *Art of War* is more popular today (with English-speaking audiences) than in Sun Tzu's own day in late sixth-century BC China. Both the paperback and audiobook versions of his military manual consistently rank high on the Amazon bestseller list.

In other words, many members of the public in antiquity and today are not done talking, reading, and of course writing about wars, ancient or modern. But the kind of reading and writing that most armchair military historians want to do glorifies war, as we saw in chapter six, when we looked at Caesar's war journals. That approach to talking about war and violence is a problem for Augustine, who certainly does not glorify the Goths' military exploits in sacking Rome. Indeed, the Greek tragedians likewise show heroes as flawed. In tragedies, the heroes' exploits on and especially off the battlefield come across as brutal and inhumane rather than praiseworthy.

But the temptation to look for heroes in military history comes easily for audiences and historians, ancient and modern alike. Indeed, Aeschylus's nameless soldier stands as a surprising foil to the dominant narrative of the Trojan War, the one presented in the Homeric epics. In the *Iliad*, heroes such as Achilles, Diomedes, and Hector are decidedly superhuman in their feats of strength. Their duels with other heroes emphasize battlefield violence in graphic ways. Gouged eyes fly, limbs are slashed, and blood pours in rivers on the ground of Homeric battlefields. Not surprisingly, the *Iliad* was a martial inspiration text in ancient Sparta and was a personal favorite of Alexander the Great, who traveled on campaign with a full set of scrolls of the epic.

But is this emphasis on glorifying battlefield violence the only way to approach military history? Augustine's narrative of the sack of Rome, focused as it is entirely on the perspective of the victims, reflects a compassionate alternative that instead sees each image bearer as precious. If our worldview does not define heroism and virtue as something that can only be won in war, and furthermore only through the killing of other heroes, it is time to consider a different outlook. That is what Augustine wanted to do in documenting the suffering of the Roman victims of the Gothic sack.

It is much easier for us to feel compassion for civilians, whom we rightly see as victims of war. This is why Augustine strikingly focuses on the non-military victims of the war. While Roman troops were engaged in fighting the Goths, Augustine's focus is entirely on the civilian residents of Rome who found their city brutally taken, their lives disrupted and perhaps ended in horrific torture and violence. Such a focus in considering war is relatable today as well. There is a reason that Anne Frank's *Diary of a Young Girl*, for instance, continues to be a bestseller. Her voice inspires readers to consider civilians' worth and preciousness in a world that challenges both. Awareness of Anne's tragic death as part of the Holocaust only makes her words, so focused on living the mundane life of a teenager, all the more powerfully poignant.

Of course, even epic heroes are not immune to loss, as has been the case for soldiers in all periods of war. Scenes of mourning and loss in the *Iliad*, whether Achilles's mourning for Patroclus or Priam's mourning for Hector, were clearly designed to appeal to the audience's emotions. Death and destruction on all sides is the defining feature of war in the epic. The contrasting scenes of war and peace on the shield of Achilles with which I opened this chapter show this well. In the city at peace, a marriage celebration is underway, and a civil arbitration of a dispute is ongoing. In the city at war, the city of this world, whether Rome or Mariupol, despair rules over the looming destruction.

Reading and writing military history as an act of compassion involves first and foremost the recognition of war as an instrument of destruction—of lives, families, civilizations—rather than a way of creating the only type of lasting glory for heroes, past, present, and future. Such a compassionate approach toward military history also involves a lot more investment of the self—whether reader or writer—in the suffering of others, embracing the literal meaning of the term *compassion* as suffering together with the goal of understanding better.

It is much easier emotionally to think of war clinically, to analyze battles, campaigns, and grand strategy of nations and empires without giving thought to the real people involved. To think of war as chess, to reduce it to a game, is intriguing. But such a denial of the reality of human suffering of both civilians and combatants is intellectually and spiritually dishonest. The people of the past, whether far removed or closer to us in time, deserve our compassion. Furthermore, what is subversive and striking about the compassion Augustine displays is that it has the ability to change us and our own outlook on war and the heroes it ostensibly creates. Aeschylus, a veteran of the Battle of Marathon (490 BC), understood this when he gave an unnamed soldier the right to criticize the greatest war in Greek imagination. Augustine understood it as well when he mourned the fall of Rome, wept with those who wept, but then told them of the glorious city of God.

Telling tales of cities at war is not easy. Nor is it easy to write them or read them. As a military historian friend once observed, "Some books cannot come into my house." I knew what she meant. Some things military historians read are simply too heavy to bring into our homes, into our own safe space, our own tiny city of life. Yet, in a world where war and suffering exist, sometimes it takes telling stories of death to show the preciousness of life. But not all tales of war and death do this. While some can orient our minds and souls toward God, others can do the very opposite.

SHAPING MINDS AND SOULS

You find yourself in an unfamiliar place. It appears to be a brick-walled dungeon of sorts or maybe an old building. All you know is that there is very little light coming from the evenly spaced sconces on the walls, the ceiling is oddly low, and it seems to have a serious mold problem—but you are not planning to be there for long. This place just oozes danger, and you are trying to figure out how to get out. Good thing you are armed to the teeth, perhaps wearing body armor to boot, though this only highlights further the danger of the situation you are in.

Suddenly, shooting explodes from just behind you. You duck just in the nick of time and return fire, perhaps killing the surprise opponent. You then strip him of his ammunition, Homeric battlefield–style, except here the point is not prestige and honor but the practicalities of survival: you know you will need every round of ammo you can get. The game will only keep challenging you further, sending more and more opponents whom you must kill or be killed yourself. At least, you can remind yourself when you take a break and realize that you have been playing now for hours, this is not real. This is just a video game. But it is so exciting, it feels so real, even if you thankfully emerge from the ordeals you experienced with nary a scratch.

In any given week, Americans spend a lot of time on streaming entertainment. According to one statistic, Netflix subscribers spend 3.2 hours per day watching Netflix.[7] It is possible that the same individuals stream other entertainment elsewhere as well or spend additional time playing video games, including first-person shooter games, which have been so popular for the past thirty years. This is time spent in an alternate reality—maybe even virtual reality—that seems convincing but is not real. Yet, it is real enough to absorb us and shape us. After all, anything we do for this large a percentage of our daily lives is bound to shape our minds and souls. In the case of violent content, such as first-person shooter games or many R-rated movies, the portrayal of violence orients us away from how God thinks of people, callously viewing people who get killed on screen as mere points to score.

It can also become addictive, to the point of interfering with the addict's ability to perform everyday tasks. I am thinking here of the stories of college-aged men who spent all of their waking hours playing video games, skipping classes and other responsibilities to do so. But modern technology is not necessary to reach this state of mind. Ancient entertainment provided a decidedly low-tech route for achieving the same result. In the fourth century AD, a young man from a small town went off to school at a larger town and . . . became addicted to watching blood sports. Every time a show was going on at the local amphitheater, this formerly promising scholar was there, absorbed utterly in the fights of men with beasts and other men,

---

[7]Frank Moraes, "Netflix During Quarantine: TV Streaming Stats That Will Blow Your Mind," HotDog, updated November 28, 2023, https://hotdog.com/tv/stream/netflix/during-quarantine/.

cheering on some to kill or be killed. Eventually, he realized that his obsession was unhealthy and quit cold turkey. But after moving to Rome a few years later, he fell back in with the old habit. Addiction is often a lifelong struggle, and the entertainment to which this young man was addicted was readily available everywhere in the Roman Empire, free of charge.

This young man was Alypius, Augustine's lifelong friend. Indeed, we know about him precisely because of Augustine, who includes his story in book 6 of his *Confessions*. Alypius's addiction story ultimately ends like that of Augustine, with a heartfelt conversion to Christianity. To be a Christian, both Alypius and Augustine conclude, is not compatible with entertainment rooted in denying the dignity of image bearers.

The violence of the arenas, in which enslaved people and convicted criminals fought to the death, served to dehumanize, degrade, and violate. But not everyone reached the same conclusion about entertainment as Alypius and Augustine. Strikingly, this entertainment, long a feature of pagan entertainment, continued to flourish in the increasingly more Christian empire. Of course, entertainment of various sorts that subtly or overtly denies the preciousness of image bearers continues to be a staple in our own world. Viewing it corrupts our very minds and souls, desensitizing us to the suffering of others.

But turning a blind eye to violence and suffering around us is not the solution either. Augustine notes as much in his reflections on horrific local violence in one city with which he was familiar:

> When at Caesarea in Mauritania I was dissuading the people from that civil, or worse than civil, war which they called *Caterva* (for it was not fellow citizens merely, but neighbors, brothers, fathers and sons even, who, divided into two factions and armed with stones, fought annually at a certain season of the year for several days continuously, every one killing whomsoever he could), I strove with all the vehemence of speech that I could command to root out and drive from their hearts and lives an evil so cruel and inveterate; it was not, however, when I heard their applause, but when I saw their tears, that I thought I had produced an effect. For the

applause showed that they were instructed and delighted, but the tears that they were subdued. And when I saw their tears I was confident even before the event proved it, that this horrible and barbarous custom (which had been handed down to them from their fathers and their ancestors of generations long gone by and which like an enemy was besieging their hearts, or rather had complete possession of them) was overthrown. (*On Christian Doctrine* 4.24)[8]

This is a story of a town where for generations there was an annual tradition of splitting the population into two murderous factions for a few days.[9] It was, it seems, a sort of entertainment, an ancient version of first-person shooter games, or a gladiatorial game that escaped from the realm of the amphitheater and engulfed the entire community for a short time, year after year. But it was very real, very dangerous, and involved relatives and neighbors killing each other, simply because this was what they had always done that time of year.

Augustine brings up this story in the final book of his four-volume work *On Christian Doctrine*, a manual for the exegetical interpretation of Scripture. While he had published the first three books of this work in AD 397, he added the fourth book, which includes the discussion of the *caterva*, in AD 426, sixteen years after the sack of Rome and toward the end of his own life. We should think of it as the second edition of the book—a greater and better version postexpansion. Augustine brings three decades of additional experience with preaching and pastoring to this revised edition. So what did he think was particularly important to add to his earlier coverage? Strikingly, in the fourth book, he focuses on the power of rhetoric and in particular the significance of emotion in achieving the right effect in reading, teaching, and preaching the Bible. When employed nobly, for just purposes, words are life giving in a culture that had previously embraced death.

---

[8]For translation, see Augustine, *On Christian Doctrine*, trans. James Shaw, *Nicene and Post-Nicene Fathers*, Second Series, ed. Philip Schaff and Henry Wace, vol. 2 (Buffalo, NY: Christian Literature, 1896), rev. and ed. for New Advent by Kevin Knight, www.newadvent.org/fathers/12024.htm.

[9]For a consideration of the *caterva* in the context of the broader story of sectarian violence in late antique African Christianity, see Brent Shaw, *Sacred Violence: African Christians and Sectarian Hatred in the Age of Augustine* (New York: Cambridge University Press, 2011), 19.

In this context of seeking to bring his audience to repentance, Augustine notes that it was when he saw tears in the eyes of those who heard his sermon at Caesarea that he knew they had repented of their generations-long communal tradition of violent sin against each other. Why? Because these were tears of those who recognized the preciousness of others around them in a new light. These tears were perhaps not so different from those Alypius or Augustine themselves had shed on those occasions, decades earlier, when they themselves first fully accepted Christ.

I do want to make one thing clear: Augustine was a flawed human being, like all believers. In fact, he did not shy from admitting this truth about his sinful nature himself. So, the goal of this chapter is not to idealize Augustine. Yet, Augustine's writing shows that, while he was often abrasive and quite argumentative with certain individuals with whom he disagreed, he also cared for people. We do not think of Augustine's caring side as much. Reading some of his letters of rebuke, in fact, we may get the opposite idea.[10] But his pastoral heart comes through in his discussion of mourning for the victims of the Gothic sack of Rome and his desire to tell difficult truths that call others to value life.

CONCLUSION: WHY WRITE?

Earlier in this book, we considered modern injunctions to women by thinkers such as Roland Barthes or Julie Phillips to place career and pursuit of creative activity at least on the same level as children. Other thinkers perhaps go further still. In an either-or choice, modern secular philosophy repeatedly emphasizes that art should win, because art (including writing) reflects true productivity, whereas children merely hinder productivity, whether creative or of more mundane sorts. I could tell you all kinds of things about my house chores that regularly pile up, but if you are a parent or have ever been around parents, you get the idea.

There is no doubt that Augustine loved writing. One does not leave the single largest corpus of writing of all ancient authors without having a

---

[10]For a study of Augustine's use of letters to correct and rebuke, sometimes quite harshly, see Jennifer Ebbeler, *Disciplining Christians: Correction and Community in Augustine's Letters* (New York: Oxford University Press, 2012).

profound passion for the written word. But Augustine did not just love writing. Augustine loved writing for the same reason he loved preaching, and we see that reason in the example he reports of a sermon that he gave a full eight years earlier in Caesarea in Mauretania—he wanted to speak words of life into a world where the default was death, whether a literal death because of war or community violence, or a spiritual death because of addiction to things that kill the mind and the spirit. Whenever we write or speak life-giving words, we are imitating God's first life-giving words as he spoke the world into being. It may seem a weak imitation, but so is everything about us. We bear the *imago Dei*, even as we are feeble and frail, mere children of dust.

Augustine wrote a lot, an abundance of pastoral words that is almost proverbially noticeable. In her Pulitzer Prize–winning novel *Gilead*, contemporary American writer Marilynne Robinson tenderly introduces John Ames, an elderly lifelong pastor. Dying slowly but surely, he is writing letters and stories to the young son of his old age, who will otherwise never get to know him or much about his family. At one point, Ames considers the sheer volume of sermons he has written and preached over the course of his life and realizes that the total of his written corpus rivals or even exceeds that of Augustine. But, he humbly adds, the quality is surely not comparable.

To repeat the sheer fact of it again, Augustine wrote a lot. But as his fictional fan John Ames reminds us, those individuals mostly likely to rival his production of words are members of his own profession even today—people who write a sermon each week. Pastors who shepherd the flock with their life-giving words are challenging the culture of death each week through the preaching of God's love, which transcends death and reminds us of the heavenly city to come.

Reflecting on what it means to speak life-giving words into a world that is defined by death has now taken us beyond conversations about valuing children and motherhood. Rightly so. As we saw in the first part of the book, the contemporary devaluing of children and motherhood is a symptom of a broader devaluing of human life. Likewise, we can see now, as we look at examples of life-giving voices, respecting the sanctity of human life means much more than treasuring children and valuing the work of mothers—although, of course, these are essential components. People do not live in a vacuum.

We live in the world that God created even before he created us to steward it. The life and well-being of this world is still inextricably connected to our well-being, long since our ancestors' expulsion from Eden. Or, more accurately, as climate scientist Katharine Hayhoe writes in her book *Saving Us*, it is our well-being that is inextricably connected to that of our world.[11] So, in the final chapter of this book, we turn to the writings of a man who has made this argument his life's mission: a farmer, poet, novelist, and advocate for human flourishing in a broken world, Wendell Berry.

---

[11]Katharine Hayhoe, *Saving Us: A Climate Scientist's Case for Hope and Healing in a Divided World* (New York: Simon & Schuster, 2021).

10

IN PURSUIT OF HUMAN FLOURISHING

And I went up, and I saw a very great space of garden, and in the midst a man sitting, white-headed, in shepherd's clothing, tall, milking his sheep; and standing around in white were many thousands. And he raised his head and beheld me and said to me: Welcome, child. And he cried to me, and from the curd he had from the milk he gave me as it were a morsel; and I took it with joined hands and ate it up; and all that stood around said, Amen. And at the sound of that word I awoke, yet eating I know not what of sweet. (*Passion of the Saints Perpetua and Felicity* 4)[1]

So wrote Perpetua in AD 203, describing the vision that presaged her martyrdom.

Whenever ancient authors imagine the ideal time and place of human flourishing, images of agricultural and pastoral prosperity and abundance predominate. We may think of the Bible's imagery of the original garden of blessings, Eden, or the land of milk and honey that becomes Israel's consolation prize, but such visions were not the purview of the Hebrews alone.

---

[1]W. H. Shewring, trans., *The Passion of Perpetua and Felicity* (London, 1931), available at https://sourcebooks.fordham.edu/source/perpetua.asp.

Scientific discussions of the agricultural revolution habitually note the population explosion that resulted, crediting it to the greater stability that the settled agricultural life allows over the nomadic pastoralism that preceded: "The planet had supported roughly 8 million people when we were only hunter-gatherers. But the population exploded with the invention of agriculture climbing to 100 million people by 5,000 years ago, and reaching 7 billion people today."[2]

The newly settled life greatly increased fertility, affecting mothers and children in obvious ways—there were now more of them. Anyone who has nursed an infant for hours each day for the first year of life knows the stability that is essential for this process. Farming was not easy, however, and crops could fail. Furthermore, the net gain in population numbers that resulted from the agricultural revolution belies the increases in human deaths from disease. It therefore should not surprise us that in the earliest world literature we already find longings for that elusive time when life was better, more harmonious, more perfect. These are instinctive yearnings for the garden where God placed his very first image bearers.

THE GOLDEN AGE OF HUMANKIND

We find traditions about the golden age of humankind in the Greek and Roman world, usually as part of narratives of decline: things started out quite well but went downhill—and fast. Some political leaders tried using this myth to their own advantage, portraying themselves as restoring that long-gone prosperity. Make Rome Great Again, if you will. In the art and literature that Augustus, Rome's first emperor, used as propaganda to support his rule, the return to this mythical golden age appears repeatedly.

Augustus invested heavily in such self-promotion, repeatedly reminding his subjects that his rule ended decades of civil war and turmoil. Never mind

---

[2]Darren Curnoe, "Was Agriculture the Greatest Blunder in Human History?," The Conversation, October 18, 2017, https://theconversation.com/was-agriculture-the-greatest-blunder-in-human-history-85898. Curnoe responds to the criticism of agriculture that Jared Diamond first presented in 1987 and expanded in greater detail in *Guns, Germs, and Steel: The Fates of Human Societies* (New York: Norton, 1999).

that he fomented the final rounds of that vicious bloodletting. His Ara Pacis, the Altar of Peace, included, among other imagery, a fertility goddess surrounded by healthy-looking children and overflowing harvest crops.[3] In the work of Vergil, Augustus's court poet, the same themes of abundances appear. Two poetry collections, the *Eclogues* and the *Georgics* idealize agricultural life and production, presenting in poetic form much of the same joyful abundance that the Ara Pacis does in sculpture. For example, we might note the fourth eclogue, with its peaceful flocks of sheep that spontaneously change their wool color, all (presumably) to accommodate the clothing preferences of the inhabitants of the new Augustan golden age. No need for hard labor to obtain that expensive Tyrian purple dye if the sheep can make it at will.

Superlative agricultural and pastoral prosperity in antiquity stood for blessing from God—or the pagan gods—on a land and its people. These last two were always connected. The health and prosperity of the land, from its crops to its bees and its fruit trees and psychedelic sheep with their color-changing wool, was inextricably connected to the well-being (and, to be sure, fertility) of its people. A blessing was a blessing on both, while curses likewise fell on both. This was a common feature of ancient oaths and treaties in the ancient Mediterranean world and the Near East: those taking these oaths or treaties invoked these blessings on themselves if obedient, and curses if not. May all the fruit trees of my land fail if I disobey this oath, people repeatedly invoked.

In the popular portrayals of Jesus in early Christian art as the good shepherd tenderly carrying a sheep, we see that same image but now made personal: this divine provision is not just care for people in general, in the abstract, but for each believer individually. God sees you, loves you, feeds you. Perpetua's vision of tasting heavenly food, that curd of milk from Jesus' own hand, fits into this ideal. This is, as even the pagans could sense at times, what a flourishing life should be about.

---

[3]For an overview of the imagery of abundance on Ara Pacis, see David Castriota, *Ara Pacis and the Imagery of Abundance in Later Greek and Early Roman Imperial Art* (Princeton, NJ: Princeton University Press, 1995). Barbette Spaeth argues that this fertility goddess is Ceres, the Roman goddess of crops, in her book *The Roman Goddess Ceres* (Austin: University of Texas Press, 1996).

Too often today, discussions of what it means to respect human life and dignity revolve around just the physical body. Yes, protecting image bearers from abortion, disease, starvation, and war, to name just a few of the threats we have considered over the previous chapters, is an essential starting point. It should not, however, be the endpoint. The embedded attacks on children and motherhood I have documented in the first two parts of this book, both in our own society and in the pre-Christian Greco-Roman antiquity, are ultimately attacks not only on human life but on human flourishing. This elusive goal, a desire to return to the conditions of life in Eden, cannot be perfectly achieved on this side of eternity. But we should at least try. This means recognizing that our flourishing does not entail merely the protection of our bodies but also our minds and souls and, last but not least, the environment in which we dwell. We are still connected to the land, even if most of us are not farming.

Thinking about these dimensions as bound together—the people and the land they inhabit as a connected whole—came naturally to the ancient world, centered as it was on agricultural life. We might note, for instance, the Athenian myth of the birth of the first Athenian spontaneously from the local land. The Athenians were not the only ones to have such a myth of origin. The Thebans had their own version: the earliest Thebans, a race of warriors, sprouted—or, more accurately, sprang up in full armor—from dragon teeth sown in the land.

Instinctive to such myths was the belief that it was somehow better to be a people who had always dwelt in a particular region than a people who were outsiders moving in. The Spartans were aware of this. Although conquerors of the region they settled, they promoted their own myth of nativity: they were the children of Heracles who returned home to the land of their origin to claim their rightful inheritance.

Emphasizing these mythologies was also a great way to justify xenophobia in antiquity, but this does not have to be part of the package. People have an instinctive desire to belong, and this means searching for roots. It is no coincidence that now, in this age of urbanization and increased mobility, companies such as Ancestry or 23andMe are doing brisk business in DNA analysis and family history. We want to know: Where are we from? Where do we belong? The where is inextricably connected to the who—who are our people, and whose cousins, however distant, are we?

Modern America has become a land of uprooted people. For so many, especially of the college-educated class, the expected life trajectory now involves moving away for college and possibly never coming back to live in one's parents' home. In many corporate jobs, promotion means yet another uprooting—you move where the job sends you. What are we losing in the process?[4] One answer only grows clearer with each passing year: the potential to flourish more deeply.

Wendell Berry, born in 1934, has had a lifelong front seat to the growth of the culture of uprootedness and the concomitant urbanization and abandonment of rural America. He has spent much of his life as a writer and a farmer in rural Kentucky, advocating in defense of more traditional forms of flourishing, pushing back against the modern treadmill life as the only option, calling instead for "Nature as Measure" not only in setting appropriate boundaries for how to treat the land but likewise for how to treat people.[5] Roots and rootedness, Berry's writings repeatedly affirm, are key to human flourishing. But what might life-giving roots look like?

THE OAK AND THE BONSAI

By the seashore somewhere outside of time, an aged oak stands planted firm, its gnarly roots extending far into the ground, reaching toward eternity. A golden chain is set on it, and a magical cat walks laps on the chain night and day. If leftward bound, he recites a poem, a song. When walking to the right, he tells a fairy tale. So goes the prologue to legendary

---

[4] See Daniel K. Williams's moving reflection on this topic: "Are Local Family Ties Worth the Sacrifice of a Career Dream? Maybe So," *Current*, May 11, 2023, https://currentpub.com/2023/05/11/are-local-family-ties-worth-the-sacrifice-of-a-career-dream-maybe-so/.

[5] A poignant essay with this title concludes Wendell Berry's essay collection *What Are People For?* (Berkeley, CA: Counterpoint, 1990), 204-10.

Russian poet Alexander Pushkin's fairy tale in poetry, *Ruslan and Lyudmila*, an epic tale of rescue, the victory of good over evil, of life over death. The immortal personification of death, Kaschey Bessmertnyi (literally, deathless!), kidnaps Lyudmila, Ruslan's wife, at the beginning of the tale, setting the stage for Ruslan's epic quest to get her back.

Is the cat walking left or right on its golden chain on the oak while telling this folktale in song? Maybe it does not matter. All that matters is the roots of such rich folktales, stories in which life always overcomes death. It is the telling of stories of life that keeps people's spirits alive generation after generation. But even if the roots do not reach centuries down into the ground, they can transform a weary soul.

> It is the telling of stories of life that keeps people's spirits alive generation after generation. But even if the roots do not reach centuries down into the ground, they can transform a weary soul.

A few years ago, I toured the Monastery of the Holy Spirit, a Trappist monastery in Conyers, Georgia. The monastic order has *stabilitas loci* as one of the vows its adherents must take. At its most basic level, this is a vow to be rooted in one place—the monastery. More than that, however, it is a vow that recognizes the soul's need for peace and stability in an uncertain world to be able to focus on God. Roots anchor us, but where?

The monk who briefly spoke to my tour group had previously had a successful career on Wall Street. Depressed and discouraged, he felt uprooted in every way, lacking a sense of peace and purpose in his life. Reaching a breaking point, he became a monk, trading a life of making a lot of money and not much else in the big city for gaining new roots in Christ and in this monastery in suburban Georgia.

One of the works of the monks at the Monastery of the Holy Spirit involves the care of bonsai trees. These are miniature trees grown in pots, with the tiniest of roots that can extend tenaciously into the depth of their small containers, but under proper care they can thrive for decades, a few even reaching the century mark. Finicky to an extreme degree, they require much closer supervision and attention than their full-sized brethren. Pushkin's large oak is free to thrive in the wild. Not so the bonsai.

They are plants, living things. Yet they are also an art form, and this is first and foremost their purpose. Their existence as laborious and difficult works of art with high stakes is a reminder of a powerful truth: growing things for people is not merely a utilitarian process to get food to survive, although it may start there. Just as our bodies need nourishment, our souls have been created to delight in beautiful things that from a strictly utilitarian perspective are utterly worthless. What is the point of a tiny tree in a pot, after all?

But then, what is the point of grown men, monks who have taken the vow of *stabilitas*, stewarding this version of the garden, a mere shadow of Eden, whose shallow roots may even seem to be a mockery of God's work? A bonsai is an art, its worth similar to the value of any art form that delights us for reasons we cannot fully articulate. A beautiful miniature of God's creation, it reflects the nature of creation itself as glorious art. Is not each of us, image bearers, a miniature version of the real one, God, reflected in the *imago Dei* that each of us bears? In the bonsai, cultivation of life and of art are inextricably bound through the knowledge that neglect or overzealous care alike will result in sure death for the tiny, vulnerable tree.

I think of these different types of roots, deep and shallow, both pointing us to God each in its own way. As an immigrant twice over, having moved first from Russia to Israel and then from Israel to the United States, I miss the imaginary homeland of my ancestors that I have never had, a homeland that has been a mirage now for a century. Long before the move out of Russia, my family was uprooted already, both by the structures of life in USSR and by the Holocaust, which wiped out much of my mother's family, centuries-long dwellers of the Jewish shtetls of Ukraine.

By God's grace, for thirteen years of my adult life, until very recently, I was in Georgia and lived in the same house for twelve years—the longest I have ever lived in any one place. The woods that teemed with poison ivy and Virginia creeper, ever creeping closer if we did not strive to beat them back, began right behind the house and extended to a small family farm an acre and a half away, down the hill, invisible for all this greenery. Massive oaks dominated the woods, extending their canopied branches over the back deck and shading the house. Their roots surrounded the house as well. A golden chain and a magical storytelling cat would not have been out of place on one of these giants. Yet it was no paradise. As a reminder of the fallen nature of this world, one summer day we found a seven-foot-long snakeskin, freshly shed, draped over the aged oak roots.

It was while living there that I learned the awful truth: I am allergic to oak.

OF ROOTS AND BRANCHES

In thinking about roots, the story of one young woman comes to mind. After growing up on a farm on the edge of a small town, she moved to the big city to attend college. There she met someone, and they got married. Both became teachers and stayed in this big city, driving daily to the different schools where they were teaching in opposite directions from their home, living their lives married but wholly apart from each other and from everyone else.

They had only one child—for how could they do otherwise, living the treadmill life that they led, wholly uprooted from anything that could ground them? Then, after more than twenty years of marriage, when their son was in his teens, the husband left the wife for another woman, someone he had met at his place of work. Years lived apart took a toll, and only when everything collapsed could they see that something had gone terribly wrong. Or, at least, the wife could see it. The husband just shrugged it off and went on with his newfound happiness.

This is the life trajectory of "little Margaret," the daughter of Hannah Coulter, the titular protagonist and narrator of Wendell Berry's novel. While Hannah was eager for each of her three children to have the opportunity to go to college, their departure from home for college turns out to be permanent, leaving her, "the last Coulter of the name in Port William," to mourn and second-guess her decision.[6] Did she equip them to flourish, or did she

---

[6]Wendell Berry, *Hannah Coulter* (Berkeley, CA: Counterpoint, 2004), 92.

set them on the road to misery? Each of the three, we learn, lives a life that is miserable in its own way. There is no escaping the treadmill, however. By contrast, she sees the different life path of the family of Danny and Lyda Branch.

Having no ambition but deep roots and love of *stabilitas loci* rivaling the most devout of monks, the Branches pass on these values to their own seven children, who all remain in Port William. And—here is the kicker—they are all happy to be there. Their name is no coincidence. Like a healthy tree left alone by an overzealous pruner, the branches grow any way nature sends them, unpredictable in all ways but one: health. This places the Branches outside time in a way that, Berry contends, is exemplary. Unlike those all around them, they are immune to the expectations of the modern treadmill lifestyle:

> Compared to nearly everybody else, the Branches have led a sort of futureless life. They have planned and provided as much as they needed to, but they take little thought for the morrow. They aren't going any place, they aren't getting ready to become anything but what they are, and so their lives are not fretful and hankering. And they are all still here, still farming. They are here, and if the world lasts they are going to be here for quite a while. If I had "venture capital" to invest, I think I would invest it in the Branches.[7]

Berry pours observations accumulated over a lifetime into *Hannah Coulter*, published the year he turned seventy. While advocating both here and throughout his life's work for respect for agrarianism and the human flourishing it fosters, he shows glimpses of ideals, like the Branches, who are decidedly not idyllic. Unlike ancient authors whose pastoral ideals harked back to that mythical ideal, Berry shows the simplicity of a present that may be in reach, just barely.

Hannah's voice as narrator, filtered through Berry's own, is in some ways profoundly modern. Yet it also echoes the themes of human flourishing that

---

[7] Berry, *Hannah Coulter*, 152.

we see already in the ancient world, including Perpetua's own vision of restored Eden in heaven. Instead of Revelation's heavenly city, this Eden is a garden, or rather a farm, with sheep and a shepherd. So are Berry's protagonists, the farmers of Port William. Their stories, never easy but always beautiful even in their heartbreaks, show that promoting a culture of life means speaking about the value of the living land as tied to our own flourishing—body, mind, and soul—with a primordial umbilical. The human race started out in the garden. Our souls yearn for it still. But our own sinful nature keeps getting in the way of this flourishing, as we keep wishing for

The human race started out in the garden. Our souls yearn for it still.

more of everything. Sometimes, Berry cautions, the enemy is our own desire to improve and innovate, perhaps in ways that seem so innocent yet prove our destruction.

The worship of progress in the modern world is not good for us as people, Berry repeatedly affirms in his critiques of innovations in farming. This subject is at the heart of *The Unsettling of America* and also comes up in the story of Andy Catlett, the protagonist of *Remembering*. Frustrated with innovations that replace people with machines, Andy is struck by the differences he finds between a thoroughly modern farmer he interviews, who lives in a constant state of debt and stress, farming an expansive land all by himself, and Amish farmers, who take genuine joy in their simple lives and flourish in friendship and relationship with each other.[8] The binary may seem at first glance to reduce both types of farmers to caricatures of themselves, but it serves a key point, as Jeff Bilbro notes: "Though such binaries run the risk of arrogant simplification, Berry uses them to draw stark moral contrasts, and to provide forms that can guide the work of life. His binaries, then, are not totalizing systems that sort a complex world into two simplistic categories; they are prophetic pry bars wielded to loosen our calcified hearts."[9]

---

[8] See Jeff Bilbro, *Virtues of Renewal: Wendell Berry's Sustainable Forms* (Lexington: University Press of Kentucky, 2019), 93-95, for a discussion of Berry's visits to Amish farms as part of his search for healthy thriving farms while writing *The Unsettling of America*.
[9] Jeff Bilbro, *Virtues of Renewal*, 73.

Progress of certain types seems to make sense in a utilitarian sense—we know which farmer grows a lot more crops!—but does not lead to human flourishing, to happiness, to health. Andy Catlett feels this particularly deeply, having lost an arm to a machine. His body has quite literally been wounded, mangled by something advertised as an instrument of progress. This progress further leads to the increasing fracturing of society and of families—isolating people instead of encouraging them to work, live, flourish together.[10] As Berry states in *The Unsettling of America*, "The terms exploitation and nurture . . . describe not only division between persons but also within persons. We are all to some extent the products of an exploitative society, and it would be foolish and self-defeating to pretend that we do not bear its stamp."[11]

As a military historian, I am reminded that there has been more progress made in military technology over the past century than in any other period of world history.[12] What is the fruit of it all? Nothing but more effective ways of killing people, cities, forests, lands. A harvest of death with seeds sown for so much more of the same. Berry, it seems, thought of this parallel as well, as toward the end of *Hannah Coulter*, a chapter on war is wedged into the story seemingly incongruously, out of place at first read.[13]

Virgil Feltner, Hannah's first husband, died in World War II. He was declared missing in action, and his body was never recovered. Such a death in a war characterized by modern technological advancements is yet another painful reminder of the fruits of such progress. A man's existence is wiped out so efficiently that there is no tangible proof even of his very death, leaving his family to mourn and grieve over this lack of closure. While her second husband, Nathan, whom she married after the war, survived Okinawa, the scars never left, Hannah thinks:

---

[10]On this topic, see Eric Miller, "Professional Disrespect," Current, January 26, 2022, https://currentpub .com/2022/01/26/professional-disrespect/.

[11]Wendell Berry, *The Unsettling of America: Culture and Agriculture* (Berkeley, CA: Counterpoint, 1977), 9.

[12]See, for example, Yuki Tanaka and Marilyn Young, eds., *Bombing Civilians: A Twentieth-Century History* (New York: New Press, 2010).

[13]Berry also considers these connections in *Unsettling of America*, 8-10, and *Imagination in Place* (Berkeley, CA: Counterpoint, 2011), 188-89.

You can't give yourself over to love for somebody without giving yourself over to suffering. You can't give yourself to love for a soldier without giving yourself to his suffering in war. It is this body of our suffering that Christ was born into, to suffer it Himself and to fill it with light, so that beyond the suffering we can imagine Easter morning and the peace of God on little earthly homelands such as Port William and the farming villages of Okinawa.[14]

The innovations of twentieth-century warfare made the destruction of life more effective than ever before. In a less visible way, Berry contends, innovations made in agriculture, replacing the love, care, and hard work of farmers with ever larger and brutal machines and chemicals, had the same effect—of erasing farmers from the landscape, and transforming people instead into the living dead. He mourns these meaningless work lives in his most recent book, *The Need to Be Whole*.[15] "And now, looking back, it seems clear that when the tractors came, the people began to go," Hannah Coulter observes matter-of-factly.[16] But no innovation can replace a deep knowledge of nature that can only come from love.

A TALE OF TWO FARMERS

There was once a farmer who wanted to create a small pond on a hillside on his property to provide water for a flock he wanted to pasture there. So, he hired someone to dig the pond. All seemed to go well for a season, but following a wet fall and winter, some of the surrounding woods slipped into the new pond. The pond and the land around it, so healthy before, became a festering wound as a result of this one foolish decision. The farmer was devastated. "Until that wound in the hillside, my place, is healed, there will be something impaired in my mind. My peace is damaged. I will not be able to forget it."[17] So wrote Berry, the farmer in this poem in prose.

---

[14]Berry, *Hannah Coulter*, 171.
[15]Wendell Berry, *The Need to Be Whole: Patriotism and the History of Prejudice* (Berkeley, CA: Shoemaker, 2022), 21.
[16]Berry, *Hannah Coulter*, 92.
[17]Wendell Berry, *What Are People For?*, 6.

It is appropriate that Berry opens his collection of essays *What Are People For?* with this cautionary tale that reflects the connection between personal well-being and that of the land for which one is responsible. The question in the title is one that could in some ways be considered the central question that he has attempted to answer in all his writing, often pointing to negative rather than positive examples. His examples show, as with the tale of the failed pond or little Margaret's failed marriage, that a solution of violence, rending something asunder, is always the opposite of wholeness. It is not what we were made for.

In the absence of wholeness we see what we are missing, and this absence is what Berry repeatedly documents in his essays, novels, and poetry. But in his most recent book, *The Need to Be Whole*, Berry has perhaps come the closest to spelling out the answer directly to that earlier question: What are people for?[18] People are for joyful community, for loving relationship, for nuanced history with each other, with their land, with their work. Families, including children, are an essential sine qua non of this wholeness.

In his review of *The Need to Be Whole*, philosopher Joshua Hochschild dubs Berry "an American Augustine."[19] This is an apt correlation. For Berry, as for Augustine, while good theology offers universal foundations for human flourishing that is rooted in Christ, any applications of these foundations must be local. There is a face, a person, attached to every generalized statement or observation. Roots must be lovingly cultivated, and the story of these roots—telling accurately the history of a place and its people—makes all the difference.

---

[18]See Eric Miller's discussion of these themes in his review essay, "A Pathway to Peace: Hope in *The Need to Be Whole*," Front Porch Republic, October 7, 2022, www.frontporchrepublic.com/2022/10/a-pathway-to-peace/.

[19]Joshua P. Hochschild, "An American Augustine," Front Porch Republic, November 18, 2022, www.frontporchrepublic.com/2022/11/an-american-augustine/.

Let us consider the story of another farmer, not Berry but one who on the surface seems like a brother. He spent his entire life on the same farm where he was born. There he was born, there he grew up, there he grew old. When he first learned to walk, his tiny toddling baby feet followed unsteadily the very same path that he followed decades later bent over with age, leaning on a stick. We can imagine his entire life as a kaleidoscopic whole, colorful pictures of similar activities done in the same place, all overlaying each other.

He has only ever imbibed water from one stream—the brook that ran through his farm. There was a big city not too far away, Verona, but he had never even made it this far away from his farm. He also had no idea what political regime was in power in the vast empire within which his little farm was but a tiny, insignificant speck. Insignificant to others, one might say, but the center of his universe. Indeed, this farm, with its boundaries, was his entire known world. But his creator, early fourth century AD pagan poet Claudian, tells us that this farmer was much happier than any other men of his age or any other—a statement that says more about Claudian's longings than about real farmers in this age of disruptions.[20]

This "Old Man of Verona," as the poem is misleadingly known—for Claudian's farmer never actually made it as far away from his farm as nearby Verona—is nostalgic but, history testifies, entirely imaginary. Nearly half a millennium earlier, the age of the late Roman Republic already was a time of consolidation of smaller farms across Italy into increasingly larger ones. Verona became from then on prime recruitment ground for the Roman military. Tombstones of Roman soldiers from across the empire show that many of these recruits from Verona and other towns in northern Italy were firstborn sons who never returned home after leaving, their bones finding their final resting place instead far away on the Danube frontier. Why did they not stay behind and farm the land of their ancestors, as we might have expected firstborn sons and heirs to do? Perhaps because there was no land left for them to inherit and farm independently.

---

[20]This section is based in part on my essay "Once upon a Time near Verona," *Plough*, July 22, 2022, www.plough.com/en/topics/culture/literature/once-upon-a-time-near-verona.

Vergil and other poets following his style were writing glorious poetry about the joys of farming, beekeeping, and ploughman garlic cheese lunches, but in reality the farmers they describe were long gone, if they ever existed. In describing the demographics of the Roman army in the Middle Republic, already back in the third century BC, Nathan Rosenstein notes that the typical Roman farmer lived a perilous existence, barely able to produce enough food to feed his family year in and year out.[21] By the time of late antiquity, four hundred years on, farmers had a very different existence from even this world of subsisting on the margins. Their lives were much more uncertain, stressful, prone to concern over crop failures that habitually happened and the invariable violence of attackers passing through—as the Goths would do to the region of Verona just a few years after Claudian wrote this poem, on their way southward to sack Rome and violently displace so many of its residents, sending some to Augustine's North Africa.

Furthermore, while Claudian seems to think it a key to happiness that the farmer has no idea what is happening anywhere around him politically, perhaps we can agree that an ignorant citizen rooted in his habitat but disconnected from society around him is not the ideal. The Old Man of Verona, living in his golden-age bubble, reminds us that such a golden age was always a myth. Once we look closely, maybe this myth should not be overly idealized. There is a right and wrong way to love rootedness, and this desire we have for stability can become an idol.

Indeed, the early Christians were people of cities, at peace with losing roots to their ancestral lands for the sake of following Jesus.[22] It was the pagans, *pagani*, by contrast, who were people of the countryside.[23] Still, the imaginary Old Man of Verona, this ideal rooted farmer, reminds us of the built-in yearning for community and for deep roots that we all have. The desire is right, but the ideal may not always be possible or worthy in the

---

[21] Nathan Rosenstein, *Rome at War: Farms, Families, and Death in the Middle Republic* (Chapel Hill: University of North Carolina Press, 2004).

[22] Wayne Meeks, *The First Urban Christians: The Social World of the Apostle Paul* (New Haven, CT: Yale University Press, 2003).

[23] Alan Cameron, *The Last Pagans of Rome* (Oxford: Oxford University Press, 2011), 14-32.

shape Claudian describes. Did Jesus not call followers to leave their nets and lands behind to follow him? But roots are not just those we put down in the land; we need relationships and connections with others. Human flourishing, as Jesus taught, never happens alone, in isolation. This is a truth that monks have understood over the centuries, as they valued *stabilitas* in community with each other.

Relationships are a marked absence in the farmer's life as described by Claudian: from the perspective of the poem, he is all alone. This reflects the artificial nature of everything about him. Not only is his farm a strange island outside time and space, but he himself seems to exist in a vacuum. There is no mention of his parents or other relatives caring for him as a little one toddling around the farm that forms his entire world. There is no mention of a wife and children with whom he shares this farm as an adult. Perhaps for Claudian these are not important, but the absences jump out. Like all humans, surely this farmer had a family that raised him; from them he inherited this family farm. Surely he himself got married and took care of this farm with the aid of his wife and children. A farm of any reasonable size cannot be run well by just one man. Farmers have always relied on families and other workers—in the Roman world, these were likely enslaved, if this farmer was sufficiently wealthy. Claudian does not care about such details, however.

The pagan hierarchy of the worth of life of different sorts of people, as we considered in chapters five and six, does not make anyone other than the farmer himself significant enough to care about. Idealizing roots in the abstract and impersonal way that Claudian does ultimately creates not a hero but an idol with clay feet. In Berry's Port William, the Branches with their large family of seven kids take this ideal and show the difference that valuing people and relationships makes in creating flourishing that gives rather than merely takes. Berry describes that as existing without a future; yet, we see their future secure. Not so with Claudian's farmer, who is presented as somehow eternal yet clearly growing old, ever closer to death. The poem ignores an obvious question: Who will inherit this farm?

In Greek mythology, the greatest curse of all was the eradication of an entire household, the erasure of an entire dynasty and its very name. It is no accident that cursed mythological families are a favorite subject of Greek tragedy. We see the inexorable curse of the gods pursue the house of Labdacus, Laius, and Oedipus, culminating with the war of the seven against Thebes. Who is left at the end? No one. We see a similar curse pursue the house of Atreus, with none but Orestes left at the end. In the process, there is much bloodshed and misery.

What causes perhaps the greatest degree of suffering is not just the horrific disregard for human life and personhood in the myths that form the subject of Greek tragedy. Rather, the worst is that before the end, those caught up in the cycle of violence know what is coming—their own death or at least the end of their line. It is the fear of that erasure of the house, as if it never existed, doomed to be remembered only for its curse, that haunts those wretches left alive at the end. The fate of Zedekiah, the last king of Judah, comes to mind— the king whose last sight in this life, before his Babylonian captors gouged out his eyes, was his own sons put to death (2 Kings 25:1-7).

The fear of this curse of extirpation has been instinctive to humanity up until recently. Now people claim the curse as a blessing. An epidemic of chosen childlessness in our society is afoot.[24] Marriage rates continue to decline as well, even in the church.[25] We feel dislocations of relationships, even if we tell ourselves that this is just how modern life is. Berry's writing and even more so his own life trajectory remind us that it does not have to be that way. Even if our roots are more like the bonsai than the oak, they matter. I think about this as I am completing this book following a cross-country move to a new home for my family. This is a time of uprooting for us, but it is also a homecoming of sorts for my husband, whose family has ties to the area. We are not making the move with the goal of making another move. God alone knows what will happen, but our hope is to put down roots and stay.

---

[24]Anna Louie Sussman, "The End of Babies," *New York Times*, November 16, 2019, www.nytimes.com /interactive/2019/11/16/opinion/sunday/capitalism-children.html.

[25]Mark Regnerus, "Can the Church Save Marriage?," *Christianity Today*, June 22, 2020, www .christianitytoday.com/ct/2020/july-august/marriage-save-church-declining-christians-global.html.

CONCLUSION: FROM DEATH TO LIFE

Perhaps emphasizing life in a world filled with death begins with speaking words of hope, words that confront what we see around and say that it does not have to be this way. This is exactly what the three thinkers who are the central case studies for these last three chapters have done.

In her journal, written as she was awaiting sure death, Perpetua challenges the devaluing of motherhood and children by showing that God's love defeats death, and the deepest love we can show our children is by loving God most. Her words aim to provide consolation in suffering, whether of the everyday variety, familiar to all parents, or of the extraordinary variety that she experienced herself. In his *City of God*, Augustine confronts the Roman dehumanization of people traditionally seen as "useless ones" especially in times of war by showing God's loving hand guiding history. Tragedies happen, but God is present even in them. Finally, Berry refutes both the ancient pagan ideal of rootedness as an idol and the secular modern glorification of machine work and, really, creative work done out of selfishness rather than love. He calls us back to who we are as created beings in need of appreciation for the beauty of the Creator's gifts.

These are all valuable reminders in our world where defending human life has too often been reduced to mere slogans and political talking points. Valuing image bearers begins with valuing mothers and children, but a consistently pro-life view requires seeing people as much more than mere bodies. The human race is resilient, and people can survive all kinds of atrocities. But flourishing rather than survival is the goal. What does it look like to be not merely pro-life but pro–human flourishing?

These are overwhelming, big-picture questions. They demand answers, but as the life stories of Berry's residents of Port William confirm, those answers cannot be grand and broad.

> Valuing image bearers begins with valuing mothers and children, but a consistently pro-life view requires seeing people as much more than mere bodies.

Rather, we must give local, concrete, rooted answers—an accounting, a reckoning—to ourselves and to others around us every day. If passive acceptance of the culture leads to death in ways documented throughout this book, to promote a culture of life means deliberately finding the countercultural joy in family, in children, in friendships, in meaningful work, and in redeeming our time to the glory of God in a decidedly utilitarian world that questions all things that do not lead to profit.

"Tell me a story," my eight-year-old son still asks my husband every morning by way of greeting. He began making this request years ago, before he could read. Now, although he reads for himself, he still wants to hear stories from his father. The stories we tell, write, and live out every day are not perfect, but they can be good, beautiful, and meaningful. But most of all, what these stories tell my son at the beginning of each day is that his life matters, that he is dear to us, that he is significant enough for his father to begin his day with a renewal of relationship.

WHO IS MY NEIGHBOR? TREASURING CHILDREN, MOTHERS, AND ALL IMAGE BEARERS

A MAN IS ROBBED AND BRUTALLY BEATEN while traveling along a busy highway. The attackers strip him of everything he has on him, then leave him for dead by the side of the road. Multiple other people then pass him by in a steady stream, all traveling along this well-trekked highway. Strikingly, all these passersby ignore the wounded man for various reasons (Lk 10:29-37). Some do not even see him, while others do not want to incur pollution or the inconvenience—cleaning up blood is so messy, you know. Besides, one might say, time is money.

This parable of the good Samaritan, one of the most universally familiar stories from the New Testament, has to do with the question of responsibility we bear to strangers, image bearers we do not know, to whom we are not directly related by familial relationship—and therefore to whom are not obviously beholden. In the pre-Christian ancient world, as I have noted throughout this book, the worth of strangers that one encountered was determined by the beholder, as it depended on a variety of factors: wealth, social status, citizenship or lack thereof, gender, ability to perform useful tasks for society, and more. Jesus challenges this utilitarian framework of thinking about image bearers in the parable of the good Samaritan.

In Jesus' parable, something striking and utterly revolutionary happens. Another traveler sees the hurt man and recognizes him as a fellow image bearer. He takes pity on him and saves him from certain death, first caring for the hurt man himself, then paying for his subsequent treatment and lodging out of his own pocket. This helper's need to move on and leave the hurt man reminds us that he too has obligations, places to be, things to do. But he was willing to disrupt them all and take on the inconvenience of caring for someone he did not even know.

We never get names in this tale. The hurt man, just as the parade of people passing him by, is simply the "everyman" around. The only fact we do get reminds us that ethnic and religious identity matters: while everyone else in this story is a Jew (including, presumably, the ruthless attackers), the kind rescuer is a Samaritan. He is therefore the only one mentioned in the story who is not at all a neighbor or ethnic kin to the man who was hurt.

There is a reason why this story strikes us so deeply, just as it did the original hearers. Jesus' audiences wondered: Just what is my obligation to complete strangers in this world we all inhabit? Who is my neighbor anyway? Can we get a sufficiently narrow definition here, so I can be off the hook for all these inconvenient things? The philosophy of "see a need, fill a need" is unpopular. We do not like to admit it, but we still ask these same questions that Jesus' audiences did whenever we are faced with suffering. Sometimes we do not even realize that we are doing it as we make ready excuses to let ourselves off the hook. This story, therefore, more than many others in the New Testament, feels like a punch in the gut for our comfortable lives. But it can be even more gut-punchy, the more we think about it—and perhaps it needs to be to convict us more fully.

In his modern rendition of this tale, Phil Christman updates it to feature "A Tradcath, an exvangelical influencer, a mainliner, and a conservative megachurch pastor," along with a couple of Duke Divinity School post-liberals, to show the extent to which Christians of different stripes have imbibed the cultural attitude of ignoring the needs of others, unless doing the opposite is convenient or fits into an obvious framework of what it means to care for others.[1] This is exaggerated satire, and yet it does not seem too far off the mark in documenting familiar excuses that some Christians use to avoid seeing the preciousness of the hurt man—or woman, or child.

The exvangelical, for instance, tells the hurt man that he is simply at capacity right now for helping anyone. Besides, he has not had a chance to talk this over with his therapist. The megachurch pastor, in the meantime, simply blames politics: "And when he saw the man, he passed by on the other side, and he said unto himself, 'This is what comes of woke politicians. Slimy dirty people everywhere. A decent person can't even ride the bus. The Uber drivers always want a tip . . .' And he passed by on the other side." The mainliner in the story notes to himself that it is always better to give directly to charity. He decides to give to a charity of some sort soon but forgets immediately. But we get the idea: out of sight, out of mind.

It is a damning witness to our lack of compassion for others and for our broader devaluing of all human beings if we cannot be moved to help someone hurt who is directly in our path. Indeed, consider this visual: the ones who did not help the hurt man, whether in Jesus' parable or in Christman's retelling, literally had to step over him in some cases to pass him by. How much easier it is to ignore the vulnerable hurt ones we do not meet, whom we never see, the ones over whose suffering, broken bodies we do not have to step over on our way to whatever else we had planned to do?

God sees, however.

Whenever we ignore the preciousness of other human beings in God's eyes, we are exhibiting the same utilitarian view of pricing human life that the ancient pagans did. Indeed, bearing responsibility for others—seeing that wounded man on the road and choosing to help him—is the ultimate pro-life statement. In chapter two, I mentioned American philosopher Judith Jarvis Thomson's famous analogy in favor of abortion rights: imagine that a

---

[1] Phil Christman, "The Effective Samaritan: A Parable," *Plough*, May 23, 2023, www.plough.com/en /topics/justice/social-justice/the-effective-samaritan-a-parable.

woman's circulatory system has suddenly and without her consent been connected to that of a famous violin player for nine months. That woman, Thomson insists, should have the right to refuse.

Thomson's analogy of refusing to save someone else is a key part of her argument for abortion rights. If a woman did not choose to sustain life for nine months, she should not have to do it. But the story she tells in this analogy is inadvertently yet another retelling of the parable of the good Samaritan. In this tale, too, there is a wounded man, one who needs another's assistance to live. Here, too, all who pass by refuse to help him. But there is a crucial difference in Thomson's analogy-turned-parable: there is no good Samaritan. The woman who was meant to play the part of the good Samaritan in this analogy is given her freedom to say no. As a result, the wounded man dies. Or it might be the unborn child. The two in this analogy are one and the same. Taken to a logical conclusion, devaluing the life of one always means devaluing the life of the other.

It is no accident that this analogy for unwanted pregnancy looks at the question of our responsibility for the lives of adults. We cannot divorce valuing unborn life from valuing the life of image bearers at every age and stage of life. Who is my neighbor? Thomson's answer is: no one, unless I decide so. It is the quintessential pagan answer. Just like that, each person gets the license to be Caesar, the one with the power to decide on the death of those whose lives are not convenient at that given moment. Is this the world we want to live in? Thankfully, the reality such a worldview presents is not the truth, even if the underlying messaging of our society accepts such a world as the default.

Thomson was not a believer. Her line of reasoning makes sense in the atheistic worldview within which she reasoned. Just as with Caesar, who had no framework for valuing the Gauls but every reason for wishing to slaughter them, we can simply accept that she was operating within a consistent, albeit immoral, framework that did not see anyone as an image bearer. But then, even faithful believers at times are guilty of similar thinking, as Christman's rendition of the good Samaritan tale reminds.

Maybe we are not literally passing by hurt people in need of immediate care on the side of the road, but we as a society choose not to provide proper health care for the poor. Yet again, this manifests itself as a devaluing of mothers and children, as too many women choose abortion simply because they find it to be their only financially viable option.[2] As for mothers who embrace pregnancy, a recent study noted that on average, one in five women experiences mistreatment from medical personnel during prenatal care or delivery. But the average does not tell the full story. It is even more disconcerting to hear that two in five women of color experience such mistreatment. This is also the group of women most likely to die in childbirth today, in the twenty-first-century United States—deaths that studies repeatedly emphasize are preventable.[3] These are not the statistics of a country that can claim to be pro-life.

We do not need to think of medical emergencies and tragedies, however, to see that opposition to motherhood and a general absence of love for human beings is deeply ingrained all around. In the week when I was finishing the first draft of this book, the following social media post from someone I do not know caught my attention, not because it is exceptionally unusual but because it is merely the latest along the same lines. A mother posted: "A lady at the grocery store today saw me with two toddlers (who were behaving) and big pregnancy belly and said 'I'm glad I'm not you.'" This story reminded me of the admittedly less appalling but similar experience I had when I first went to the grocery store with all three of my children after the birth of my daughter. An acquaintance saw us, her eyes got wide upon seeing my newborn, and she blurted, "You had another one?!" Awkwardly in that moment, I quipped something about doing my part to ensure that the family name of Williams will not die out.

Our culture devalues life in the simplest everyday ways, such as these grocery-store conversations. This messaging is having its effects; according

---

[2]Daniel K. Williams, "Abortion and the Class Divide," Current, July 30, 2021, https://currentpub .com/2021/07/30/abortion-and-the-class-divide/.

[3]Roni Caryn Rabin, "One in Five Women Feels Mistreated During Maternity Care, C.D.C. Reports," New York Times, August 22, 2023, www.nytimes.com/2023/08/22/health/pregnancy-mistreatment -health-care.html.

to the US Census Bureau, for the first time ever in this nation's history, "older adults are projected to outnumber children by 2034."[4] But just because this is the current status quo does not mean that it must remain so. The point of the parable of the good Samaritan is of course that Jesus calls all of us to claim all image bearers as our neighbors, whether it is convenient or not, costly or not. By the way, doing what Jesus calls us to do usually will be inconvenient and financially costly, as we see in the parable. Christians today should, as many in the ancient Mediterranean world were, be distinguished from the culture around by being the people who "rescue the perishing, care for the dying" near and far, showing our love for all image bearers in daily action.[5] We claim to be a people who are pro-life, but American Christians' witness on issues of life, outside support for pro-life legislation, desperately needs improvement.

We claim to be a people who are pro-life, but American Christians' witness on issues of life, outside support for pro-life legislation, desperately needs improvement.

While it is easy to criticize Christians today for failing to follow their own values, we saw in chapter seven that at times the early Christians, too, lamentably failed to do likewise. The point of this book is not to idealize early Christians as unquestioned pro-life heroes, just as I am not idealizing believers today. Rather, the story that emerges is that whatever our failings are at times in treasuring others, Christ always treasures us. That has always influenced the way that at least devoted Christ-followers viewed other human beings. Without knowing Christ, one has no reason to tell someone such as Thomson that her view of human life, whether fetal or grown, is wrong, just as without Christ, Julius Caesar's view of the Gauls as worth more dead than alive makes sense.

---

[4]Jonathan Vespa, Lauren Medina, and David M. Armstrong, "Demographic Turning Points for the United States: Population Projects 2020 to 2060," U.S. Census Bureau, revised February 2020, www .census.gov/content/dam/Census/library/publications/2020/demo/p25-1144.pdf.
[5]Fanny Crosby, "Rescue the Perishing" (1869), https://hymnary.org/text/rescue_the_perishing_care _for_the_dying.

Where does this leave us? It leaves us with the gospel of Jesus Christ—the good news of the only one who is the same yesterday, today, and every tomorrow yet to come. Interwoven through the gospel is the story of the preciousness, the infinitely and unconditionally priceless nature, of each and every human being who has ever existed and will ever exist. It is the most incredible and beautiful love story—of God's love for every mother, child, and image bearer not because of what they can do, have done, or have the potential to become but because of who they are already as image bearers. The knowledge of this love should empower us to embrace a culture of life in a world that too often chooses death.

Most of us will never encounter a dramatic variation of the good Samaritan scenario. But there are many ordinary ways in which we are called into such care. Too often, because these ways of displaying care for the life of others do not seem glamorous enough, or perhaps because they do not look like what we had in mind (like for Christman's satirical Christians), we are likely to say no. One practical way in which all Christians have the opportunity to live out their love for mothers and children in the church involves participating in teaching children's Sunday school and volunteering in the church nursery instead of placing these responsibilities solely on mothers and women in the congregation.[6] Agnes Howard lists other such ways of caring for new mothers and their children in the conclusion to her book. Not only does a pro-life ethic of this sort require a change of heart from us, but also it changes us ourselves in the process of action.[7]

Wendell Berry's rewriting of the Samaritan's tale in his short story "The Hurt Man" offers a striking call to love our neighbor. In this story, set in the familiar (to Berry's readers) Port William in 1888, Mat Feltner, a mere child of five at the time, observes an unusual incident on an otherwise ordinary day.

---

[6]Nadya Williams, "Pro-Life? Then You Should Teach Sunday School and Volunteer in Your Church Nursery," Anxious Bench, June 13, 2023, www.patheos.com/blogs/anxiousbench/2023/06/pro-life-then-you-should-teach-sunday-school-and-volunteer-in-your-church-nursery/.

[7]Agnes Howard, *Showing: What Pregnancy Tells Us About Being Human* (Grand Rapids, MI: Eerdmans, 2020), 181-201.

A man, seriously hurt and dripping blood from his wounds, runs into his family's home with a crowd of other men in hot pursuit. Mat's mother not only lets him inside but takes care of this hurt man, whose name Berry never provides but notes that Mat himself never knew it either. The most important detail about this man, indeed, is that he is hurt, defined by not being whole: "He might have remained nameless to Mat because of the entire strangeness of the look of him. He had shed the look of a man and assumed somehow the look of all things badly hurt."[8]

We are not our own; we are part of communities. So, while the story is about the hurt man in the title, it is no less so about those who care for such as these and what such care means in a cosmic sense—a bold act of love that is greater than any other. Through Mat's five-year-old eyes we get to see how his mother perceived this man:

> What he saw in her face would remain with him forever. It was pity, but it was more than that. It was a hurt love that seemed to include entirely the hurt man. It included him and disregarded everything else. It disregarded the aura of whiskey that ordinarily she would have resented; it disregarded the blood puddled on the porch floor and the trail of blood through the hall. . . . It was as though she leaned in the black of her mourning over the whole hurt world itself, touching its wounds with her tenderness, in her sorrow.[9]

A Christlike love and care for the sorrow and pain of others cannot help but transform us too. There is indeed something remarkably Christlike in Berry's description of a widowed young mother, who has buried a husband and several children, who now thinks with sorrow of the preciousness of all of their lives as she takes care of a man whom she has never met before, whose name she does not know, but whose blood has spilled on the floor of her home. "And this was a part, and belonged to the deliverance, of the town's hard history of love."[10]

---

[8]Wendell Berry, "The Hurt Man," in *That Distant Land: The Collected Stories* (Berkeley, CA: Counterpoint, 2005), 8-9.

[9]Berry, "Hurt Man," 10.

[10]Berry, "Hurt Man," 10.

The overall story that I tell in this book is how much such care for the weak, the helpless, those who need our care and compassion, is not something that comes naturally to our sinful nature since expulsion from Eden. Indeed, such care and love for the hurting did not come naturally to people in the Greco-Roman pagan world. Rather, the love for every human being, hurt or whole—man, woman, child—regardless of age, gender, social or marital status, wealth, ability or disability, is the revolutionary fruit of two things. The first of these is the Judeo-Christian doctrine of the *imago Dei*. The second is the faith that so many have accepted—which includes belief in the *imago Dei* alongside God's other promises to us in the Bible. This truth calls us to extraordinary, lavish action. It calls us to love.

GENERAL INDEX

"In this moving, pastoral book, Nadya Williams plumbs the long history of assumptions and practices that culminate in what Pope Francis has termed our 'throwaway' culture. In the same way that the early Christian church dismantled the Roman Empire's commodification of human persons, so the gospel continues to bear witness to the intrinsic value of all humans, even those society deems useless. Williams wears her considerable learning lightly, and readers will find her narrative brings both illumination and conviction."
Jeffrey Bilbro, associate professor of English at Grove City College and editor in chief at Front Porch Republic

"Nadya Williams has the great ability to bring together good history and contemporary application without being cheesy or ignoring nuance. In this volume, she ably helps us see how both a Judeo-Christian account of the *imago Dei* and the gospel's call to radical and sacrificial love were revolutionary in the ancient Greco-Roman world, and how these two realities remain revolutionary in our own dehumanizing world. Read Williams not simply to learn about the past but to be inspired for the present!"
Kelly M. Kapic, professor of theological studies at Covenant College and author of *You're Only Human*

"Parents tempted to optimize every aspect of children's experiences, beware. Those very efforts may make us complicit in devaluing human life, especially of mothers and children. Nadya Williams warns that few Americans are exempt from cultural imperatives assigning a price to everything—even human beings. The author's deep knowledge of the history and poetry of the pre-Christian Roman world makes her a perceptive guide through its brutalities too, some of which bear disturbing likeness to our own. Then Jesus came, and the soul felt its worth: the author reminds us that the gospel recognizes every soul as precious. Williams bids readers to transform pro-life concerns into commitment to full human flourishing."
Agnes Howard, author of *Showing: What Pregnancy Tells Us About Being Human*

"I read *Mothers, Children, and the Body Politic* in fits and starts, exhausted because my baby has adopted a new (worse) sleep schedule and my own schedule has yet to adapt. But it seemed an apt method for engaging Nadya Williams's work here, a scholarly yet conversational and timely examination of how Christianity transformed a casually cruel culture, how our society increasingly resembles its pagan past, and how we can better value mothers, children, and indeed all image-bearers of God."
Bonnie Kristian, editorial director of ideas and books at *Christianity Today* and author of *Untrustworthy* and *A Flexible Faith*

"In this far-seeing, deeply personal book, Nadya Williams offers the gift of intelligent, alert, learned conviction—a beam of light aimed at dark corners of our lives and our world, past and present. She not only exposes us for who we're not, but she also shows us who we might yet become. It's a vision no Christian can afford to miss."
Eric Miller, professor of history and the humanities at Geneva College

"In this deeply learned and readable book, Christian classicist Nadya Williams takes readers on a tour of pre-Christian societies and the ideas that animated them. Exposing their views about and treatment of women and children, Williams uncovers just how revolutionary the Judeo-Christian worldview—in particular, the *imago Dei*—has been for the equal dignity of women. Those on both the left and right today who wish to trade in Christianity for the paganism of the pre-Christian world—and think women and children will be just fine—would do well to heed Williams's cautionary tale. I pray it gets a wide reading."

Erika Bachiochi, ethics and public policy legal scholar and author of *The Rights of Women: Reclaiming a Lost Vision*